Cracks in

'Ben White has written a book which provides valuable and profound insights into the present apartheid reality of Israel as a "Jewish state" and contributed to our understanding of the international dimensions of the Palestinian struggle. This is not just sharp analysis but an urgent call to action.'
Member of Knesset Hanin Zoabi

'Ben White follows up his 2009 book 'Israeli Apartheid: A Beginner's Guide' with a look to the future and the implications of the legal and moral contradictions at the heart of current Israeli policy towards the Palestinians. He correctly identifies the best way forward as resting on the principles of equality and self-determination.'
Crispin Blunt MP, Foreign Affairs Select Committee chair 2015–17

'In the midst of a torrent of competing facts, and often dense and bewildering arguments, we are fortunate to have the steady, clear, and utterly principled voice of Ben White ... If you are coming to the issue of Palestine for the first time, or simply wish to learn more, there is nowhere better to start. This book vividly captures the myriad debates, the complex struggles, and an extraordinary cause, bringing into view the world of Palestine that lies hidden behind the headlines.'
Karma Nabulsi, Fellow in Politics, St Edmund Hall, University of Oxford

'Ben White's book will be important, essential reading for all who care about the rule of law and the rights of Palestinians.'
Ken Loach, film director

'Ben White's eagerly awaited book analyses important trends that are no longer moving in Israel's favour, trends that will shape a more hopeful future for Palestine/Israel, and is a must read for all those who might despair of ever seeing peace, let alone justice, come to this tormented land.'
Nadia Hijab, co-founder of Al-Shabaka, the Palestinian Policy Network

'Ben is a professional and perceptive journalist with a deep commitment to human rights. His latest book will no doubt prove to be a vital contribution to the Palestine/Israel debate.'
Tommy Sheppard MP

'Thoroughly-researched and precisely formulated, this is an important book that clarifies the nature of Israeli apartheid, identifies hopeful forms of growing opposition to it, sheds important light on the BDS movement, and makes a powerful case for a one-state solution.'
**Professor John Chalcraft, Department of Government,
London School of Economics**

'In this important book, Ben White has captured several elusive phenomena: the discriminatory one state reality that has existed in Palestine for some time, the growing divisions in the American Jewish community over Israel's behaviour, and the beginning of the end of bi-partisan support for Israel as Republicans support, and Democrats recoil from, the hard-right policies of the Israeli government, and its treatment of the Palestinians.'

Rashid Khalidi, Edward Said Professor of Modern Arab Studies, Columbia University

'I've long relied on Ben White's books for smart, unflinching insights into the struggle for justice in Palestine. With *Cracks in the Wall* he goes even deeper into the ideological history of Zionism and what it has wrought for Palestinians in the twenty-first century. Anyone seeking a hopeful and humane vision of a future for all the inhabitants of this land would do well to read this book.'

Rabbi Brant Rosen, founding rabbi of Tzedek Chicago

'With a brilliant combination of a bird's-eye vision and a forensic examination of the facts, Ben White has shown prominent cracks in Israel's wall of impunity that may augur the end of its apartheid system ... White argues, a single democratic state in historic Palestine that offers equal citizenship to all and enables the Palestinian refugees to return may finally be born.'

Omar Barghouti, co-founder, BDS Movement

'With his usual incisive gaze, Ben White unfolds for us the Palestine/Israel reality as it is and cuts through the layers of misinformation, deceit and ignorance ... White points to the drastic erosion in Israel's international standing and calls upon us to seize this historical moment and search more energetically for a just solution within a one democratic state all over historical Palestine.'

Ilan Pappe, Director of the European Centre for Palestine Studies, University of Exeter

'Ben White smashes through stifling conventional wisdom that there's no prospect for justice and peace in Palestine. He is clear-eyed about the grinding apartheid Israel is determined to cement and mask from view ... White debunks Israel's propaganda and acts as a guide through a political landscape that shows many green shoots of hope in Palestine and around the world for a just and equal future sooner than we might think possible.'

Ali Abunimah, author and co-founder, *The Electronic Intifada*

'*Cracks in the Wall* presents a wealth of information, clearly, concisely, and accurately, on the narrowing of support for Israel among Western liberals, the rise of pro-Israel sentiment on the right, and the new coalition of support for the Palestinians ... The book should appeal to those who need a short introduction to these issues, and to those who follow them obsessively. A highly useful resource ... engaged writing at its best.'

Charles H. Manekin, Professor of Philosophy and Jewish Studies, University of Maryland

Cracks in the Wall

Beyond Apartheid in Palestine/Israel

Ben White

First published 2018 by Pluto Press
345 Archway Road, London N6 5AA

www.plutobooks.com

Copyright © Ben White 2018

The right of Ben White to be identified as the author of this work has been
asserted by him in accordance with the Copyright, Designs and Patents Act 1988.

British Library Cataloguing in Publication Data
A catalogue record for this book is available from the British Library

ISBN   978 0 7453 3762 3   Hardback
ISBN   978 0 7453 3761 6   Paperback
ISBN   978 1 7868 0251 4   PDF eBook
ISBN   978 1 7868 0253 8   Kindle eBook
ISBN   978 1 7868 0252 1   EPUB eBook

Typeset by Stanford DTP Services, Northampton, England

Simultaneously printed in the United Kingdom and United States of America

Contents

For Mum and Dad

Foreword

Diana Buttu

The years 2017 and 2018 were the years of Palestinian anniversaries – or, more aptly, commemorations of Palestinian tragedies. Beginning in 1917 when Arthur Balfour, an Englishman with no ties to Palestine, declared his support for the 'establishment in Palestine of a national home for the Jewish people', Palestinians have endured – and resisted – one hundred years of colonial arrogance.

This colonial arrogance has taken different shapes and forms over the years. This notably included the 1947 Partition Plan, in which the UN tried to, once again, give away parts of Palestine without consulting Palestinians. More notorious yet was the 1948 Nakba, during which Israel forcibly ethnically cleansed us from our homeland to fulfil Balfour's promise. That brazen taking evidently fuelled further takings and the 1967 Naksa in which Israel took over the remaining parts of Palestine. Israel's unstoppable and insatiable appetite for Palestinian land has continued apace since as evidenced by the ever-accelerating settlement project.

The commemoration of tragedies is incomplete without reference to the current 25th anniversary since the 1993 signing of the Declaration of Principles, which launched the disastrous Oslo negotiations process. In those 25 years, Palestinians have witnessed the number of settlers in the West Bank (excluding Jerusalem) rise from 52,000 to an astonishing 400,000, an onslaught that evidently hastened Israel's division of the West Bank into cantons surrounded by walls and checkpoints, the cooptation of Palestinian resistance through the formation of the Palestinian Authority, in particular its security forces, as well as the burgeoning growth of

NGOs, UN agencies and an unbridled overall assistance paradigm that serves to gloss over Israel's efforts to effectively emasculate Palestinian ambitions for the realisation of our self-determination. In the Gaza Strip, the Oslo process served as cover for Israel to the world's largest open-air and largely refugee inhabited prison. With the water supply undrinkable, electricity available for only a few hours a day, soaring unemployment and poverty rates and a brutal, crippling Israeli siege, Gaza today is both unliveable and in an infinitely more dire situation than it was two decades ago. An entire generation of Palestinians have grown up under Oslo's strangulation, cut off from one another and from the rest of Palestine, living under Israel's oppressive rule and Palestinian Authority repression. A Gazan child more than nine years old today has survived three brutal military assaults.

It is in this context that US President Donald Trump emerges promising the 'deal of the century' but instead dealing the final – and wholly predictable – blows to Palestine. Within the first year of his term, Trump took the decision to embolden Israel's settler movement through the appointment of Jared Kushner and David Friedman, as envoy and ambassador respectively. Both men have a history of strong ties to Israeli settler organisations and helped press for Trump's recognition of Jerusalem as Israel's capital. These Trump administration measures were, in part, facilitated by the Palestinian Authority's longstanding determination to pursue negotiations (and only negotiations), even in the face of successive Israeli governments that have made clear that their vision is for Palestinians never to be free and for Israel to swallow many more vast tracts of Palestinian land to make way for Israeli settlers. Trump's election simply removes the mask of the US being the 'honest broker' and of bilateral negotiations being a credible path toward Palestinian liberation.

Yet while the political picture appears bleak, Palestinians remain strong, defiant and unwilling to submit to Israeli, or other, colonial diktats. Despite that a mealy-mouthed international community continues to flail and crumble in the face of Israeli pressure, we continue to show the world that stateless, dispossessed, refugee-camp-dwelling Palestinians are stronger than superpowers. Whether defying Israeli checkpoints, rebuilding homes and villages destroyed by Israel or refusing to compromise on our rights and principled demands for liberation, equality and return, Palestinians increasingly make Israel uncomfortable, leading to the very rapid rise in Israeli fascism in recent years. So terrified is Israel of the growing BDS movement – a grassroots movement that has still not been endorsed by the Palestinian Authority – that Israel has invested substantial resources in an effort to malign the movement, deport its leadership, criminalise its activities and bar its supporters from entering the country. In the past few years, the Israeli Knesset has passed successive racist laws targeting Palestinians while also openly promoting myriad annexation and transfer schemes. Palestinians are routinely arrested for writing poems or Facebook posts and for speaking out against Israel's apartheid. We will persist nevertheless and with ever greater clarity and determination.

It is in this context that Ben White's *Cracks in the Wall* is important. For while Israel may have erected a Wall, Palestinians have succeeded in making many increasingly visible cracks in it – and one day it, like Israel's apartheid regime, will crumble.

Acknowledgements

A project like this is impossible without the input, advice, guidance, and kindness of far too many people to mention, going back more than a decade. To all those – especially in Palestine and the diaspora – whose wisdom, intellectual labour, commitment, courage, and hospitality, I am fortunate enough to have experienced, drawn on, and been inspired by, thank you. I am deeply grateful.

Thank you to David Shulman at Pluto Press, and all his colleagues, who have helped make this book the finished product that it is.

Thank you to Alaa, Paul, and Tony, for the time and effort you graciously gave.

Thank you to all those who have kindly endorsed this book – and a huge thanks to Diana Buttu, for the sacrifices made to contribute a wonderful foreword.

Thank you to Bella and Daniel, for your patience and thoughtfulness.

And thank you to Julia, for all your love, support, and encouragement.

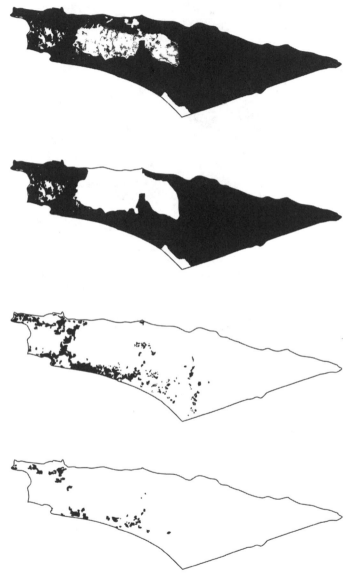

Jewish-owned land 1918, 1947, Israeli 'state land' 1960, today. (arenaofspeculation.org, based on Malkit Shoshan, B'Tselem)

Introduction

It was a Senate hearing like no other.[1] David Friedman, US President Donald Trump's nominee for the position of ambassador to Israel, had been speaking for about 20 seconds when he was loudly interrupted by a man holding a Palestinian flag. 'Mr. Friedman also said that Palestinian refugees don't have a claim to the land, don't have a connection to Palestine,' the man shouted. 'My grandfather was exiled, was kicked out by the State of Israel.' As he was led out by police officers, Taher Herzallah, of American Muslims for Palestine (AMP), managed one last parting shot. 'We aren't going away, Mr. Friedman. We were there, we are there now, and we will always be there. Palestinians will *always* be in Palestine!' After an awkward silence, Friedman resumed. But this was just the first of a series of interruptions; two minutes later, fellow AMP staffer Kareem El-Hosseiny stood up and protested Friedman's support for Israel's illegal settlements in the West Bank. Waving a Palestinian flag, El-Hosseiny was also removed and arrested.[2]

Before Friedman could get to the end of his opening statement, he was subjected to an equally dramatic interruption by three members of IfNotNow, a group started in 2014 by young Jewish Americans in the context of 'Operation Protective Edge'.[3] The activists stood after blowing a shofar, 'a ram's horn used in the Jewish tradition to call our community to action in times of crisis', before denouncing Friedman's track record in the strongest terms. 'You promote racism, fund illegal settlements', one man shouted. 'We will not be silenced. You do not represent us, and you will never represent us.' Another activist stood and stated loudly: 'Israeli occupation is an injustice against Palestinians, and a moral crisis for American Jews. Moral American Jews stand against occupation and against Friedman.' As they were taken out, the activists 'sang

1

Olam Chesed Yibaneh, a Hebrew song about building the world with love'.[4]

So why exactly was Friedman so controversial?[5] As a December 2016 piece in *The New York Times* summarised it:

> he is president of the American fund-raising arm for a yeshiva [Jewish religious school] in a settlement deep in the West Bank [Beit El] headed by a militant rabbi who has called for Israeli soldiers to refuse orders to evacuate settlers. He writes a column for a right-wing Israeli news site in which he has accused President Obama of 'blatant anti-Semitism', dismissed the two-state solution to the Israeli-Palestinian conflict, likened a liberal American-Jewish group to 'kapos' who cooperated with the Nazis, and said American Jewish leaders 'failed' Israel on the Iran nuclear deal.[6]

In fact, Friedman's financial ties to the settlement movement 'run deeper than Beit El' – he also 'made contributions over the years to Ateret Cohanim, a right-wing organisation that buys land in the Muslim Quarter of Jerusalem's Old City and Arab East Jerusalem for creating a "Jewish presence" there'.[7]

After an opening statement punctuated by protests, the rest of Friedman's confirmation hearing proceeded without interruption. But Trump's nominee did not have an easy time of it from many of the senators themselves. Friedman was repeatedly challenged over his rhetoric regarding Obama, the State Department, and liberal American Jews, including the frequency with which he had levelled the charge of anti-Semitism at even moderate critics of Israeli policies. Senator Tim Kaine (D-VA) led Friedman through a careful series of questions, courtroom-style, eliciting an affirmation from the nominee that the US could 'never support a solution where Palestinians are deprived of equal rights'. Another senator, Tom Udall (D-NM), stated plainly and bluntly that he was 'strongly opposed to this nominee' on the basis that 'Mr. Friedman is completely unfit for this, or any other, diplomatic office.'[8]

Despite such misgivings about his suitability for office – including from five former US ambassadors to Israel – the Senate Foreign Relations Committee voted on 9 March 2017, to approve Friedman's nomination. As Reuters reported at the time, the 12–9 vote 'was largely along party lines, a contrast with strong bipartisan support for past ambassadors to Israel'. All eleven of the committee's Republican senators voted for Friedman, along with Bob Menendez (D-NJ); the remaining nine Democrats all voted against the nomination.[9] Though Friedman's nomination continued to be opposed by groups like Jewish Voice for Peace (JVP), as well as by senior political figures such as veteran Democratic Senator Patrick Leahy (D-VT), on 23 March 2017, the Republican-controlled Senate duly confirmed Friedman's nomination in a 52–46 vote.[10]

Friedman's tumultuous confirmation hearing, and the storm surrounding his nomination was more than just a dramatic bump in the road on his way to the ambassador's residence in Israel; it was representative of deeper processes underway in the US, which are now accelerating under a Trump presidency. One of those developments is widening splits in the American Jewish community over Israel and US policy in the region. As an Associated Press report in December 2016 observed, Friedman's nomination had 'sharpened a growing balkanization of American Jews, between those who want the U.S. to push Israel toward peace and those who believe Obama's approach abandoned America's closest Mideast ally'.[11]

Nathan Guttman, the *Forward*'s Washington bureau chief, described it as 'a Jewish battle royale for supporters and detractors of the two-state solution', while for some observers – like *Haaretz* journalist Judy Maltz, writing before Friedman's confirmation hearing – 'America's Jewish organizations ... [had] rarely been more split'.[12] Groups like the Zionist Organisation of America, the Conference of Presidents of Major American Jewish Organizations, Jewish Federations of North America, and the Orthodox Union, all backed Friedman's appointment. Opponents, meanwhile, included J Street, Union for Reform Judaism, Americans for Peace Now, Ameninu, and JVP. Some notable groups kept silent prior to Friedman's appointment, including the American Israel Public Affairs Committee and American Jewish Committees.

Friedman's opponents represented different, though related, phenomena – from a policy establishment-focused, liberal Zionist group like J Street, to the far more radical campaigning organisation JVP, and the smaller – and younger – direct action-focused activism of IfNotNow. Their tactics also varied (and reflected their origins, goals, and constituents): J Street, for example, sent more than 600 members to Capitol Hill in order to hand-deliver a petition signed by 40,000 people against Friedman's nomination to Senate offices.[13] IfNotNow, on the other hand, vocally disrupted Friedman's confirmation hearing, and denounced his nomination as representing 'the moral failure of the Jewish communal establishment'; Trump and Netanyahu, they declared, are 'two sides of the same coin'.[14] The emergence of this, very public, 'American Jewish conflict over Israel' – including similar developments elsewhere, like in Britain – is examined in more depth in Chapter 3.

Another significant subject highlighted by Friedman's nomination is Israel's transformation into a partisan issue in US politics. This was made plain in both the Senate confirmation hearing – where the ambassador-to-be was repeatedly and strongly criticised by Democrats – as well as during the wider debate surrounding his nomination. It wasn't just the Foreign Relations Committee that divided along partisan lines: the Senate's final confirmation of Friedman was a roll call vote, described by news website *Politico* as 'an unusual step', since US ambassadors 'have traditionally been approved by voice vote or through unanimous consent' because of the 'strong bipartisan support' for Israel.[15]

Concerns over the end of such bipartisan unity over Israel were explicitly expressed in the confirmation hearing itself. In explaining why many of the senators were posing 'detailed questions' to Friedman about his past statements, Chris Murphy (D-Conn.) bemoaned the fact that 'Israel has become another political football'.[16] He went on: 'What was most important in the past was keeping our support of Israel out of the political playing field and today that is not the case'. In the 'short time' he had been 'in public service', the senator continued, 'Israel has gone from being an issue that unites us to an issue that is used in political campaigns in order to divide us'. The worry for the likes of Murphy then, was that Friedman – through his public positions and past rhetoric – was both part of the problem, but could also hinder efforts to stop or slow this trend.

The fight over Friedman was only the latest episode to suggest that Israel no longer enjoys the bipartisan consensus in US politics that many had assumed was unshakeable (and this will be examined further in Chapter 4). Recall the very public fight over the Iran deal in 2015, which saw the Israeli prime minister directly fighting a foreign policy goal of the US president, or the way in which Bernie Sanders' leadership bid in the Democratic primaries acted as a megaphone for those within the party who want a tougher line when it comes to Israeli policies. Meanwhile, polls suggest the partisan divide is here to stay: in a February 2017 Gallup survey, 61 per cent of Democrats backed 'establishing an independent Palestinian state on the West Bank and Gaza Strip', compared to just 25 per cent of Republicans.[17] That same month, the results of a national poll by YouGov was published, in which American adults were asked to rate whether a country was an ally or enemy of the US on a five-point scale. Israel dropped to 16th place from sixth in 2014, a significant enough development – but even more striking was the vast disparity between Republicans and Democrats, who placed Israel fifth and 28th respectively.[18]

Israel's deteriorating image amongst the liberal left, or progressives, is a phenomenon that looks impossible to reverse – not least because of a catalysing factor in the aforementioned processes of fracture and partisan divides: Donald Trump.[19] Speaking to the *Jerusalem Post* in April 2017, Israel's Consul-General in New York, Dani Dayan, told the paper that the divisions in US society post-Trump's election victory were impacting on Israel's status as a bipartisan issue. 'It's more challenging these days than ever', he said, 'because everything is partisan in this country now: abortion is partisan, guns are partisan, capital punishment is partisan and lately even the weather [global warming] became a partisan issue in America.' He added: 'In this landscape, keeping Israel as virtually the only nonpartisan issue in American politics is tremendously challenging.'[20] That same week, writing in *Newsweek*, Dayan acknowledged 'the perception that Israel is increasingly becoming an exclusive cause of the political Right.'[21]

The 'Trump factor' is not just about the more general polarisation in US politics; it is also about the support for Israel expressed by the president and his close advisers during the US election campaign, and since Trump took office. While Trump has not, thus far, given Israel carte blanche in the way that some on the country's nationalist far right had hoped, his administration – both in policy and personnel terms – is sympathetic to Benjamin Netanyahu's coalition government. From Trump's December 2017 recognition of Jerusalem as Israel's capital, to the focus on 'economic peace' rather than territorial concessions, even the modest amount of diplomatic pressure applied by Barack Obama on the Israeli government is, for now, a distant memory. But the apparent common cause between Trump's White House and the Israeli right is not all good news for Israel's supporters: as Brandeis University professor Jonathan Sarna told Deutsche Welle, 'there is fear that people will say "I hate Trump, Trump loves Israel, therefore I hate Israel".'[22] Though this is too simplistic, as I will argue in Chapter 4, the Trump presidency both represents and will serve to accelerate growing divisions in the American Jewish community and amongst progressives over Israel.

I chose to begin this book with the story of Friedman's nomination, confirmation hearing, and approval, because of the way in which it was a microcosm of the important trends and developments in Palestine/Israel and in the US that are the focus of this book: a confident, Israeli right wing consolidating a de facto, single apartheid state; fragmentation amongst the US Jewish community over Israel and Zionism, and the end to bipartisan support for Israel. However, there is one final element to this story

I wish to highlight. Discussions about an increasingly divided Jewish community – in the US, UK and elsewhere – over Israel, as well as Israel's deteriorating 'brand' amongst liberals, are often characterised by the exclusion of Palestinian voices.

Though that may sound counter-intuitive, in reality, Palestinians are still all too often absent from these conversations, whether they are conducted in the op-ed pages, academia, or the corridors of Capitol Hill. In recent years, however, Palestinians – students, scholars, and activists – have forced themselves on to the agenda, through organising, determination, intelligence, creativity, and moral clarity. At Friedman's confirmation hearing, Palestinian voices *were* heard – an interruption that embodied the way in which marginalised history and experience can force itself into view. On one level, Friedman's appointment as American ambassador to Israel was a grim reminder of the power enjoyed by the practitioners of contemporary colonialism and their allies; below the surface, however, it was also a story about cracks in Israel's international pillars of support that, should they widen, could be instrumental in the move towards a Palestine beyond apartheid. But first, we must take stock of the grim situation on the ground at it stands today.

1

Reality check: Palestine/Israel is already a single (apartheid) state

Once we recognize that the situation in the [occupied Palestinian] territories is one of de facto annexation, it becomes clear that Israeli rule there is no longer temporary ... A situation that was meant to be temporary has become indefinite in duration.[1]

– Aeyal Gross, *Haaretz*, 27 October 2015

The people of Israel ... ask to empower settlements all over Israel – in the Galilee, the Negev and in Judea and Samaria [the West Bank] – and we will keep on doing so.[2]

– Member of Knesset Moti Yogev, 2 February 2017

It was 4.30am on 27 July 2010 when 1,300 armed Israeli police officers descended upon al-Araqib, a small, impoverished Bedouin Palestinian village in the Negev region of southern Israel.[3] After blocking the entrance to the village, Israeli forces – including mounted cavalry, bulldozers, and helicopters – forcibly removed residents from their homes, including 'children and elderly people'.[4] By the end of the raid, the Israeli authorities had destroyed some 45 homes, leaving more than 300 people homeless, half of them children under 16-years-old. The bulldozers did not spare animal pens and chicken coops, and hundreds of trees were uprooted (for 'replanting elsewhere').[5]

According to one resident, the police officers and inspectors smiled as they demolished the village, and 'made victory signs with their hands after the destruction'.[6] A village spokesperson told the media: 'Today we got a close glimpse of the government's true face. We were stunned to witness the violent force being used. The black-clad special unit forces are the true face of [then Minister of Foreign Affairs, Avigdor] Lieberman's democracy'.[7] Eyewitnesses told CNN that they saw 'busloads of civilians who cheered as the dwellings were demolished'.[8] Just two days before the pre-dawn raid on al-Araqib, Israeli Prime Minister Benjamin Netanyahu told government colleagues that a Negev 'without a Jewish majority' could constitute a 'palpable threat' to the state.[9]

The story of al-Araqib's residents is an all too familiar one for many Palestinian citizens of Israel: forcible displacement from their ancestral lands in the years after the creation of the State of Israel, broken promises by the state, land appropriation for 'security purposes', and a bureaucratic system designed to thwart any attempts by the indigenous population to claim their rights.[10] In more recent times, Israeli authorities have ramped up their efforts at preventing al-Araqib's residents from returning to their land, including by spraying toxic chemicals on cultivated fields and ploughing up crops. In addition, the state and Jewish National Fund (JNF) have spearheaded a foresting project intended to plant 'one million trees on the western land of the village'.[11]

Some 90,000 Bedouin Palestinians live in dozens of so-called 'unrecognised' villages across the Negev. Though they constitute 25 per cent of the population of the northern Negev, Bedouin 'occupy less than 2 percent of its land'.[12] Meanwhile, in recent years, Israeli authorities 'have allocated large tracts of land in this region, and public funds, for the creation of private ranches and farms'.[13] According to a Human Rights Watch (HRW) document in 2010, out of 59 such 'individual farms' in the Negev, only one is 'allocated to a Bedouin family and the rest to Jewish families'.[14] In the words of HRW researcher Joe Stork, 'Israel employs systematically discrimin-inatory policies in the Negev. It is tearing down historic Bedouin villages before the courts have even ruled on pending legal claims, and is handing out Bedouin land to allow Jewish farmers to set up ranches'.[15]

Just a few days before the bulldozers went to work in al-Araqib, a similar scene had played out in the West Bank, as Israeli authorities tore down Palestinian homes en masse in al-Farisiya, a herding community in the northern Jordan Valley. On 19 July, Israeli forces invaded the village and destroyed more than 70 structures in one fell swoop, including 'homes, stables, sheds, water tanks, two tons of animal fodder, fertilizer and wheat'.[16] Israeli authorities also targeted eight kitchens and ten bathrooms.[17] The mass demolitions left more than 100 Palestinians homeless, half of whom were children. Among the items destroyed were water tanks and irrigation pipes donated by global charity Oxfam; at the time, its advocacy officer Cara Flowers said the area looked like 'a natural disaster had taken place'.[18] Flowers added: 'With no access to shelter, water or fodder for their goat and sheep herds, an entire community is being forced to leave their land'. Just over two weeks later, Israeli forces returned and destroyed 27 tents provided by the Red Cross to residents who had been left homeless by the initial demolition raid on 19 July.[19]

Israeli authorities targeted al-Farisiya on the grounds that the structures had been built 'illegally', that is to say, without an Israeli-issued permit.[20] Under the Oslo Accords, the West Bank and Gaza Strip were divided into so-called Areas A, B and C, as a way of delineating where the Palestinian Authority could exercise limited autonomy over civil affairs. In Area C, the Israeli military retained full control of security and civil affairs. Therefore, in Area C – where al-Farisiya is located – Palestinians must obtain building permits from the Israeli occupation authorities. The catch? These permits are almost impossible to come by. In July 2016, European Union diplomat Lars Faaborg-Andersen told the Israeli parliament that out of 2,000 permit applications by Palestinians from 2009 to 2013, only 34 were granted – less than 2 per cent.[21] During 2016, according to the Office of the UN Special Coordinator for the Middle East Peace Process (UNSCO), 91 per cent of 'applications for building permits in Palestinian communities in Area C were rejected'.[22] Meanwhile, UNSCO reported in May 2017, out of 94 submitted outline plans for Palestinian communities in Area C, only five have been approved by Israeli authorities.[23] The 'cumulative area' covered by Israeli-approved plans – where Palestinians can 'legally' build – is thus less than 1 per cent of Area C.[24]

In the Jordan Valley specifically, Palestinians are denied access to and/or use of 78.5 per cent of the entire area on various pretences: the municipal areas of illegal settlements, closed military zones, so-called 'state lands', and so on.[25] According to a 2017 report by The Aix Group, the Palestinian cultivated area in the Jordan Valley is only 37–40 per cent of the total, 'due to extensive cultivation' carried out by Israeli settlers.[26] The average Israeli settler, moreover, 'has almost 10 times more available water than the average Palestinian living in the area'.[27] Speaking to Oxfam, Ali Zohdi, a herder and resident of al-Farisiya, explained the difficulties faced by the villagers: 'Every time the army comes and demolishes the houses and animal pens here we rebuild, but they come and demolish again. Our life is the goats and the sheep, and without this source of income we lose our life'.[28] Meanwhile, as Oxfam noted, 'the nearby Israeli settlement of Rotem thrives'.

The piles of rubble and twisted metal left in al-Araqib and al-Farisiya over a few days in the summer of 2010 were a microcosm of the grim reality that has taken shape in Israel and the occupied Palestinian territory (oPt). For both Palestinian citizens in the Negev, and Palestinians in the West Bank under military rule, Israeli authorities carry out displacement and dispossession with a rubber stamp of 'due process'. The Green Line, the post-1949 armistice line that distinguishes between territory held by Israel before and after 1967, has been erased in practical terms; the reality on the ground is that of a single regime. In this territorial unit, Palestinians are subjected to institutionalised discrimination, whether they have Israeli citizenship or are under military occupation. Note the similarities between the events and their context in al-Araqib and al-Farisiya; indigenous Palestinian communities struggle for their very survival thanks to a legal system and bureaucratic apparatus shaped by Israel's explicitly discriminatory political priorities: Jewish homes are built, Palestinian homes are torn down.

*　*　*

June 2017 marked 50 years since the beginning of Israel's military occupation of the West Bank, including East Jerusalem, and the Gaza Strip (the constituent parts of the oPt). According to the International Committee of the Red Cross, this is the longest running military occupation in modern times.[29] Israel's military rule of the oPt has lasted for the vast majority of the state's entire, 70-year existence. Over the last five decades, Israeli authorities have pursued a de facto annexation of the oPt, advancing 'facts on the ground' even as various diplomatic initiatives have come and gone. Central to this long-term project of incorporating the territory conquered in 1967 into the fabric of the Israeli state are the settlements.

Today, there are more than 200 Israeli settlements in the oPt, including 137 state-sanctioned colonies (twelve of which are in East Jerusalem), and some 100 or so 'outposts', technically unauthorised settlements that have nevertheless benefitted from varying degrees of state support – and in some cases, received retroactive 'legalisation'.[30] *All* Israeli settlement activity in the oPt is a violation of international law, since the Fourth Geneva Convention prohibits an occupying power from transferring its citizens into the territory it occupies, an act proscribed as a war crime by the Rome Statute of the International Criminal Court. This has been the position of the United Nations Security Council, United Nations General Assembly, the International Criminal Court at The Hague, the High Contracting Parties to the Fourth Geneva Conventions, and others. Indeed, just a few weeks after the West Bank had been conquered in 1967, an Israeli government legal adviser explicitly stated that to colonise the occupied territory with civilians would contravene international law.[31]

There are now more than 400,000 Israeli settlers in the West Bank, and more than 200,000 in East Jerusalem.[32] Revealingly, the settler population has more than doubled since 1993, when the Oslo Accords were signed by Israel and the Palestine Liberation Organisation (PLO), with more than 50,000 settlement units built in the West Bank since 1995.[33] Even just during US President Barack Obama's two terms in office, a time when the White House invested a good deal of energy in the peace process, the West Bank settler population grew by more than 100,000 – a 20 per cent increase.[34] In 2016, the last year for which there are complete figures, construction on new settlement homes in the West Bank rose by 40 per cent compared to the previous year.[35] 2016's total of 2,630 housing units was the second highest number of construction starts for 15 years.[36]

In 2017, Israeli authorities proceeded with the establishment of a brand new settlement, in what was the first such move since 1992 (excluding the retroactive authorisation of outposts). The new settlement was established for settlers removed from the Amona outpost following a lengthy court battle, and, according to Israeli NGO Peace Now, is located 'deep in the West Bank', in a region that 'serves as focal point of settler land takeover and settler violence'.[37] Peace Now added: 'the message that is being conveyed by the government of Israel is that it seeks to heighten its control over the West Bank and that it has whatsoever no intentions of ever evacuating the territories and achieving a political agreement with the Palestinians'. This move followed other steps intended to facilitate settlement expansion in recent years, such as the declaration in 2014 of almost 1000 acres near Bethlehem as so-called 'state land'.[38] In 2015, a total of 15,300 acres in the West Bank were 'ratified' as state land, the largest total since 2005.[39]

The approval of a new settlement followed hot on the heels of an even more significant move in February 2017, when Israel passed a new law designed to 'retroactively legalize the expropriation of privately owned Palestinian land'.[40] The so-called 'Regularization Law' was intended to pave the way for Israel to 'recognise thousands of illegally built Jewish settler homes', including in outposts.[41] Even *before* the law was passed, Israeli authorities had been trying to legalise about a quarter of the 100 or so outposts, effectively creating new settlements under the radar.[42] The new law was passed a mere six weeks after the adoption of UN Security Council Resolution 2334, condemning Israeli settlements in the oPt and other related violations of international law. Yet in the three months following Resolution 2334, Israel announced plans to build more than 5,000 settlement housing units, including 'deep inside the West Bank', in addition to building permits for 566 settlement units in East Jerusalem.[43]

One of the less well understood aspects of Israel's colonisation of the oPt is the size and significance of the settlements' physical footprint.[44] For while the built-up area of residential colonies constitutes 'only' 2 per cent of the West Bank, a full 39 per cent comes under settlement local authorities' jurisdiction – land which, according to UN OCHA, Israel has 'consistently refused to allocate … for Palestinian use'.[45] Palestinians in the oPt are also impacted by 'de facto settlement expansion' carried out by settlers, processes which typically 'lack official authorization', yet take place 'with the acquiescence, and at times the active support, of the Israeli authorities'.[46] Nor is it just about the settlements and their local authorities; the de facto annexation of the West Bank is also about transport networks, water resources, telecommunications infrastructure, and more. As Israeli journalist Uri Misgav wrote in March 2017, if an alien landed in the oPt 'and you told it that this was not part of Israel, it wouldn't understand what you were talking about'.[47] He continued:

> Two Supreme Court justices live there [the West Bank], as well as cabinet ministers, the Knesset speaker and other Knesset members, as well as a host of government officials. The Electric Corporation provides electricity, the Mekorot national water company supplies water, the National Roads Company looks after roads and the National Lottery erects and manages public

buildings. Factories, businesses and services operate there without limits, including schools and a university that are under the Ministry of Education's supervision. State-funded cultural institutions are compelled to perform in every settlement.

Palestinians, meanwhile, in 'those [same] areas', are 'also subject to Israeli law, but Israeli military law with military courts and directives issued by the regional military commander'.[48] It is this 'two-tier system of laws, rules, and services' (HRW) that places Israeli settlements in the oPt at the centre of an 'inherently discriminatory' system (Amnesty International), whose related human rights violations include 'arbitrary movement restrictions, demolitions, forcible transfer of Palestinian communities, [and] restricted access to natural resources for Palestinians'.[49] As of December 2016, the UN counted 682 physical obstacles to Palestinian movement in the West Bank, an extraordinary figure for an area smaller than Delaware.[50] These obstacles included checkpoints, earth mounds, road blocks, road gates, and trenches. The settlements are, in other words, at the very heart of Israel's military regime in the oPt; at any given time, more than half of the Israeli army's regular forces are in the West Bank – of whom, almost 80 per cent 'are involved in direct protection of the settlements'.[51] It is a picture of pure colonialism.

*   *   *

Israel's de-facto annexation of the oPt has proceeded over the past half century at varying speeds, and through different mechanisms. The only explicit act of annexation that has taken place (thus far) with respect to the territory conquered in 1967 – excluding the Occupied Syrian Golan Heights – was the area that became known as East Jerusalem, and this occurred almost immediately. In the first few weeks following the Six-Day War, Israeli officers 'toured' the area, 'maps in hand', in preparation for drawing Jerusalem's 'new borders'.[52] They had one clear goal: 'include the maximum territory with the minimum Palestinian population'. In total, Israel annexed 70 square kilometres to the municipal boundaries of Jerusalem, the vast majority of which was land that 'belonged to 28 villages in the West Bank' as well as 'to the municipalities of Bethlehem and Beit Jala'.[53] In 1968, more than 4,200 dunams – over 4 square kilometres – was expropriated from 'mainly Palestinian owners'.[54] Two years later, in August 1970, eight separate orders saw 10,000 dunams (10 square kilometres) of land in East Jerusalem confiscated and used to establish the settlements of Ramot, Gilo, East Talpiot and others.[55]

Yet even this act of annexation, further confirmed by a Basic Law adopted in 1980, was conducted in a way that sought to obfuscate the nature of what was taking place.[56] The relevant legislation, passed less than three weeks after the Six-Day War, was 'conducted in coded language', with the 'annexation directive ... integrated into an obscure statutory text' rather than being 'set forth in a special law'.[57] As related by veteran Israeli journalist Uzi Benziman, 'the Knesset procedure [similarly] bore an extremely low public profile', all of which was done 'in order to keep that act hidden from the international community'.[58] Indeed, the Foreign Ministry instructed its ambassadors and diplomats around the world to describe the annexation laws as 'municipal fusion', merely 'a practical necessity stemming from the desire to run the whole city properly'.[59] Nevertheless, on 4 July, the UN General Assembly condemned 'the measures taken by Israel to change the status of [Jerusalem]', measures it deemed 'invalid' and which it urged Israel to 'rescind'.[60]

In the West Bank, meanwhile, the establishment of civilian colonies began slowly. The first handful of settlements, located in the 'Gush Etzion' area of the West Bank south of Jerusalem, in Hebron, and in the Jordan Valley, were established by the Labor party.[61] By the time that Menachem Begin's Likud came to power in 1977, there were some two dozen settlements in the West Bank (excluding East Jerusalem), home to around 4,500 residents.[62] In 1981, by the end of Likud's first term in office, the number of settlements had more than doubled to 68, and the number of settlers quadrupled to 16,200.[63] During that period (1977–81), around 13 per cent of the West Bank was 'transferred to Israeli administrative control … through closure, requisition, or expropriation', as well as a third of the Gaza Strip.[64] A road network was constructed – 94 kilometres between 1979–81 – linking Jewish settlements up to one another and with Israeli communities inside the Green Line, while the Likud government also expanded 'the number of legal and administrative services which Israeli settlers in the territories could enjoy'.[65]

By the first half of the 1980s, some believed that the steps being taken by Israeli authorities in the oPt were leading to an irreversible fait accompli. In April 1982, former Arab affairs advisor to the Israeli PM, Shmuel Toledano predicted that 'within a few years, if anyone were to suggest giving up any part of the [occupied Palestinian] territories, the suggestion would be regarded as no different than that of giving up part of the Negev or the Galilee'.[66] A few months later, former deputy mayor of Jerusalem Meron Benvenisti warned that the settlement enterprise in the oPt was already so well advanced that it was 'five minutes to midnight' in terms of preventing an irreversible Israeli hold on the West Bank.[67] In 1983, Israeli journalist Amos Elon declared that, 'for all practical purposes [the oPt] have already been annexed to the State of Israel, perhaps irrevocably'.[68] Not all such predictions were warnings, of course: that same year, Likud deputy minister Michael Dekel vowed that 'within two years there will be 100,000 Jews in Judea and Samaria [the West Bank], then no Israeli Government will be able to agree to return that area to Arab control'.[69]

As the years went by, observers and journalists continued to repeat the same message. Shortly after the First Intifada had erupted in December 1987, Thomas Friedman observed in the *New York Times* how, 'for the past 20 years many Israelis have insisted on referring to the West Bank by its Biblical names "Judea and Samaria" and on viewing these occupied territories as integral parts of a Greater Israel. The Green Line, many Israelis said, did not exist for them anymore'.[70] More than a decade later, in June 1999, the same newspaper published an op-ed by journalist Anthony Lewis, who questioned what kind of Palestinian 'state' was emerging as a result of the Oslo Accords.[71] 'There will almost certainly be a Palestinian state', he wrote, 'but it will be a state of a peculiar kind.' Highlighting Israel's domination of the territory, Lewis referred back to the warnings of Benvenisti, noting that, while 'in formal terms … Israel will not govern all of historic Palestine', in terms of 'the realities on the ground … Benvenisti was right.'

And on it went – in 2006, Israeli NGO B'Tselem declared that Israel had 'de facto annexed the Jordan Valley', having 'instituted a regime of permits and harsh restrictions on the movement of Palestinians' in the area.[72] More recently, the organisation highlighted 'an Israeli policy to concentrate Palestinian activity in enclaves throughout the West Bank and de-facto annex the rest of the land to Israel proper'.[73] In 2007, the *Financial Times* presented a map of the West Bank it said showed a territory 'in which 2.5m Palestinians are confined to dozens of enclaves separated by Israeli roads, settlements, fences and military zones'.[74] In 2009, former director of the Institute for Jewish Policy Research, Antony Lerman, writing in the *Guardian*, urged readers to acknowledge that 'one state exists'.[75] He added: 'It has not been formally proclaimed. It has no legal status. No one wants to acknowledge it. But it's hard to see Israeli control of the area of the pre-1967 state, the West Bank and Gaza as constituting anything other than one, de facto state.'

For some Israeli leaders and politicians, even this de-facto single state reality is not enough; they want the official annexation of some, or even all, of the West Bank. Israeli economy minister Naftali Bennett, head of the Jewish Home party, is one of the most well-known, and outspoken, advocates of such an approach, but he's not alone.[76] In December 2016, Israeli public security minister Gilad Erdan said Israel should 'announce a full annexation of settlement blocs' in response to the passing of UN Security Council Resolution 1443.[77] In February 2017, Israeli justice minister Ayelet Shaked expressed opposition to annexing the entirety of the West

Bank, but affirmed that 'we definitely need to annex Area C', some 60 per cent of the West Bank.[78] Her government colleague, deputy foreign minister Tzipi Hotovely, has no such qualms; that same month, she recommended that Israel work towards officially annexing all of the West Bank: 'It can be done in a gradual manner', she said, 'starting with the greater Jerusalem area and from there applying Israeli law on the entire settlement enterprise and later to sovereignty from the sea to the Jordan.'[79]

This type of 'creeping annexation' is exactly what some fear – and others hope – has been unfolding in the last few years. According to Michael Schaeffer Omer-Man, editor in chief of +972 *Magazine*, the likes of Ayelet Shaked 'make no secret of their intentions to annex the West Bank to Israel – slowly.'[80] He went on: 'They recognize that neither mainstream Israel nor the international community is ready to accept sweeping annexation; incremental annexation is a far more effective, and achievable goal.' Before noting some recent legislative developments, however, it is important to note that Israel has long used 'different instruments' in order to apply 'parts of its domestic legal system to the territories occupied in 1967'.[81] These have included the Supreme Court's exercise of jurisdiction over the oPt, as well as the application of 'a significant bulk of Israeli domestic law' to the oPt through both military order and legislative action. As 'The Nakba Files' blog noted, 'because these laws mostly apply to people rather than territory, Israel preserves the fiction that it is not engaged in annexation by arguing that if the settlers were to be evacuated there would no longer be any basis to apply these laws in the territories'.[82]

The first half of 2017 witnessed an acceleration of legislative efforts at creeping annexation. The aforementioned settlement 'Regularisation Bill', for example, was not just a significant land grab – it was also 'the first time since Israel annexed East Jerusalem in 1967 that Israel has acted to extend Israeli law to the occupied West Bank'.[83] Then in June, Israeli justice minister Ayelet Shaked announced that all government-sponsored legislation will 'henceforth explicitly mention applicability to residents of West Bank settlements', justifying the move in the name of 'equality' for settlers (compared to other Israeli citizens).[84] Praising the law, Israeli minister Yariv Levin said 'we are not seeking "creeping annexation"; we are looking for justice for the residents'. But, he then added, 'if there are those saying that through legislation we are advancing "creeping annexation" – we won't argue'. Shaked and Levin's move was described by the *Jerusalem Post* as a 'loophole' enabling 'the bulk of new Israeli laws [to be applied] to Area C of the West Bank without formally annexing the region to sovereign Israel'.[85]

The picture I have sketched out thus far, that of five decades of colonisation of the oPt and incremental, de facto annexation, has led many – for a while now – to assert that the so-called 'two-state solution' is imperilled, or mortally wounded. Putting aside for the moment the fact that different people mean different things by a 'two-state solution' (I will address this in the next chapter), it is clear that the goal of a sovereign Palestinian state in the oPt is, at the very least, complicated by Israel's 'facts on the ground'. Indeed, it can be argued that actions taken and policies adopted by various Israeli governments since 1967 have been pursued specifically in order to *thwart* the emergence or viability of an independent, sovereign Palestinian state. There is, however, an important piece of the puzzle that is often neglected in a debate focusing on practicalities and settlement expansion, and on whether there is some kind of cut-off point beyond which Israel's de-facto annexation of the West Bank is a fait accompli from which there is no coming back.

In 1985, Professor Ian Lustick – a renowned Middle East scholar – wrote a report commissioned by the US government's Defense Intelligence Agency titled 'The "Irreversibility" of Israel's annexation of the West Bank and Gaza Strip: Critical Evaluation'.[86] It is an extraordinary read, not least because of the ways in which many of the key arguments are still repeated more than 30 years later. At the time, there were some 40,000 settlers in the West Bank, in addition to more than 100,000 in East Jerusalem.[87] It is tempting, in light of the fact that the West Bank settler population has increased 10-fold since then, to conclude that, if Israel's 'annexation' of the territories was debateable in 1985, it is certainly a done deal in 2018. But there is, perhaps, a more instructive lesson from Lustick's report.

Lustick argued that 'approaching the problem with the image of a single dramatic "point of no return" obscures more than it illuminates', adding that the notion of some single such point 'is more important for the role it plays as a polemical device, to exhort or discourage opponents of annexation (depending upon the speaker), rather than a useful conceptual category for discussing the likely or possible future of the areas'.[88] Rather, Lustick argued, 'Israel's relationship to the West Bank and Gaza Strip is plotted along a continuum interrupted by two thresholds, an "institutional" threshold and a "psycho-cultural" threshold'. It is the latter that is more significant, since it represents 'the point at which the absorption of the territory ceases to be problematic for the overwhelming majority of citizens of the central state, i.e. when the question of the "future" of the territory is removed from the national political agenda, when no ambitious politician would consider questioning the permanence of the integration of the territory'.

Polls in recent years suggest that the 'cultural threshold' is being, or has been, crossed. In one survey conducted in October-November 2016, among a representative sample of 1,027 Israeli Jews, respondents were asked 'whether to the best of their knowledge Israel has formally declared its sovereignty over Judea and Samaria [the West Bank]'.[89] Only about half of those polled correctly answered 'no' (and only 40 per cent of those aged 18–29), with the other half split between 'yes' and 'don't know'. The poll also asked Israeli Jews 'whether they believe certain settlements in the West Bank lie within the territory of the State of Israel'. The eight settlements selected varied in terms of size and location – some 'lie deep in the West Bank' while 'others are more proximate to the Green Line'. Strikingly, 'there was not a single settlement which a majority of respondents thought was outside the territory of the State of Israel'.

21

In May 2017, ahead of the fiftieth anniversary of the Six-Day War, the respected 'Peace Index' poll conducted by Tel Aviv University asked: 'In your opinion, should or should not Israel's control of Judea and Samaria [the West Bank] be defined as an occupation?'[90] Only 31.1 per cent of Israeli Jews replied in the affirmative. A year earlier, the poll produced a similar result; asked 'is it right or not right to define Israel's control of the territories as an "occupation"', only 22.7 per cent answered 'yes', while 71.5 per cent responded 'no'.[91] By way of giving a different angle, in 2015, a poll specifically of Israeli teachers discovered that 57 per cent of them did not know about the Green Line 'or how it was determined'.[92] When asked, however, whether the time has come to *officially* annex *all* the territories conquered in 1967, Israeli Jews – according to the May 2017 poll – are divided: 44.4 per cent said 'yes', and 45 per cent said 'no'.[93]

*   *   *

For now, at least, neither Israeli politicians, nor the public, are decisively in favour of formal annexation (as we will explore further in the next chapter), and thus the status quo remains a de facto apartheid, one-state reality in all of historic Palestine. Inside the pre-1967 lines, Palestinian citizens of Israel face 'institutional and societal discrimination' (the words of the US State Department) that affects them in areas of life as diverse as land ownership and housing, through to education budgets, family life, and political expression.[94] In East Jerusalem, Palestinian 'residents' are subject to home demolitions and settler takeovers, and discrimination in municipal services. Throughout the West Bank, meanwhile, Palestinians are subject to a military regime that facilitates land colonisation by the state and settlers, restricts the indigenous population's freedom of movement, and convicts hundreds each year in sham courts. In the Gaza Strip, meanwhile, almost 2 million Palestinians are fenced-off and blockaded, cut off from Palestinians in the West Bank, after years of deliberate de-development and bloody assaults.[95]

This de facto single state exists for, and preserves the ability of Israeli Jews to enjoy rights and privileges denied to Palestinians. The laws and policies differ, but from the Negev to the southern Hebron hills, from the Galilee to the Jordan Valley, and from East Jerusalem to the Gaza Strip, Palestinians confront, in law and in practice, a political system defined by their dispossession, segregation, exclusion, and brutalisation. Let's zoom in for a moment, to understand what this de facto single state reality looks like on the ground. Take Umm al-Hiran, a Bedouin Palestinian village in the Negev targeted for destruction by Israeli authorities in order to implement a long-standing plan to expel its residents and replace the village with a Jewish community.[96] Umm al-Hiran's residents, remember, are Israeli citizens – and yet they find themselves dispossessed in what Israeli legal advocacy organisation Adalah called 'a clear case of dispossession and displacement for strictly racial reasons'. On 18 January 2017, hundreds of Israeli police officers descended on the village in order to carry out an initial round of demolitions; during the raid, they shot and killed local resident Yaqub Abu Qi'an while he was driving in his car.[97]

Not far from Umm al-Hiran – about a dozen or so kilometres north-east – is another Palestinian village threatened with destruction, but this time in the southern Hebron hills area of the West Bank.[98] All of Susya's homes have been deemed to have been built 'illegally', thanks to its location in 'Area C' of the West Bank, where Palestinians find it almost impossible to obtain the required permit from the Israeli occupation bureaucrats. In other words, as HRW has described, 'in both the Negev and the West Bank, Israel authorities apply zoning laws in a discriminatory manner that frequently restricts the ability of Arabs to build lawfully'.[99] So, while there are indeed important differences between the plight of Umm al-Hiran and Susya – and those differences matter, not least with respect to options of and strategies for resistance – they are part of the one, same story: namely, an Israeli government policy that 'comes at the expense of the people who live in those spaces, their homes destroyed in order to make room for the expansion of Jewish-only communities'.[100]

The stories abound. In the Jordan Valley, which runs all the way down the eastern most flank of historic Palestine, in today's West Bank, Israeli authorities are displacing Palestinians while Jewish settlements flourish. In 2016, Israeli occupation forces conducted dozens of 'destructive [demolition] raids' in the Jordan Valley, targeting not just homes and agricultural facilities, but also 'water networks'.[101] As Palestinian homes are torn down, meanwhile, Israeli colonies continue to flourish: in December 2017, the Israeli government released a plan to build three brand new settlements in the Jordan Valley, expand pre-existing ones, and triple the region's total settler population.[102] Or take Silwan, a Palestinian neighbourhood of East Jerusalem, where eviction cases have been filed against 67 households (as of November 2016), threatening more than 300 with displacement.[103] In parallel to these disturbing developments, settler groups, with the backing of various government bodies, are expanding their presence in the area through 'tourism' and 'archaeology' projects, in addition to fortified housing.[104]

The Gaza Strip, of course, is unique – but it is a mistake to consider it outside of the framework of this apartheid regime. Its isolation goes back some three decades, when, in 1989, 'Israel introduced a system whereby only Palestinians vetted by the Shin Bet security service and in possession of magnetic cards were permitted to travel to the West Bank via Israel'.[105] By the mid-1990s, under then Prime Minister Yitzhak Rabin, a perimeter fence had been built around the Gaza Strip, a precursor to the Separation Wall that would follow, some years later, in the West Bank. Since Israel's unilateral removal of settlers and troop redeployment in 2005 (the so-called 'disengagement'), the Gaza Strip has remained under Israeli military occupation, a position affirmed by the UN Security Council, UN General Assembly, and Office of the Prosecutor of the International Criminal Court.[106] It remains, with respect to international law, part of the single territorial unit that is the oPt. As part of historic Palestine, it has become a way for Israel

24

to fence off some 2 million Palestinians, the majority of whom are children, and 1948 refugees. 'I would like Gaza to sink into the sea,' Yitzhak Rabin famously said, and Israel has settled for the next best thing; trapping its unwanted Palestinians – and the 'demographic threat' they represent – behind fortified fences, watchtowers, and automatically triggered machine guns.[107]

* * *

The reality sketched out in this chapter is not new, nor did it emerge overnight; it developed steadily, openly, and indeed, has been copiously documented by Palestinians, Israelis, and international observers and human rights groups. Israel's incorporation of the oPt – its land and resources, at any rate, not its Palestinian inhabitants – into the fabric of the state and its infrastructure, the successive Israeli governments' policies that de facto annexed territory seized in 1967, has proceeded in plain view. In 2009, almost a decade ago now, Israeli political geographer Oren Yiftachel wrote how 'persisting colonial and oppressive practices are working to further Judaise contested space and deny Palestinians – on both sides of the Green Line – their legitimate rights.'[108] Yiftachel called this process 'creeping apartheid', which he defined as 'an undeclared yet structural process through which new, oppressive sets of political geographic relations are being institutionalised for Jews and Palestinians living under the Israeli regime between Jordan and the [Mediterranean] sea'. This process has, he said, led to 'the merging of the colonised West Bank, the besieged Gaza Strip and Israel proper into one system, ultimately controlled by the Jewish state'.

Israel has undeniably benefitted from the fact that, while the oPt has been *de-facto* annexed to form part of a single regime, there has been no *formal* annexation (excluding East Jerusalem). This is no accident – it is a 'deliberate ambiguity' based on 'creating a framework of temporary military occupation that falls in line with international law (and as such is considered a legitimate occupation), but which de facto promotes permanent control and annexation'.[109] International law scholar Valentina Azarova has described the situation in the oPt as one of 'an unlawfully prolonged occupation', which 'arises when an occupying state seeks to permanently transform the international status, government or demographic character of a foreign territory, including through de jure or de facto annexation'.[110] In October 2017, senior UN human rights expert Michael Lynk used a periodic report on the situation in the oPt to similarly declare that Israel's occupation had 'crossed a red line into illegality'.[111]

But the fact that, until now, the West Bank remains de facto, rather than de jure, annexed, is – paradoxically – one of the reasons why Israel has been able to advance its colonisation project so effectively. As Israeli international law expert Aeyal Gross wrote in his recent book, 'The Writing on the Wall', 'Israel acts in the OPT as a sovereign insofar as it settles its citizens there and extends to them its laws on a personal and on a mixed personal/territorial basis.'[112]

> Yet, insofar as the territory has not been formally annexed and insofar as this exercise of sovereignty falls short of giving the Palestinian residents citizenship rights, Israel is not acting as a sovereign. In the OPT, then, Israel enjoys both the powers of an occupant and the powers of a sovereign, while Palestinians enjoy neither the rights of an occupied people nor the rights of citizenship. The implication is a matrix of control whereby Israel acts as both occupier and non-occupier, and as both sovereign and non-sovereign, one of the ways wherein *legal indeterminacy itself serves as a form of control.*[113]

A situation where 'a state, although empirically sovereign in a territory, deliberately abjured a claim to be the juridical sovereign precisely in order to avoid the international obligations that would pertain if it were' is unusual, perhaps unique.[114] But over the last half century, Israel has exploited the 'difference between empirical and juridical sovereignty' for its own 'strategic advantage'.

Another seeming paradox is that Israel has been aided in its creation of a de facto, single regime in all of historic Palestine by the peace process, which – dating it from the Madrid Conference and Oslo Accords of the early 1990s – has existed in various forms for a quarter century; half the entire duration of the military occupation of the oPt. The almost three decades of (primarily US-managed) talks and diplomacy have played a crucial role in helping Israel pursue de facto annexation by effectively neutralising any potential international opposition to such a process. As Israeli journalist Chemi Shalev wrote in 2014:

> with the benefit of hindsight it is hard to counter the argument that the perennial search for a two state[sic] solution has served as a cover for a de-facto annexation of the West Bank that absolves Israel of the need to grant the Palestinians full civil rights. Without the dangled promise of eventual peace, it would be much harder for Israel to look in the mirror and rebuff the claims of apartheid.[115]

This point is ably illustrated by recalling the warnings issued by senior international diplomats – and even Israelis – in recent years, about the supposed dangers posed to Israel by a failure to achieve a two-state solution with the Palestinians. During a March 2017 visit to the region, British foreign minister Boris Johnson told local media that 'you have to have a two-state solution or else you have a kind of apartheid system'.[116] Johnson, a declared friend of Israel, was echoing a similarly-expressed warning by John Kerry, who, as US Secretary of State in 2014, described the two-state solution as the only viable option: 'Because a unitary state winds up either being an apartheid state with second-class citizens – or it ends up being a state that destroys the capacity of Israel to be a Jewish state'.[117] Even former Israeli premier Ehud Barak, speaking in Herzliya in 2010, had said much the same: 'as long as in this territory west of the Jordan river there is only one political entity called Israel it is going to be either non-Jewish, or non-democratic', adding: 'If this bloc of millions of Palestinians cannot vote, that will be an apartheid state.'[118]

Yet what is important to note here is that this picture painted of a single political entity in which millions of Palestinians cannot vote actually describes the *status quo* (of some time now), not a future scenario. And one of the key ways in which this artificial distinction between status quo and future is maintained, a crucial part of how the illusion of impermanence with respect to Israel's hold on the oPt is preserved, is the politics of the peace process. Even though Johnson, Kerry, and Barak are describing a situation that – regardless of the lack of Israel's *formal* annexation of the oPt – corresponds to the reality on the ground, it is the prospect of a 'two-state solution', the idea that Israel's presence and control over the oPt still have to be determined or are, in some way, temporary or negotiable, which keeps the same international diplomats from denouncing Israeli apartheid as it exists *today*.

This illusion is now proving increasingly difficult to uphold, for a combination of reasons. First, the collapse of US-supervised talks between Israel and the Palestinians in 2014 – and the failure ever since to recommence anything like as substantial an effort – has threatened the very credibility of the peace process itself. The absence of talks imperils Israel's strategic ambiguity with regards to the status of the oPt, and also threatens to create an atmosphere where punitive measures are on the table; as Tzipi Livni instructively argued in 2011, 'restarting negotiations would stop the snowball rolling towards us at the UN and in general'.[119] She added: 'The diplomatic impasse is leading to diplomatic isolation.' Second, at the time of writing Benjamin Netanyahu has been prime minister of Israel since March 2009 – almost a decade. Netanyahu has, at most, paid lip service to a 'two-state solution' (more of which in the next chapter), and a number of his government ministers over the years openly and proudly opposed Palestinian statehood, backing partial or total, formal annexation of the oPt. Finally, a series of recent, significant anniversaries, have highlighted the length of time that Israel has held the oPt, and drawn attention to the plight of the Palestinians more generally: 2017 saw the 50th anniversary of the Six-Day War, the centenary of the Balfour Declaration, and the 70th anniversary of the UN's Partition Plan for Palestine.

This combination, of a comatose peace process, a rejectionist and intransigent Israeli government, as well as a succession of significant anniversaries, has made it harder to deny the obvious – that Israel has, in the last 50 years, established a de facto, apartheid regime in historic Palestine – and indeed, that reality has been laid increasingly bare. Such a perspective also changes how one views the aforementioned developments that some have called 'creeping annexation', instead characterising such steps as 'just the latest attempts to renegotiate and redraw the lines between legal regimes to consolidate conquest and demographic transformation'.[120] Ultimately, however, the key to understanding how – and why – Israel has established this de facto, apartheid single state can be found in remarks by former premier, and then foreign minister, Yitzhak Shamir, when discussing in March 1983 the status of the oPt, Israel, Shamir said, 'did not conquer the territories from their legal owners, but liberated them from countries that conquered them in 1948. We have not "annexed" them, and shall not "annex" them. They are part of Eretz Yisrael [the Land of Israel], and what is part of your country you do not annex.'[121]

It is impossible to understand Israel's approach to the oPt, and the trajectory that successive governments have taken over the last half-century, without placing such developments in the wider context of the Zionist movement's efforts to create a 'Jewish state' in Palestine. While for its founding thinkers and activists, Zionism was about Jewish nationalism and self-determination, for Palestinians it was experienced from the very beginning as displacement, discrimination and dehumanisation. In 1897, when the first Zionist Congress was held in Basle, the population of Palestine was approximately 96 per cent Arab and 4 per cent Jewish.[122] Even by 1947, after waves of Jewish immigration, Palestinian Arabs still constituted two-thirds of Palestine's population. There was, inevitably, only one way of establishing a Jewish state in Palestine; removing the land's non-Jewish inhabitants. Such a step, in the words of Palestinian historian Nur Masalha, was 'the logical outgrowth of the ultimate goal of the Zionist movement, which was the establishment of a Jewish state through colonization and land acquisition – in other words, through a radical ethno-religious-demographic transformation of a country, the population of which had been almost entirely Arab at the start of the Zionist venture'.[123] Masalha's conclusions are echoed by Israeli journalist and historian Tom Segev: '"disappearing" the Arabs lay at the heart of the Zionist dream, and was also a necessary condition of its realization'.[124]

Over a period lasting roughly two years, bisected by the establishment of the State of Israel in May 1948, around 85–90 per cent of Palestinians who lived in what became the new 'Jewish state' were expelled (some 700–800,000).[125] Around four out of five Palestinian towns and villages were destroyed (or repopulated by Jewish Israelis), while in cities such as Haifa and Acre, Palestinian neighbourhoods were emptied, and resettled.[126] 'Beyond the hypocritical rhetoric and naïve phraseology', Israeli scholar Ze'ev Sternhell wrote, 'one basic fact stands out: the significance of Zionism was the conquest of land and the creation of an independent state through work and settlement, if possible, or by force, if necessary'.[127] In his seminal essay, 'Zionism from the Standpoint of Its Victims', Edward Said noted how 'all the constitutive energies of Zionism were premised on ... the functional absence of "native people" in Palestine'.[128]

> Institutions were built deliberately shutting out the natives, laws were drafted when Israel came into being that made sure the natives would remain in their 'nonplace', Jews in theirs, and so on. It is no wonder that today the one issue that electrifies Israel as a society is the problem of the Palestinians, whose negation is the most consistent thread running through Zionism.

Said was writing in the late 1970s, but, sadly, his diagnosis rings all too true some 40 years on, as we shall see in the next chapter.

2

The impasse in Israel

The maximum we are willing to give is far from the minimum the Palestinians are willing to take.

– MK Yoav Kish, May 2017[1]

We have to go from solving the problem, to living with the problem.

– Israeli economy minister Naftali Bennett, June 2013[2]

In Chapter 1, we took a hard look at the reality on the ground in Israel and the occupied Palestinian territory (oPt), an area which, over the last five decades, has been incrementally but undeniably fashioned into a single, apartheid regime by successive Israeli governments and state institutions. We looked at the facts; the history of settlement establishment and expansion, the means by which Israel has colonised and incorporated the oPt into the fabric of the state, and how the dispossession, displacement, and segregation of Palestinians is an ongoing process across the entirety of this de facto, single state. But how did we get here? And what are Israel's political leaders proposing by way of a solution? These are the questions that we will address in this chapter.

In Israeli politics today, there is an impasse with respect to the Palestinian question. It is a deadlock born out of one simple fact: the Israeli maximum on offer does not meet the Palestinian minimum, or the demands of international law. There are, of course, profound divisions amongst Israel's political parties about the best way forward – and we shall consider some of those disputes shortly. But before doing so, it is of vital importance to bear in mind the *commonalities* that unite Israel's main political leaders and factions, namely the belief in the *right* of the Jewish people to the entire land of *Eretz Yisrael* (Israel and the oPt, all of historic Palestine), and the denial of the right of the Palestinian people to self-determination. It is impossible to understand how we got to where we are today without grasping this uncomfortable truth, and nor is it possible to grasp why successive attempts at peace talks have failed without facing up to this reality.

Israeli politics is notoriously volatile; fragile coalitions can reach crisis point and collapse, new splinter factions and personality-driven parties can emerge – then disappear – and anyone making predictions about the longevity of a particular government can be made to look very foolish indeed. With those caveats in mind, it is, however, possible to paint a picture of the current, principal political forces in the Knesset based on the kind of solutions or framework with which they view the Palestinian question. Individuals and party leaders, governments and coalitions can change; but it is possible to identify broader categories of strategy and vision, with respect to the Palestinians, within which you will find the main Israeli political streams and parties.

Maintain the status quo

At the time of writing, Israeli prime minister Benjamin Netanyahu has been in power since 2009, in addition to the three years he served during his first term as premier 1996–9. His approach to the Palestinian issue has thus had a significant impact on the trajectory of Israel's apartheid regime over the past decade, and even earlier. Netanyahu clearly opposes a sovereign Palestinian state in the oPt; his approach is best summarised as a desire to maintain the status quo – and (his own) power. His position is a matter of record, both in terms of rhetoric, and policy. In the final days of campaigning before the March 2015 election, for example, Netanyahu declared: 'We won't divide Jerusalem, we won't make concessions, we won't withdraw from land.'³ The next day, Netanyahu told an interviewer that a Palestinian state will not be established with him as PM.⁴

While such remarks could be downplayed as last-minute campaign trail bluster, Netanyahu made a more instructive comment in early 2017, when he told colleagues that what he was 'willing to give to the Palestinians is not exactly a state with full authority, but rather a state-minus, which is why the Palestinians don't agree [to it]'.⁵ Soon after, Michael Oren, a deputy minister in the prime minister's office, suggested that 'alternative solutions' should be looked at, including a scenario which 'may not conform to what we know as a two-state solution, but would enable the Palestinians to lead their lives in prosperity and security'.⁶ In May 2017, an unnamed Netanyahu aide affirmed this, telling *Foreign Policy* that '[Netanyahu] has always said it will be a state-minus'.⁷ There are echoes here of an interview Netanyahu gave to CNN in 2014, when he noted drily: 'I think we have to adjust our conceptions of sovereignty'.⁸

All of which is more than enough to cast into doubt Netanyahu's sincerity when expressing support for a Palestinian state in his oft-quoted Bar Ilan speech of 2009 – or, perhaps more instructively, raise significant questions about what exactly he envisages, or means, by a Palestinian 'state'.⁹ In that speech, the Israeli premier backed a 'Palestinian state', provided that the state would be demilitarised, and, 'if the Palestinians recognise Israel as the Jewish state'. Netanyahu has repeatedly insisted that 'Israel must retain the overriding security control over the entire area west of the Jordan River' *forever*.¹⁰ Netanyahu has also made clear that he sees Israel retaining all of Jerusalem as its 'undivided capital', in addition to major, so-called 'settlement blocs' (more on which later) in the southern, central and northern West Bank (Gush Etzion, Ma'ale Adumim, and Ariel respectively). Taken together, this is a blueprint for Palestinian cantons – combined with the demand for recognition of Israel as a 'Jewish state', this recipe for reservations is intended to be impossible for a Palestinian leadership to accept.

Netanyahu's position on the Palestinians is consistent with his Likud party's positions. In 1999, for example, Likud explicitly 'reject[ed] the establishment of a Palestinian Arab state west of the Jordan river', adding: 'The Palestinians can run their lives freely in the framework of self-rule, but not as an independent and sovereign state', with 'their activity … [to be] limited in accordance with imperatives of Israel's existence, security and national needs.'[11] In 2006, the Likud constitution affirmed 'the right of the Jewish people to the Land of Israel as an eternal, inalienable right, working diligently to settle and develop *all parts of the land of Israel*, and extending national sovereignty to them [my emphasis]'.[12] On 31 December 2017, the Likud Central Committee adopted a resolution urging unrestrained construction in settlements, and the annexation of West Bank land.[13]

Over the last decade, Netanyahu-led governments have pursued policies consistent with such a vision, expanding settlements all over the West Bank, including in more isolated colonies, and working to retroactively-approve settler 'outposts'. Before Netanyahu returned as premier in 2009, according to a settlement watchdog, the percentage of new housing starts on the eastern side of the Separation Wall was some 20 per cent of total settlement construction. Since then, however, that proportion has increased to 35 per cent (as of October 2016).[14] In June 2017, the Netanyahu government was reported to be set on advancing 2,500 housing units, 98 per cent of which were also east of the Wall, with 75 per cent 'located deep within the West Bank'.[15]

Such policies have only ever been – modestly and temporarily – diluted or held back when Israel has been required to demonstrate a show of 'restraint' for the sake of the peace process charade. While Netanyahu may have, begrudgingly, been forced to express verbal support in 2009 for a Palestinian state, the 'state' he has in mind is, in essence, a permanent version of the status quo. In other words, there are plenty of good reasons to believe Public Security Minister Gilad Erdan when he stated in February 2017: 'all the members of the cabinet oppose a Palestinian state, and the Prime Minister first among them.'[16]

Formal annexation (total/partial)

While Netanyahu is happy with the apartheid status quo, some of his ministerial colleagues, as well as influential movements both inside and outside of the Knesset, advocate the formal Israeli annexation of some, or even all, of the West Bank. In both cases, an important role is envisaged for Jordan, whether in terms of some kind of confederation with the West Bank cantons of Palestinian 'autonomy', or even with respect to some proposals for Palestinians in the West Bank to actually vote in Jordanian elections. Another important point to note about the pro-annexation camp is that the Gaza Strip is left out of the equation entirely, thus 'solving', so the thinking goes, one of the main challenges presented by annexation of all or part of the West Bank: demographics. Absorbing hundreds of thousands of Palestinians in the West Bank – with or without offering them Israeli citizenship – is one matter; but the annexationists do not even consider taking into account the two million Palestinian residents of the Gaza Strip.

Supporters of annexation can be found amongst Netanyahu's ministers – including from his own Likud party. In early 2017, Intelligence and Atomic Energy Minister Yisrael Katz urged the annexation of 'dozens of settlements in the Jerusalem area', including Ma'ale Adumim.[17] A few weeks later, Likud minister Ayoub Kara declared that 'Israel shouldn't apologize for intending to annex Judea and Samaria [the West Bank]. We should be determined to implement our right to these historic areas of our homeland.'[18] Minister Chaim Katz (no relation), meanwhile, was even blunter, speaking in December 2015: 'The land of Israel is whole. There is no Palestine,' he said.[19] 'Let the Palestinians go to Jordan, to Gaza, to Saudi Arabia, to Kuwait, to Egypt and to Iraq.' Perhaps one of the most vocal, pro-annexation voices within Likud is deputy foreign minister Tzipi Hotovely, who for years has urged the government to 'apply Israeli sovereignty over Judea and Samaria', giving its Palestinian residents 'full Israeli citizenship'.[20] In November 2016, she urged the annexation of 60 per cent ('Area C') of the West Bank, rather than its entirety, and a few months later, returned to a more comprehensive language: 'We need to go to a million settlers in Judea and Samaria – with a US embassy in Jerusalem. We need to think of new ways of thinking that will include Judea and Samaria under Israeli sovereignty forever,' she told a receptive audience in Washington DC.[21]

One of the most high-profile and consistent supporters of annexation is Jewish Home leader Naftali Bennett, whose party platform ahead of the 2015 elections backed the annexation of Area C of the West Bank. Bennett had attracted international attention as early as 2013, for his pro-annexation positions, and view that 'Palestinians living in Area C could either take Israeli citizenship or relocate to the Palestinian-governed 40% of the West Bank.'[22] His understanding of 'self-government' is, in his own words, 'autonomy on steroids'.[23] In 2014, Bennett explained how the unilateral annexation of Palestinian land could be enacted in stages: first the Gush Etzion so-called 'bloc' south of Jerusalem, 'and then to Ariel and Ma'ale Adumim and the Jordan Valley' – and finally 'all the Jewish communities in Judea and Samaria'.[24] Bennett has continued to share his annexation proposals to anyone who will listen, telling Al Jazeera English in February 2017 that Israel's right to the West Bank derives from nothing less than the Bible itself.[25] Bennett's colleagues in Jewish Home, like ministers Uri Ariel and Ayelet Shaked have also explicitly rejected Palestinian statehood, with the latter telling a DC conference in October 2015: 'There is not and never will be a Palestinian state.'[26]

Unilateral annexation – even of portions of the West Bank – would constitute a measure that the Western sponsors of the peace process could not ignore, and its likely diplomatic impact means that – for now, at least – an Israeli government headed by a status quo proponent like Netanyahu is unlikely to formally implement such a step. However, even if the annexationist camp's vision is not being implemented in full, their very existence and relative strength, both inside and outside the Likud party, is enough to hamper the willingness or ability of someone like Netanyahu to establish even a canton-style Palestinian 'state-minus' (and note that, as of June 2016, only four ministers in the Israeli cabinet were on the record in support of a Palestinian 'state' in any shape or form).[27] That is to say, putting aside Netanyahu's own views, he is aware of how much he owes politically to the pro-annexation constituency.

The 'separation' camp

Against Netanyahu's policy of maintaining the status quo, and the pro-annexation positions of members of Likud, Jewish Home, and non-parliamentary activists, is an Israeli opposition that unites behind one, main call: separation from the Palestinians. Regrettably, such an approach not only offers little by way of optimism but even represents a particularly deleterious assault on Palestinian rights in and of itself. Let us begin with Israel's Labor party, which in the 2015 election ran under the banner of the Zionist Camp (sometimes translated as the less militaristic-sounding 'Zionist Union'), together with Tzipi Livni's small Hatnuah party. While railing against Netanyahu's approach to the Palestinians, the Zionist Camp's manifesto was, in reality, a blueprint for a Palestinian Bantustan that would be a 'state' in name only.[28] According to the Zionist Camp, under any 'final status agreement', the future Palestinian 'state' would be demilitarised, 'the settlement blocs in Judea and Samaria [the West Bank]' would be 'under Israeli sovereignty', and Jerusalem would remain 'the eternal capital of the State of Israel'.[29] On the campaign trail, the then leader of Labor and the Zionist Camp, Isaac Herzog, declared that the Jordan River – i.e. the West Bank's entire eastern flank – would be Israel's 'security border'.[30] He also singled out Gush Etzion, Ma'ale Adumim, and Ariel – located in the south, centre, and north of the West Bank respectively – as so-called 'settlement blocs' that Israel would keep in perpetuity, noting: 'in the ideal world, I would like to keep it all'.

37

A year later, and Labor officially kicked the 'two-state solution' into the long grass, adopting a platform at its party conference which urged Israel to pursue unilateral withdrawal from areas of the oPt in order to 'separate' more effectively from the Palestinians.[31] According to Labor's platform, Israel would complete the Separation Wall, hold on to the 'settlement blocs', and reassign portions of Area C to full Palestinian Authority 'control'. A few weeks prior to the Labor conference, Herzog put it plainly, when he declared that he 'wish[es] to separate from as many Palestinians as possible, as quickly as possible'.[32] In February 2017, a few months before he was removed as Labor leader, Herzog laid out a 'road map' for Israel's relations with the Palestinians, which had, as its primary framework, a period of ten years during which Israel would de facto annex the 'settlement blocs', and the Israeli army 'would continue acting throughout the West Bank up to the Jordan River'.[33] Only after this period would 'direct negotiations' begin – *if* the decade 'passed without violence' (as defined, of course, by Israel). Herzog's successor as Labor chair, Avi Gabbay, meanwhile, has hailed West Bank settlements as 'the beautiful and devoted face of Zionism', and insisted that even isolated colonies may not need to be removed as part of a 'separation' plan.[34]

The above proposals are neither the parameters of a genuine Palestinian state, nor a million miles away from what we can deduce Netanyahu imagines a Palestinian 'state' to look like. So why do the likes of Herzog and Livni get so furious with what they describe as the prime minister's refusal to 'separate' from the Palestinians? In essence, the dispute boils down to the following. While Netanyahu believes in Israel's ability to continue with the status quo ad infinitum – and also lacks the political base from which to pursue an alternative path – Herzog and his like-minded colleagues in the Zionist Camp believe that Israel's strategic interests are best served by both the existence of some kind of 'peace process', as well as by a unilaterally defined 'separation' from Palestinian population centres in the oPt that can, if the Palestinians want, be called a 'state'. But make no mistake, this recipe, with its commitment to the 'settlement blocs', a 'unified' Jerusalem, and Israel's control of the Palestinian entity's eastern border, is as much an obstacle to the realisation of Palestinian rights as the annexation vision of the likes of Bennett and Shaked. The latter may get the headlines for their brand of rejectionist nationalism but Herzog likewise is dedicated to ensuring that Jerusalem will 'remain Jewish' and 'whole'.[35]

Labor – and its temporary alliance, the Zionist Camp – is not the only political party advocating for 'separation' from the Palestinians. This is also the approach of self-styled 'centrist' Yair Lapid, and his Yesh Atid party, who told Israeli television in 2016: 'We need to remove the Palestinians from our lives – we need to do this by building a high wall and making them disappear' – or as another translation put it: 'Get them [the Palestinians] out of our sight'.[36] Lapid had said similar things before: in 2015, he said: 'We need to separate from the Palestinians and to make sure there's a higher wall between us – not a smaller wall'.[37] In its platform, Yesh Atid spells out what this means in more detail; the party supports 'two states for two people as part of which the major settlement blocs (Ariel, Gush Etzion, Maale Adumim[sic]) will remain as part of Israel'.[38] As Israeli political scientist Neve Gordon noted in 2013, it was 'telling that Yesh Atid launched its election campaign in Ariel, a settlement located in the heart of the occupied West Bank. Ariel was thus constituted as an eastern suburb of Tel-Aviv, part of normal Israel, rather than an illegal settlement'.[39] For Yesh Atid, a permanent deal will also 'guarantee Israel's right to act to defend itself and against any terrorist threat without limitations, as well as the demilitarization of the Palestinian state'.[40] Lapid also remains within the consensus that includes Netanyahu and Herzog when he insists that 'Jerusalem will not be divided and will remain the capital of Israel' (Ramallah will be the Palestinian 'capital').[41]

Labor and Yesh Atid self-consciously position themselves as responsible, or pragmatic, centrists, but the principle of 'separation' is also to be found on the right, in the form of Avigdor Lieberman, head of Yisrael Beiteinu. Lieberman, who has served as a government minister in a number of different coalitions, rejects both the position of the annexationists, as well as what he sees as the international community's understanding of the 'two-state solution'. In February 2017, Lieberman elaborated on his position at the Munich Security Conference.[42] 'I believe that what is necessary for us is to keep the Jewish state', he said, continuing: 'My biggest problem is that today on the table we have a proposal (which) will establish a very homogenic Palestinian state without even one Jew [referring to removal of West Bank settlers] and we will become a bi-national state with more than 20 percent of the population Palestinians.' For Lieberman, then, 'two-states' means an 'exchange of land *and population*' (my emphasis), whereby West Bank settlements become part of Israel, while communities of Palestinian citizens would be inside the borders of the Palestinian state. This idea of 'two states', which prioritises a goal of maximum ethno-homogeneity, is often presented as 'extreme', but in fact, merely makes explicit the racism of the 'separation' discourse long advanced by so-called Israeli moderates – it was Tzipi Livni, who in 2008, told high school students in Tel Aviv that 'once a Palestinian state is established', Palestinian citizens can be told that 'the national solution for you is elsewhere'.[43]

One final group merits a mention, with respect to the call for separation, and that are various former Israeli military, security and political figures who have, in recent years, advocated for 'two states for two peoples' as a way of protecting Israel as a 'Jewish state'. One such group is Blue White Future, which describes itself as 'a non-partisan political movement' committed 'to securing the future of Israel as a Jewish and democratic state'.[44] Only a 'two state solution', says the group, can guarantee Israel's existence 'as a democratic state with a significant Jewish majority, define permanent and secure borders, [and] strengthen Jerusalem's position as the capital city of Israel' – which gives you a clue as to the kind of Palestinian 'state' they envisage (in a 2017 piece, the group's co-chairs repeatedly referred to the Separation Wall as a future border).[45] Years earlier, Blue White Future used unintentionally instructive language when they warned that '[Israel] cannot remain a Jewish democracy without disengaging from 2.5 million Palestinians', thus evoking the 2005 redeployment from Gaza that Israel used to deny its continued responsibilities as occupying power.[46]

Another prominent group is Commanders for Israel's Security who, like Blue White Future, describe themselves as 'non-partisan', and are made up of senior, retired officers from the Israeli army, Shin Bet, Mossad, and police.[47] The group promotes 'a political agreement with the Palestinians as part of a regional framework', on the basis of safeguarding '[Israel's] future as the national home of the Jewish People'. Until conditions 'ripen' for such a deal, 'Israel must take independent action to restore security to its citizens, improve its standing regionally and internationally and preserve conditions for a future agreement'. In 2017, the group sponsored billboards featuring images of Palestinians and the words, in Arabic, 'Soon we shall be a majority'.[48] The adverts also included a telephone number which, if rung, played a recording of former Israeli general Avi Mizrahi saying: 'Are the billboards bothering you? They will disappear in a few days. Those who won't disappear are two and a half million Palestinians in the West Bank. They want to be the majority – and this is who we want to annex? If we don't separate from the Palestinians, Israel will be less Jewish and less secure. We need to separate from the Palestinians now.'

Movement within, rather than between, 'blocs'

Over the last three elections (2009, 2013, 2015), the voting patterns of the Israeli electorate have remained generally consistent with respect to the principle 'blocs' in the Knesset, namely the division between the right-wing and Haredi parties on the one hand, and the so-called centrist parties on the other.[49] In the 2009 election, right-wing and Haredi parties secured 52.4 per cent of the vote, while 32.4 per cent went to centrist parties.[50] Arab parties got 9.2 per cent of the vote, while left-of-centre Meretz got 3 per cent. In the 2013 election, right-wing and Haredi parties secured 46.37 per cent of the vote, while centrist parties achieved 32.79 per cent.[51] Meretz secured 4.55 per cent, while the Arab parties again got 9.2 per cent combined. Two years later, in the 2015 election, the electorate divided along similar lines: the right and Haredi parties got 45.97 per cent, centrist parties got 34.98 per cent, the Arab parties combined under the Joint List to get 10.61 per cent, while the Meretz-dominated Israel's Left got 3.93 per cent.[52]

It is important to note, however, that the Haredi parties, Shas and United Torah Judaism (UTJ – itself an amalgamation of two smaller parties, Degel HaTorah and Agudat Israel) are not *automatic* coalition partners of the Israeli right. Shas, for example, which has traditionally represented the interests of Sephardic and Mizrahi Haredim, went into coalition with Ehud Olmert's government in 2006, and in 2013 chose to sit on the opposition benches, rather than join Netanyahu's government (though re-entered government in 2015).[53] More recently, Shas minister Aryeh Deri indicated that the party's more natural home *is* with the right, telling the pro-settler media outlet *Arutz Sheva* in July 2017: 'As long as the system works the way it does and we have to endorse a candidate for prime minister, we will endorse the right-wing candidate.'[54] Affirming good relations with all the coalition partners, Deri added: 'Everyone understands that there's no better government.' UTJ, meanwhile, though in principle 'non-Zionist', is happy to use its position in government to work for the interests of Haredim with respect to welfare and significant issues such as military service.

Parties representing Palestinian citizens of Israel, are simply not considered as coalition partners by the vast majority of other parties, and their (unlikely) inclusion in any government would likely be a deal breaker for other members of such a coalition. Indeed, no Arab party has *ever* been part of a ruling coalition, and there have only ever been three non-Jewish ministers from any party since 1948. In 2015, the United Arab List, Hadash (a joint Jewish-Arab party), and Balad, combined to form the Joint List, which secured 13 seats, making them the third largest party (though it should be noted that this only represented an increase of two seats when compared to the Joint List's constituent members' combined total in 2013). Yet even before the election, Moshe Kahlon – who left Likud to head the 'centrist' party Kulanu – declared that he 'would not sit on a government that relied on the Arabs'.[55] In 2013, during post-election horse-trading, Yair Lapid similarly vowed that he would 'not be part of an obstructionist bloc with the Hanin Zoabis' (a reference to a prominent Palestinian politician whose views and activities turned her into somewhat of a bete noire amongst Jewish Israeli parliamentarians).[56]

In summary, recent elections have shown that shifts in votes tend to be *within* the right or centrist blocs (by any reasonable interpretation of the term, there is no left-wing bloc), rather than across or between those blocs. That is to say, in general, while some voters may switch between Likud and Jewish Home, and others may cross between Labor and Yesh Atid, there has not been, and there is no imminent sign that there will be, a seismic shift in the size of these blocs. The upshot of this, in addition to the role played by the Haredi parties, and Palestinian legislators, is that it remains far easier to form a right-wing coalition government, than a centre, or centre-left, one. Thus, with respect to the Palestinians, this means that the aforementioned pro-status quo and pro-annexation camps are likely to remain in power, versus the pro-separation camp.

The death of the peace process – and the elephant in the room

Israeli-Palestinian negotiations of any serious nature ground to a halt after the collapse of talks led by the then US Secretary of State John Kerry in April 2014.[57] Many analysts and politicians have sought to understand the failure of these talks, as well as previous rounds, by focusing on the temperament of the individuals involved, or the minutiae of the exchanges of offer and counter-offer. Yet one critical point is routinely omitted: the Israeli maximum on offer has never met either the Palestinian minimum or the standards of international law. And the reason for that is something that has been almost entirely neglected by policymakers and experts: ideology.

Speaking at a conference organised by UK-based Israel advocacy organisation The Britain Israel Communications and Research Centre (BICOM) in March 2017, Professor Galia Golan, a former consultant to the Israeli government, acknowledged that 'Israeli negotiators go into negotiations with the idea that it's ours. It's all ours ... And that's a very, very basic attitude.'[58] This idea that 'it's all ours' is shared across the Israeli political spectrum. When the Knesset passed the settlement 'Regularisation Bill' in February 2017, a government minister said: 'The argument tonight is about who this land belongs to and about our basic right to our land. Tonight, we are voting on our right to the Land [of Israel].'[59] The likes of Naftali Bennett explicitly grounds his exclusivist claim to all of historic Palestine in religious terminology: 'If you want to say that our land does not belong to us, I suggest you go change the Bible first' (or even more pithily on another occasion: 'the Land of Israel is ours. Period.').[60] Netanyahu confidante Tzachi Hanegbi, for example, declared in March 2017 that Israel is 'committed to living in our regional land'. Land, he added, 'that was given to us not by Google or Wikipedia but by the Bible'.[61] A few months later, Netanyahu protested a UNESCO decision to make Hebron a World Heritage site in 'Palestine' by reading from Genesis during a cabinet meeting.[62] Shas's Aryeh Deri has also stated: 'We believe Israel is ours because God gave it to us. I don't believe I am an occupier.'[63]

But note that Golan did not distinguish between Israeli negotiators from the right or centre – and indeed, the most serious attempts at talks (Camp David, Taba, Annapolis) were held when Israel was led by centre or centre-left governments. Thus you will find the same ideology also informing Israel's so-called moderates, whether it is Tzipi Livni – 'this is our land' – or Yair Lapid's Yesh Atid who, in their 2015 platform, explained their support for 'separation from the Palestinians' as a means of avoiding 'a state for all its citizens' or a bi-national state.[64] 'The dilemma between keeping *sections of the land of Israel* and maintaining a Jewish majority', Yesh Atid stated, 'requires us to *give up Israeli territory*' (my emphasis), adding: 'The concessions of *some of the territory of the historic land of Israel* is a necessary part of the fight for the survival of a Jewish state in the land of Israel with a Jewish majority' (again, my emphasis). Yesh Atid, like the pro-separation current represented by Labor and other 'pragmatic centrists', see the Palestinian population as a problem to be got rid of – this is what motivates their desire to 'separate', not a recognition of Palestinian self-determination or rights.[65] The pro-separation centrists are part of a milieu described perceptively by the Associated Press as 'the more sophisticated nationalists [who] profess to support a partition – albeit on terms the Palestinians aren't likely to accept'.[66]

In October 2016, Israeli newspaper *Haaretz* published minutes of a secret meeting between then Israeli premier Menachem Begin and Shimon Peres, head of the opposition at the time.[67] The discussions took place on 31 August 1978, ahead of Begin's talks with Egypt's leader Anwar Sadat at Camp David. The minutes shed valuable light on how what distinguishes Israeli 'hawks' from 'doves' – the journey Peres is typically said to have made – is less about ideology, and more about strategy. According to Peres in 1978, 'Jordan is also Palestine,' adding: 'I'm against … another Palestinian country, against an Arafat state [in the oPt].' Yet, at the same time, Peres told Begin that there was 'no choice but a functional compromise' in the West Bank. Or, as he put it: 'I do think that one of these days there will be a need for a partition because we won't know what to do with the Arabs.' He continued:

We'll reach 1.8 million Arabs and I see our situation as getting very difficult and not a matter of police or prison … I see them eating the Galilee and my heart bleeds, because I was one of the founders of Ramot Naftali [a moshav] and I see 300 houses bought by Arabs and that's the beginning of the process. They live in houses in Afula and in Acre and they take over entire streets. The moshavim are full of Arab laborers and Jews sitting in their houses and playing tennis and the Arabs are working in the fields. That doesn't seem right to me.

Thus, Peres 'the hawk' already believed that some kind of 'partition' of the land would be necessary, due to the problem of 'what to do with the Arabs'. Peres 'the dove' came to see the Oslo peace process, and even support for a Palestinian 'state' (or an 'Arafat state', as he ironically and presciently put it in 1978), as the answer to the question that had bothered him years earlier. The minutes also show that the parameters for an 'Arafat state' barely changed over the years, with Peres telling Begin: 'We don't agree to return to the 1967 borders, Jerusalem must remain unified and the defence of Israel must begin from the Jordan River with an IDF presence in Judea and Samaria [the West Bank].' In 1995, shortly before he was assassinated, then Israeli premier Yitzhak Rabin told the Knesset that the Oslo Accords would produce 'a Palestinian entity ... which is less than a state', with Israel retaining major settlements, a 'united Jerusalem', and the Jordan River becoming a 'security' border in the 'broadest meaning'.[68]

The essence of the impasse

Ahead of Benjamin Netanyahu's visit to the White House, not long after Donald Trump's inauguration, an administration official told reporters that 'peace is the goal, whether it comes in the form of a two-state solution ... or something else' (and it was at the joint press conference with Netanyahu where Trump famously said: 'I'm looking at two-state, one-state, and I like the one that both parties like ... I can live with either one').[69] But the unnamed official also made quite a perceptive comment, observing: 'If I ask five people what a two-state solution is, I get eight different answers.' While Netanyahu has been quite explicit in how he has drained the 'two-state solution' concept and Palestinian 'statehood' of real meaning, he was not the first to do so – and others have performed the same trick with more subtlety, thus avoiding provoking a similar level of international disquiet. The grim reality is that *none* of the Israeli political parties who are either part of the current ruling coalition, or who could feasibly form part of an alternative one, support a two-state solution based on international law and the Palestinian people's right to self-determination and sovereignty. It is crucial to understand how this rejectionism encompasses both *explicit* opponents of Palestinian statehood, as well as those who express support for a 'two-state solution' but whose parameters are unviable; Netanyahu seeks a 'state-minus', Rabin sought an 'entity which is less than a state'.

In June 2017, an article was published in the *New York Times* on the prospects of a two-state solution. 'The Israeli idea of Palestinian statehood never included all of the attributes of full sovereignty,' wrote the paper's correspondent Isabel Kershner.[70] 'Israel insists on a demilitarized state, and Mr. Netanyahu says the Israeli military has to keep overall security control.' She continued: 'Together with other so-far-intractable issues – like the fate of Jerusalem and of Palestinian refugees – many experts have long said that the maximum Israel can offer does not meet the minimum Palestinian requirements.' It is rare for such a clear acknowledgement of the yawning chasm between Israel's maximum and the Palestinian minimum to appear in such a prominent forum. Even the headline was, unintentionally, instructive: 'Is 2-State Solution Dead? In Israel, a Debate Over What's Next.' In this colonial conflict, Israel is still debating – as Peres put it – 'what to do with the Arabs'. Some Israelis are now openly saying, in the words of former defense minister Moshe Ya'alon, that 'Israel should manage the conflict rather than trying to solve it'.[71] Micah Goodman, an Israeli philosopher and West Bank settler (a description he is not fond of – 'It's where I live, not who I am'), published a runaway success of a book in 2017, in which he argues that 'there is no solution', and that the 'conflict' with the Palestinians is destined to be 'one that will be [always] part of our life, like car accidents and crime and poverty'.[72]

The Israeli right represented by Netanyahu wants the status quo for as long as possible, a permanently temporary occupation. The

Israeli right of Bennett wants to take steps such as annexation of all or part of the West Bank. The Israeli centrists, the 'moderate' opposition represented by Labor and Yesh Atid want separation through the form of a Palestinian Bantustan. The international community must understand that these are the Israeli options on the table. The fact that Israel's maximum does not meet the Palestinian minimum (or the standards of international law) has long been obscured, in party, thanks to a quarter century-long peace process which has fuelled the illusion that – in the words of Trump – a solution can be found that 'both parties like'.[73] The peace process has also obscured the fact that the majority of Jewish Israelis have chosen the status quo, as Israeli journalist Noam Sheizaf has written: Israel gains strategically from the existence of a 'peace process', with respect to 'international legitimacy', but 'has to give nothing, or very little, in return'.[74] It has thus been in 'Israel's interest … to sit around the negotiating table forever.' This illusion is, slowly, coming to an end. The two-state solution is dead, but the unsettling truth is that it was never really alive – at least in terms of what Israel's leaders were ever prepared to allow, without the international pressure that, to date, has never materialised.

Daniel Levy, head of the US Middle East Project and a former Israeli adviser to negotiations, was discussing the plausibility of a two-state solution with me in early 2017 when he made this perceptive point. 'There are creative solutions to various problems,' he said. 'But creative solutions can't paper over a gap that is so huge, because one side simply does not accept the legitimacy of the independent sovereign existence of the other.'[75] Yet the significance of ideology, when it comes to understanding Israeli politics and society, and identifying obstacles to establishing a Palestinian state, has been neglected by Western policymakers and analysts. You can locate this ideology not only – or perhaps not even primarily – in the rhetoric of Israeli leaders, but in their policies, their maps, in legislation – in the *material*. The ideology is expressed in speeches and statements – but also in bulldozers and cranes, fences and walls. The de facto, single apartheid state that exists today is a testimony to the existence and impact of this hegemonic ideology amongst Israel's military and political leaders, and it explains the impasse reached with the Palestinians. Yet, away from the headlines, opposition to these discriminatory policies is growing – including amongst a particularly key constituency: American Jews.

3

Jewish communities divided

Anti-Zionism and opposition to a Zionist state has been – and is … a legitimate position in Judaism. There were – and are – Jews who, far from incorporating political Zionism as part of their faith, have regarded it as a moral imperative to stand in opposition.[1]

– Elmer Berger, 1989

Support for Israel is no longer the great unifier of American Jewry that it was after 1967. Israel is now actually becoming a divisive, rather than a unifying force in American Jewish life.[2]

– Professor Dov Waxman, 2016

Zionism emerged in the context of the serious questions and challenges facing Jews in Europe and Russia in the nineteenth century. It was one answer to, and offshoot of, the social and political developments that had flowed from the Enlightenment and the French Revolution, and a response to the pogroms in the Pale of Settlement and the anti-Semitism found in Vienna and Paris. The rise of assimilation amongst Jews in Western and Central Europe, and even in the Russian empire, was also a major cause of concern for the early Zionists. Some emphasised the need to save Jews as *individuals* (from anti-Semitism); some argued the need to save the Jews *as a nation* (from assimilation). Thus, for its adherents, Zionism was a positive response to the challenges of emancipation and anti-Semitism, an expression of Jewish national-ism rooted in the fertile soil of a century or more of philosophical innovation and activism.

There were two, broader ideological and political currents, whose existence was instrumental to the emergence of Zionism, and the success of its project in Palestine. First, mainstream political Zionism was 'part and parcel of the history of late-nineteenth-century ethnic nationalisms' – like other European nationalisms of its time, the Zionist movement embraced a 'vision of ethnonational citizenship'.[3] The second element at play was European colonialism. Theodor Herzl, who published the seminal essay 'The Jewish State' in 1896 and convened the First Zionist Congress the following year, knew that the Zionist project could only be realised under the protection of an imperial power. But this was not just an issue of practicalities; it was also a reflection of how 'European supremacy' had fostered 'the idea that any territory outside Europe was open to European occupation'.[4]

Zionist thinkers and factions diverged over strategies, political traditions, economics, and religion: there was Herzlian Zionism, Labour Zionism, Revisionist Zionism, Socialist Zionism, Religious Zionism and Cultural/Spiritual Zionism. Ultimately, however, all these variations shared some fundamental ideas in common: the solution to anti-Semitism was Jewish nationalism; Jews had a right to the land of 'Eretz Israel' (Palestine); the necessity of mass emigration to, and the establishment of a Jewish majority in, Palestine; and the legitimacy, and need for, a Jewish state/sovereignty in Palestine. As Israeli historian Ze'ev Sternhell put it, 'the historical struggle between the labour movement and the revisionist Right was a struggle over the *methods* of implementing national objectives, *not over the objectives themselves*' (my emphasis).[5] 'The real content of the Zionist idea is political,' declared Israel's first prime minister, David Ben-Gurion, in 1924: 'Zionism is the desire for a Jewish state, a country and authority in that country [Palestine].'[6]

Today, a majority of Jews in Western Europe and North America self-define as Zionists, a small, but significant, number of whom actively mobilise to advocate for Israel's (perceived) interests (from varying perspectives).[7] The ideas developed by those early Zionist thinkers and activists were, in other words, eventually embraced by a majority of Jews worldwide. The support offered to Israel by American Jews in particular developed into a core 'strategic' interest for Israel, less in terms of donations and more with respect to the role it plays in helping to shape US foreign policy. Yet it was only after the Six-Day War in 1967, 'some two decades after Israel's founding', that 'the American Jewish pro-Israel establishment was built'.[8] Furthermore, the support offered for Israel by the majority of today's main Jewish communal bodies in the US and Europe can overshadow both an oft-forgotten and suppressed history of Jewish opposition to Zionism, and a contemporary surge in dissent. This fragmentation within the organised Jewish community, especially in the US, and the growth in opposition to not just individual Israeli policies but to Zionism itself, is the first 'crack in the wall' whose significance this chapter will hopefully make clear.

A forgotten history of opposition

For some time, the pioneering Zionist thinkers and activists struggled to capture the imagination of most, or even many, Jews in Europe and the Russian empire. For example, only a small number of Jewish emigrants who left the Russian Empire following the pogroms of the late nineteenth and early twentieth centuries went to Palestine 'out of a firm, coherent ideological motive'.[9] Indeed, 'among the masses of Jews who left Eastern Europe in the thirty or forty years prior to the passing of the [restrictive] American immigration laws in 1922, only about 1 percent or slightly fewer came to Palestine'.[10] Nor was it just a question of apathy or lack of support – the Zionist movement faced explicit and often fervent opposition from many groups, and for different reasons.

One source of opposition can be found in those Jews committed to various forms of left-wing and socialist political organising and activism. Perhaps the most prominent example of this was the Jewish Workers Association (*Bund*). With its base in the Jewish working class of Russia and Poland, for a time, the *Bund* boasted the largest membership of any socialist organisation in the Russian empire. For the *Bund*, 'the future was perceived ... as the integration of the Jewish proletariat, conscious of its own cultural heritage, within the general revolutionary proletarian movement.'[11] The *Bund* were also fierce opponents of Zionism and efforts to establish a Jewish political entity in Palestine. 'We are asked why we are opposed to Zionism,' *Bund* leader Vladimir Medem stated in 1920.[12]

> The answer is simple: because we are socialists. And not merely socialistically inclined or socialists in name only, but active socialists. And between Zionist activity and Socialist activity there is a fundamental and profound chasm ... Across that chasm there is no bridge ... A national home in Palestine would not end the Jewish exile ... The Jewish exile would exist as before. All that would change would be the belief of Jewry in its future – the hope of the Jews in exile – the struggle for a better life would be snuffed out.[13]

Other opponents of Zionism could be found among those Jews for whom the whole enterprise was seen as a threat to integration in their respective societies. For these Jews, Zionism was even seen as an aid to the anti-Semites, by promoting the concept of the Jews as a separate nation. This point of view was expressed, notably, by Edwin Montagu, the only British government cabinet minister to oppose the Balfour Declaration, and the cabinet's only Jewish member. Montagu's strident opposition, expressed in a memo to the rest of the cabinet, was primarily based on what he felt would be the consequences for Jews in Britain (and elsewhere) of a Jewish state being established in Palestine: 'When the Jews are told that Palestine is their national home, every country will immediately desire to get rid of its Jewish citizens,' he wrote.[14] Montagu also rejected an even more fundamental premise of the Zionist movement, asserting that Jews around the world were linked by religion, rather than nationhood ('the members of my family ... have no sort or kind of community of view or of desire with any

Jewish family in any other country beyond the fact that they profess to a greater or less degree the same religion').

But it wasn't just socialists and the more elite 'integration-ists' who resisted Zionism; perhaps the most significant form of opposition was religious. Indeed, in the words of Israeli professor and expert Yosef Salmon, of the 'several far-reaching religious crises' experienced by 'traditional Jewry in Europe [in the course of the modern era]', it was 'the Zionist threat that offered the gravest danger'.[15] Salmon continued: 'Zionism challenged all the aspects of traditional Judaism ... The Zionist threat reached every Jewish community. It was unrelenting and comprehensive, and therefore it met with uncompromising opposition'. The Zionist movement was seen as

> a rejection of that age-old desire for the Jews to return to the Land of Israel, and not its linear fulfilment ... because that tradi-tional 'yearning for Zion' was tied inexorably to the belief in the advent of a messiah chosen and anointed by God – and by God alone – who would initiate the 'ingathering of the exiles'.[16]

Religious opposition to Zionism came from both Reform and Orthodox Judaism. 'A sober student of Jewish history and a genuine lover of his co-religionists sees that the Zionist agitation contradicts everything that is typical of Jews and Judaism,' remarked a professor at Hebrew Union College, the Reform movement's rabbinical school in the US, in 1889.[17] Amongst Orthodox Jewish leaders in Europe, meanwhile, 'rejection of Zionism united otherwise disparate Judaic groups because all of them drew on a deep-rooted tradition that antedates Zionism'.[18] In 1900, for example, the rabbis of Lithuania 'published their collective condemnation of Zionism' in a compilation called *Or la Yesharim* (Light for the Upright).[19] In Germany, 'Orthodox Jews in Germany were no less determined to reject Zionism than their brethren in Eastern Europe'; it was opposition from German Jews that forced the first Zionist congress to be held in Basle, rather than in Berlin.[20]

In his book 'What is Modern Israel?', University of Montreal-based professor Yakov Rabkin describes how Zionism, 'at its inception', was very much 'a marginal movement'.[21]

Most practicing Jews, both Orthodox and Reform, rejected Zionism, referring to it as a project and an ideology that conflicted with the values of Judaism. Jews who joined various socialist and revolutionary movements saw Zionism as an attack on equality and as an attempt to distract Jewish masses from pursuing social change. Finally, those who, thanks to the Emancipation, had integrated into the broader society and become dedicated liberals were convinced that Zionism was, no less seriously than anti-Semitism, a threat to their future. Jewish nationalism was thus rejected because it was seen to imperil not only Judaism but also the social status and political values of the emancipated Jews.[22]

Over time, however, 'the rising tide of anti-Semitism in Europe diluted opposition to political Zionism'; it was 'anti-Semitism and compassion for its victims' that 'were the principal factors leading Orthodox, Reform, Conservative and secular Jews into the Zionist fold'.[23] But the opposition never fully faded away – many Ultra-Orthodox Jews, for example, remain opposed to Zionism even while adapting to the practical reality of the State of Israel – and the historical perspective is a vital backdrop for examining the contemporary fragmentation and fresh shoots of dissent.

Growing fragmentation

One of the reasons why this past opposition is so easily forgotten, or suppressed, is that for most of the last half century, fervent support for Israel has characterised the main Jewish institutions and communal bodies in the US. 'For decades, especially after the Six-Day War in 1967', Dov Waxman has described, 'the American Jewish relationship with Israel was largely character-

ised by unwavering support for Israel by most American Jews ...
It was also a central component in American Jewish identity.[24]
That era is well and truly over, with 'a historic change' taking place
'in the American Jewish relationship with Israel' – 'the pro-Israel
consensus that once united American Jews is eroding, and Israel is
fast becoming a source of division rather than unity for American
Jewry'. Put simply, 'a new era of American Jewish conflict over
Israel is replacing the old era of solidarity'.[25] Various phenomena
have contributed to these changes: in Israel, thirty years of Labor
domination was followed by the return of Revisionist Zionism and
the growth in popularity of Likud and other right-wing factions;
decades of military occupation in the oPt; the invasion of Lebanon
and First Intifada of the 1980s. But the fragmentation is not just a
product of events in the Middle East – it has also been driven 'by
changes within the American Jewish community itself', including
'a broader process of polarisation between non-Orthodox and
Orthodox Jews'.[26]

In June 2017, the fiftieth anniversary of Israel's military
occupation of the West Bank and Gaza Strip provided an insight
into elements of the current divide. For some, it was an occasion of
'unabashed celebration', while for others, the anniversary marked
'the start of the occupation and remains a deeply complicated and
conflicted milestone' – and some saw 'nothing at all to celebrate'.[27]
On the one hand, 4 June saw a 'New York Celebrates Israel Day',
with a parade down Fifth Avenue, and a 'Celebrate Israel Festival'
sponsored by the Israeli American Council.[28] On the other hand,
the young Jewish American group IfNotNow organised 'public
demonstrations all across the country' designed to 'force the
American Jewish community to reckon with what it means to
have supported the occupation for the past 50 years'.[29] Two very
different delegations were also a microcosm of this divergence.
One saw the former British chief rabbi Jonathan Sacks lead a trip
that included participation in the notorious 'March of the Flags'
on so-called Jerusalem Day, and a dance with Israeli soldiers 'in
the radical settler enclave inside the city of Hebron'.[30] That same

summer, more than 100 activists from Jewish communities abroad, mainly the US, participated in a 'Sumud Freedom Camp' to rebuild a demolished Palestinian community in the West Bank.[31]

These are relatively small-scale examples, but this fragmentation has also taken place at an institutional level. In 2008, a group of American Jews frustrated with the approach taken by the likes of the American Israel Public Affairs Committee (AIPAC), who offer uncritical support for Israeli government policy, established J Street, a more liberal, centrist pro-Israel lobby organisation that has since gone from strength to strength. Five years after it was established, J Street had 180,000 registered supporters and 20,000 donors.[32] At its sixth and then largest conference in early 2017, some 3,500 delegates attended.[33] J Street has positioned itself as a left-of-centre friend of Israel: it supports Israel as a 'Jewish state' and has explicitly and repeatedly opposed the Boycott, Divestment, Sanctions (BDS) Movement. Yet even its very modest criticism of Israeli government policies – often framed less in terms of respect for Palestinian rights and more with regards to Israel's interests – has been enough to make it beyond the pale for some (including, notoriously, the US's now ambassador to Israel, David Friedman).[34] Despite J Street's pretty conservative (with a small 'c') agenda, it has played a critical role in the growing divide amongst American Jews towards Israel (as well as reflecting an approach that did not, until recently, have a high-profile platform from which to express itself). It is also possible that some members of J Street, perhaps especially its younger members, will come to chafe at the organisation's liberal Zionist approach, and seek a more critical, and radical, politics. 'If Palestinians in the occupied territories are to be denied self-determination in a state of their own', said Bernie Sanders at the aforementioned 2017 J Street conference, 'will they receive full citizenship and equal rights in a single state, potentially meaning the end of a Jewish majority state?'[35] He went on: 'these are very serious questions with significant implications for America's broader regional partnerships and goals'.

What Israel worries, of course, are the answers Jewish Americans might have to such questions – and especially young Jewish Americans. The Open Hillel movement, for example, 'a network of student groups that promotes open dialogue about Israel on college campuses', has 'struck a nerve with the pro-Israel establishment in the US' for creating a space for Jewish students where questions like BDS and Zionism can be discussed, not policed or repressed.[36] In June 2017, a report appeared in the *Times of Israel* under the headline ' "Devastating" survey shows huge loss of Israel support among Jewish college students'.[37] Describing a 'dire' picture amongst 'the next generation of potential Jewish leadership', the piece reported on how polling showed Jewish college students drop 27 percentage points on the question of whether they 'lean towards the Israeli side' between 2010 and 2016. American Jewish commentator Peter Beinart, noting how some scholars believe the 'gap' in attitudes towards Israel among American Jewish generations 'will close over time', has argued that the evidence does not support such a conclusion: 'were that the case', he wrote, 'surveys would show rising attachment to Israel as American Jews enter their thirties and forties and a flattening after that. Instead, the data shows a straight drop.'[38]

Some of those observing these trends, like Beinart, believe they can be arrested and reversed by promoting and defending a form of 'liberal' Zionism that, its proponents believe, marries progressive values with support for the existence of Israel as a 'Jewish state'. So-called liberal Zionism backs a 'two-state solution' on the basis that dividing the land is the only way to preserve Israel as an ethnocracy. For this pro-'separation' constituency, the Zionist gains secured in 1948 are safeguarded by relinquishing some of the territory conquered in 1967. Even the mere *prospect* of a 'two-state solution' has had its uses as 'a kind of comfort zone'. In the words of British journalist Jonathan Freedland: 'Jews could have a state of their own, without depriving Palestinians of their legitimate national aspirations.'[39] The two-state formula, in other words, helped ease (but not remove, of course) the inherent tension in the liberal Zionist identity; as the two states framework grew imperilled, those tensions have become increasingly public, and unbearable.

Alienation and dissent

The division over Israel amongst Jewish communities in the US, UK and elsewhere is not just a question of alienation, apathy, or even divergence over how best to advance Israel's 'interests' (or disagreement about what those interests are). Increasingly, American Jews in particular are mobilising in solidarity with the Palestinian people's struggle for self-determination and liberation, and in opposition to not just Israeli policies, but to Israel's identity as a 'Jewish state'. An instructive example of this growing phenomenon, and certainly one of the most influential, is the American organisation Jewish Voice for Peace (JVP), 'a diverse and democratic community of activists inspired by Jewish tradition to work together for peace, social justice, and human rights'.[40] At the time of writing, JVP boasted 65 chapters across the United States, some 210,000 online supporters, and around 10,000 dues-paying members.[41] JVP also has a Rabbinical Council, an Artist and Cultural Workers Council, an Academic Advisory Council, a Labor Council, and works in partnership with a Jews of Colour/Mizrahi and Sephardi Caucus. Its 2017 national conference saw more than 1,000 JVP members and partners gather in Chicago.[42] It is, in other words, a force to be reckoned with.

The group's mission is both local and Palestine/Israel-focused: its website states that JVP 'opposes anti-Jewish, anti-Muslim, and anti-Arab bigotry and oppression', and 'seeks an end to the Israeli occupation of the West Bank, Gaza Strip, and East Jerusalem; security and self-determination for Israelis and Palestinians; a just solution for Palestinian refugees based on principles established in international law; an end to violence against civilians; and peace and justice for all peoples of the Middle East'.[43] JVP's work includes campus organising, interfaith work, legislative advocacy, arts and culture, and 'Jewish community transformation' – 'challenging institutional Jewish communities to act on values of justice, and our Rabbinical Council and Open Synagogue Network are paving the path to justice-centred Jewish communities'.[44] In addition, a core part of JVP's work is support for the Palestinian-led BDS campaign.

A September 2017 article by long-standing JVP executive director Rebecca Vilkomerson gave a valuable insight into her personal trajectory, as well as that of her organisation.[45] 'I joined Jewish Voice for Peace, then just a small Bay Area organization, in 2002', Vilkomerson wrote. 'The first time I wore a JVP t-shirt, one that said "Jews Say End the Occupation Now", I felt vulnerable and unsure about professing such a sentiment loudly and publicly. Fast forward 15 years, and expressing opposition to the occupation is now the norm in most liberal Jewish communities.' According to Vilkomerson, throughout its history, JVP has 'played the role of pushing and challenging the boundary of the conversations on Israel that are possible in the American Jewish community'. But, as Vilkomerson acknowledges, JVP itself has been challenged on and moved its own boundaries. 'Surprising as it may be to some', she related, 'JVP did not always fully support BDS.' She continued:

> We supported forms of economic pressure on Israel, including ending military aid, but it took us a full 10 years from the initiation of the call from Palestinian civil society for us to sign on as an organization. We endorsed the full call for BDS, including the Palestinian right of return, in 2015, following a multi-year organization-wide process of study and discussion.

Behind that decision, Vilkomerson relates, was the emergence of a 'collective understanding that recognizing the trauma of the Nakba, the displacement of Palestinians and the ongoing inability of many Palestinian families to unite in their homeland is a core obstacle to moving towards justice'. Perhaps even more significantly, she wrote, 'we don't see the right of Palestinians to return to their homeland as a threat'. Vilkomerson acknowledges that 'we often hear the critique that embracing the right of return is akin to the destruction of Israel', but, she adds, 'I disagree.'

> What we are seeking is the full rights and equality of all people living in Israel/Palestine. This would transform the State of Israel, but in the long-term has a better chance of protecting the safety and the possibility of a just future for all people. For liberal Zionists who hear this aim as destructive, I would invite them to think more deeply about how liberal values are compromised by the reality of the Israeli state.

Vilkomerson added a final insight into her own journey. 'The back of that t-shirt I wore in 2002 read: "Security for Israel Requires Justice for Palestinians"', she wrote.

> Then, advocating for the rights of Palestinians solely for the purpose of making Israeli lives better felt like a radical act. But I've changed too. Justice for Palestinians is an imperative in its own right, not merely a tool or a condition of security for Israeli Jews. We all need to be able to examine our internal biases and assumptions. The collective vision of equality and justice for all people that we are building depends upon it.

For Rabbi Brant Rosen, co-chair of the JVP Rabbinical Council and rabbi of newly founded congregation, Tzedek Chicago, Vilkomerson's story is far from unique. According to Rosen, writing in March 2016, 'growing numbers of Jews and others identify as anti-Zionists for legitimate ideological reasons. Many profess anti-Zionism because they do not believe Israel can be both a Jewish and democratic state.'[46] Some, meanwhile, 'don't believe that the identity of a nation should be dependent upon the demographic majority of one people over another.' Others 'choose not to put this highly militarized ethnic nation-state at the centre of their Jewish identity'. Such beliefs, he continued, 'are motivated by values of equality and human rights for all human beings'. In March 2017, three Jewish students at Columbia University, and Jewish Theological Seminary, published an eloquent expression of these kinds of shifts, again, in very personal terms.[47] 'Nearly two years ago, the three of us arrived on this campus as Jewish teens inoculated with an intense fear of the Israeli/Palestinian debate,' they wrote. 'We had been told for years in day school and summer camp that we would be provoked by anti-Semitic and anti-Israel rhetoric – presented to us as synonymous – and warned that we would be made to feel ashamed of our Jewish identities.'

Instead, they continued,

what we actually found ourselves confronting when we arrived at Columbia, however, was the way our education and socialization in the mainstream Jewish world hadn't prepared us for the conversations about Israel/Palestine happening on college campuses. We had been lied to and deceived by our teachers, parents, camp counsellors, role models, and community leaders. We came to realize just how much the Jewish community has yet to reckon with the violence and dispossession that American Jews are complicit in perpetuating.

What we hadn't learned from our combined 26 years of Jewish day school, countless hours spent in Hebrew school and synagogue, and years of Jewish summer camp, was that Judaism could flourish without the need for ethnonationalism – the supremacy of Jewish ethnic identity in the State of Israel – or racist apartheid policies. We hadn't learned that those policies were being enacted in our name and in the name of all Jewish people.

'We must be better than this,' they continued. 'Our history is one that is rooted in dispossession, fear, loss, and diaspora. We are Jews with lasting generational trauma. We must confront this and reckon with it; we must work with those facing similar traumas of dispossession, similar fears, similar losses, and similar diaspora today.' Palestine solidarity events like 'Israeli Apartheid Week' are not 'an insult to our identities as Jewish people', the students insisted. 'It's a week dedicated to demanding that our Judaism be a Judaism of morals, that our Judaism not be tied to ethnic nationalism, and that our Judaism be a religion and culture of liberation and redemption for all.'

Similar, though naturally smaller-scale developments are taking place elsewhere, including in the UK. Jews for Justice for Palestinians, for example, has been protesting Israeli policies and organising in support of Palestinian rights since 2002, defining itself as a 'network' that 'bring[s] together Jews from across the religious and political spectrum and value[s] contributions to the struggle for justice for Palestinians by Jews from every background, in Britain, Israel, and across the world' (it is not, as an organisation, 'anti-Zionist').[48] Independent Jewish Voices, meanwhile, was launched in 2007 'out of a frustration with the widespread misconception that the Jews of this country speak with one voice – and that this voice supports the Israeli government's policies'.[49] The goal was to 'create a climate and a space in which Jews of different affiliations and persuasions can express their opinions about the actions of the Israeli government without being accused of disloyalty or being dismissed as self-hating'. That same year, Jews for Boycotting Israeli Goods published its founding statement in support of the BDS campaign.[50] A different kind of organisation, but a notable one, is the Jewish Socialists Group, whose history dates back to the 1970s, and which defines itself as 'socialists, diasporists and secularists'.[51] While their work is broader than Palestine-related campaigning, their position represents an important element in Jewish opposition to Zionism; in their own words:

> as diasporists we celebrate the fact that the Jews are an international people. We support the right of Jews and other ethnic minorities to live in security and harmony with other communities wherever they are in the world, and to be free to express and

develop their historical and cultural identities. In the diaspora we are at home, not in exile. We reject the negative ideology of Zionism, which subordinates the political, social, economic and cultural needs of diaspora communities to the demands of the Israeli state.[52]

In recent years, there have been various expressions of dissent amongst young British Jews. In 2016, the Union of Jewish Students' (UJS) election was unprecedented in recent years for the inclusion amongst the three candidates for president an avowedly anti-Zionist candidate. Eran Cohen, who was born in Israel, also openly backed the BDS Movement.[53] To be able to run for president, Cohen had to secure ten nominations from members of at least five campus Jewish societies. At the time, Cohen told the *Jewish Chronicle*: UJS should represent all Jewish students – Zionist or not,' adding: 'I am a diasporist – I believe the focus of Jewish life is wherever Jews live, and excessive focus on Israel damages the UK Jewish community'[54] In his campaigning, Cohen cited a 2015 poll where 24 per cent of British Jews said they 'would be prepared to support some sanctions against Israel if I thought they would encourage the Israeli government to engage in the peace process'[55] In the same poll, only 59 per cent said that they consider themselves to be a 'Zionist'. Cohen cited such figures to substantiate his argument that the views of Jewish students about Israel and Zionism were more diverse than represented by a body like UJS; one of his supporters said that his campaign had demonstrated 'that I am not the only one who feels pushed out of the Jewish community'[56] Always a rank outsider, and smeared during the campaign as a 'self-hating Jew', Cohen eventually came last out of the three candidates, winning 8.5 per cent of the vote.[57]

The months following Cohen's run for president provided further examples that there is a growing disillusionment with and opposition towards the State of Israel amongst young British Jews. In March 2017, a Jewish student wrote a blog post on the *Times of Israel*, positioning herself as 'part of a generation of young Jews who have been on a journey of learning a more complete truth about Israel-Palestine's past and present'.[58] Describing a personal journey from support for Israel to opposing the occupation, and from opposing boycotts to supporting them, the author wrote: 'Not so long ago, we were in the minority, fighting for the ability for Jews to be critical of Israel in our UK Jewish community. The people who dismissed us then have now taken up the anti-occupation role for themselves.' However, she continued,

> while it's becoming increasingly acceptable for Jews to speak out against the State of Israel, boycotting Israel is still a red line for our community. I know many young Jews who have confided in me their support of boycotts, yet are too scared to speak out. Their fear is not unjustified, pro-boycott Jews face intimidation and harassment by many in our community, and are constantly having their Jewishness questioned.

Around the same time, a former President of Edinburgh University's Jewish Society (2012–13) wrote about 'the growing frustration felt by many millennial Jews about the default positioning that support for Israel receives amongst Jewish civil society organisations.[59]

In October 2016, an article was published in *Haaretz* by Sara Yael Hirschhorn, then the Sidney Brichto Fellow in Israel Studies at the University of Oxford.[60] The title was striking: 'Liberal Zionists, We Lost the Kids'. The piece was based on an afternoon that Hirschhorn spent with 'a group of teenagers in my community here in Oxford, leading a session about Zionism'. The aim 'was to talk about what Israel means to 14 to 18 years olds', but, as it turned out, the answer was that 'it really doesn't mean much at all'. Within this group, 'the majority children of the stalwarts of this proudly Zionist community which ranges from Reform to Orthodox', not a single one 'would self-identify as a Zionist'. Hirschhorn was keen to point out that the problem was not issues like Israel's settlements in the West Bank, but rather 'the very premise of a self-defining State of the Jews' – to them, she wrote, 'the State of the Jews was synonymous only with xenophobia, colonialism, displacement, chauvinism, fundamentalism, and illiberalism'. In fact, as Hirschhorn relayed, when she 'asked them pointedly if it would alter their Jewish identity if the State of Israel was wiped off the map tomorrow', she was 'met with shrugged shoulders and then more adamant statements that Israel was not relevant to their understanding or expression of Judaism'.

The era of Trump and Bibi

Worryingly, from the point of view of the State of Israel and its allies, the Trump era is set to be a catalyst for these processes of fragmentation and growing dissent. As JVP's Vilkomerson wrote in a recent volume on anti-Semitism, 'the acquiescence and even support for Trump and his appointments by a number of mainstream Jewish institutions is opening a new conversation about how support for Israel and support for Jewish people are not only not equivalent, but sometimes at odds'.[61] In fact, she added, 'a noxious stew of Islamophobia, antisemitism, and racism is emerging that remarkably converges on one point: support for Israel'.[62] A piece in the *Forward* in November 2016, following Trump's election, put it like this: 'Just as the US starts mimicking Israel, most Jews have become deeply uncomfortable.'[63] Moreover, Trump arrived in the White House as many American Jews were already feeling the strain over a different, ongoing era – that of Netanyahu.

In June 2017, two decisions by the Israeli authorities 'sparked outrage in the Jewish world'.[64] First, the Israeli cabinet voted to suspend its own plan 'to create a new and permanent space for egalitarian prayer at the Western Wall'. That very same day, 'a ministerial committee voted to move forward a bill that would deny recognition of conversions performed in Israel but outside the state-sanctioned Orthodox system'. These developments, the *New York Times* reported, prompted 'an emotional debate' over Israel's relationship with the world's Jews, 'at a time when a right-wing Israeli government, under increased international criticism, has relied on support among the generally more liberal Jewish diaspora in the West.[65] 'To the casual observer, Israel has never looked more secure and prosperous,' wrote Thomas Friedman in the same paper.[66] 'In fact', he continued, 'the foundations of Israel's long-term national security are cracking', as,

> under the leadership of Prime Minister Bibi Netanyahu, Israel is … drawing a line between itself and the Jewish diaspora, particularly the U.S. Jewish community that has been so vital for Israel's security, diplomatic standing and remarkable economic growth.

Half a century ago, just after Israel had conquered the West Bank and Gaza Strip, American journalist I. F. Stone reviewed an issue of Jean Paul-Sartre's journal *Modern Times* dedicated to the 'Israeli-Arab conflict'.[67] 'Israel is creating a kind of moral schizophrenia in world Jewry,' Stone wrote in the *New York Review of Books*.

> In the outside world the welfare of Jewry depends on the maintenance of secular, non-racial, pluralistic societies. In Israel, Jewry finds itself defending a society in which mixed marriages cannot be legalized, in which non-Jews have a lesser status than Jews, and in which the ideal is racial and exclusionist.

Fifty years on, and as American Jewish commentator Peter Beinart has put it, 'maintaining this moral distinction' between support for liberal politics and democratic values in the US and support for occupation and illiberalism in Israel has only 'grown harder' for 'organised American Jewish life' – and it is a distinction that is now 'fading' entirely.[68] The overlap in Trump's occupancy of the White House and Netanyahu's premiership is pushing a long-standing, often below-the-surface tension into the public eye, and possibly to breaking point.

In an August 2017 piece for *Haaretz*, veteran commentator Chemi Shalev pointed out how, as Dov Waxman's scholarship among others has demonstrated, 'the erosion of American Jewish solidarity with Israel didn't start with Donald Trump'.[69] Rather, 'the identification of the Jewish community with the Jewish state reached a zenith in the 1967 Six-Day War and has been going downhill ever since, in spurts and bursts'. Though Israel continues to 'enjoy the support of an overwhelming majority of American Jews, divisions about peace, the occupation, religious pluralism and Israel's increasingly right-wing character' have grown 'steadily'. Shalev continued:

> When the presidency of Barack Obama pitted his adoring Jewish supporters against a right-wing Jewish establishment and an Israeli prime minister that reviled him, many people thought the rupture couldn't get worse. But that was before anyone imagined that Trump could be elected president.

For many Jews, Chalev explained, 'Trump is the worst thing that has happened to America in their lifetimes'. At the same time,

> Israel's tepid reaction to the neo-Nazi show of force and violence in Charlottesville … casts Israel as a country that continues to curry favour with Trump despite his flirtation with anti-Semitic scum. It portrays Netanyahu as a leader willing to sacrifice American Jews in exchange for continued support for his policies and for the occupation.

Thus, Chalev concludes, 'the delineation between the two opposing Jewish camps has never seemed clearer'.

> On one side we have Netanyahu, many of his colleagues, the pro-settler lobby, an unfortunate proportion of Orthodox Jews, supporters of Jewish settlements, Obama and/or Muslim-hating Israelis along with hyper-hawks and ultranationalists such as Sheldon Adelson. On the other side there are Israeli doves along with American Jewish liberals, Reform and Conservative Jews

and other Trump-haters. And increasingly it seems that never the twain shall meet.

Conclusion

In March 2017, Israeli think tank the Reut Institute warned of a 'perfect storm' brewing for Israel's relationship with Jews around the world, citing 'several indicators', and in particular, 'an increasingly complex relationship between Israel and the younger generation of American Jews'.[70] The think tank suggested that 2017 would represent a symbolic watershed, 'a critical year for Israel-Diaspora relations' and 'the site of a convergence of worrying events and trends'. So, what was so special about 2017? First, the Institute explained, 2017 was a year of key anniversaries, including the Balfour Declaration centenary, and 50 years of Israeli control of the occupied Palestinian territory. 'The convergence of these events', Reut wrote, would 'further highlight the Israeli-Palestinian conflict and its implications for Israel-Diaspora relations'. Specifically, 'a decline in the prospects for a Two-State Solution, and the lack of an agreed upon alternative' has meant that leading American Jewish organisations 'increasingly struggle to deal with a complex Israeli reality'. Second, the think tank argued, 2017 was set to be 'the site of renewed conflict around the status of Progressive Judaism in Israel', referring to issues such as access to the Western Wall mentioned earlier in this chapter. 'Conflicts such as these negatively affect the ability of a growing number of individuals, as well as Jewish communal organizations, to maintain a meaningful connection to Israel', Reut observed.

Finally, and significantly, 2017 was a year where Israel and the American Jewish community had to 'deal with the repercussions' of Donald Trump's presidential victory, 'in the face of strong opposition of progressive Jews in the United States'. Their stance is in strong contrast to 'the present Israeli government's strong support for the Trump Administration' which, along with 'the lack of progress in negotiations with the Palestinians', was 'likely to place most American Jews and the Israeli government on two different sides of the political arena'. As a result, 'American Jewish organizations will be compelled to take clear sides on Israeli political issues', developments which 'will create significant organizational dilemmas where every outcome comes with significant costs'. Overall, the think-tank concluded, while 'the veteran leadership of American Jewry seeks to contain and ease these contradictions', in contrast, 'many young American Jews show signs of polarization in relation to Israel'.

Two months previously, on the eve of Trump's inauguration, another think tank, The Institute for National Security Studies (INSS), published a similar warning.[71] 'The Jewish communities in Israel and the US, which constitute about 80 per cent of the world's Jewish population, are already tested by their divisions over religion and politics,' the report noted, highlighting the familiar disputes over worship at the Western Wall and the policies of Israel's Orthodox state rabbinate. The INSS noted further, 'significant gaps between the US and Israeli Jewish communities in attitudes relating to politics', pointing to surveys that show while '49 percent of US Jews describe themselves as liberal, only 8 percent of Israelis identify similarly' (separate recent research showed a 'wide rift' in attitudes between young American Jews and young Jewish Israelis).[72] The INSS also cited other surveys indicating that 'the younger generation in the United States, Jews and non-Jews alike, supports Israel less than its predecessors did'. Meanwhile, 'the growing hate speech and incitement towards foreigners and minorities evident after Trump's victory may well distance the US Jewish community from the incoming administration, at the same time that the incoming President's pro-Israel positions could lead to closer ties between Jerusalem and Washington'. In the context of 'pre-existing tensions', INSS concludes, 'these different attitudes toward the Trump presidency ... could easily deepen the divide between American Jewry and Israel'.

The Reut Institute was careful to frame such developments as strategic concerns, on the basis that the relationship between

Israel and Jewish communities worldwide 'serves as a central pillar of Israel's national security', and, more broadly, 'fundamentally relates to the essence of the State of Israel, its vision, mission, and purpose'.[73] Former, and even current, Israeli officials have discussed the growing crisis in similarly serious terms. During a June 2017 discussion by a Knesset subcommittee on 'trends in American Jewry and their impact on relations with Israel', senior Likud parliamentarian Avi Dichter described 'the connection between American Jewry and the State of Israel' as 'a strategic-to-existential asset; strategic turbo'.[74] He added: 'The weakening of this asset is a real threat to the State of Israel'. That same month, a former Israeli ambassador, Arthur Koll, who also served in senior positions within the Ministry of Foreign Affairs, penned a similarly troubled op-ed: 'the strategic alliance with the US is a central pillar in the very foundation of the national security of Israel, and its international standing', Koll wrote.[75] 'The bond between the Jewish State and American Jewry has been a central component in nourishing and forging this unique alliance'. However, he continued, 'we are now reaching a stage in which decisions by the Israeli government win support by American Jews who support Trump, and at the same time, they tangibly harm the position of liberal American Jews, who – it so happens – are Democratic supporters'. These 'partisan reverberations' mean that, ultimately, 'these [Israeli government] decisions undermine the traditional Israeli interest of securing bipartisan support of Israel'. What Koll did not address, however, is that Israel's star has been waning for some time amongst the Democratic base and left-liberals more generally – and this is the 'crack in the wall' we will look at next.

4

Progressive alienation,
far-right embrace

The fact that an overwhelming majority of Democrats voted
against Israel on a matter that it described as existential doesn't
bode well for the future.

– Chemi Shalev, September 2015[1]

Yet we cannot just shuck off the sense that there's a real affinity
here as well. Far-right nationalists often see Israel, particularly
its current far-right government, as an ally.

– Asher Schechter, October 2017[2]

For decades, support for Israel has been a bipartisan issue in US
politics; that is to say, both Republicans and Democrats have seen
the US's strong relationship with Israel – manifesting in military
aid, diplomatic protection, and more – as an unquestioned good.
Resolutions on Capitol Hill declaring support for Israeli military
offensives have been passed without a single dissenting vote.
During Barack Obama's two terms in office, the US signed a
new Memorandum of Understanding (MOU) for military aid to
Israel worth $38 billion over a ten-year period ('the single largest
pledge of military assistance in U.S. history', boasted the White
House).[3] The Obama administration also resolutely defended
Israel's assaults on the Gaza Strip, and shielded Israel in international fora, such as the United Nations; though the US declined
to veto Security Council Resolution 2334 in December 2016, the
first time that Obama used its veto power at the Security Council
was to thwart a 2011 resolution condemning Israeli settlements.
However, it was also during the Obama years that signs started to

appear that the era of rock solid bipartisan support for Israel was ending, a process that has continued – and looks set to accelerate – under the Trump presidency. More on some of those signs in a moment, but first, let's recap the events discussed in the book's introduction; the Senate confirmation hearing of Trump-nominee and now-Ambassador to Israel, David Friedman.

On 9 March, after a highly contentious public debate about the suitability of Friedman for the post, the Senate Foreign Relations Committee approved the bankruptcy lawyer's nomination in a 12–9 vote. Only one Democrat joined 11 Republicans in backing Friedman. In the final, full vote, the Senate was split 52–46 in a roll call vote, described by Politico as 'an unusual step' since US ambassadors 'have traditionally been approved by voice vote or through unanimous consent', on account of 'strong bipartisan support' for Israel.[4] The words of Chris Murphy (D-Conn.) during the confirmation hearing bear repeating. Warning that 'Israel has become another political football', the senator claimed that in the 'short time' he had been in public service, 'Israel has gone from being an issue that unites us to an issue that is used in political campaigns in order to divide us'.[5] Friedman's tumultuous nomination was just one recent episode to suggest that Israel no longer enjoys the bipartisan consensus in US politics that many had assumed was unshakeable (and was itself representative of the shift). Another example was Bernie Sanders' candidacy in the Democratic primaries, a leadership bid that shed light on those within the party – especially amongst the grassroots – and amongst progressives more broadly, who want a tougher line on Israel.

Like Friedman, Sanders is both a symptom and an accelerant. At a debate with Hillary Clinton in Brooklyn in April 2016, an exchange took place that is worth reproducing verbatim from the transcript.[6] Asked about comments he made regarding 'Operation Protective Edge' in 2014 – an unprecedentedly brutal assault on the Gaza Strip by the Israeli military – Sanders doubled down on his (admittedly mild) criticism of the offensive.

SANDERS: But – but what you just read, yeah, I do believe that. Israel was subjected to terrorist attacks, has every right in the world to destroy terrorism. But we had in the Gaza area – not a very large area – some 10,000 civilians who were wounded and some 1,500 who were killed.

AUDIENCE MEMBER: Free Palestine!

SANDERS: Now, if you're asking not just me, but countries all over the world was that a disproportionate attack, the answer is that I believe it was, and let me say something else.

(APPLAUSE) (CHEERING)

SANDERS: And, let me say something else. As somebody who is 100% pro-Israel, in the long run – and this is not going to be easy, God only knows, but in the long run if we are ever going to bring peace to that region which has seen so much hatred and so much war, we are going to have to treat the Palestinian people with respect and dignity.

(APPLAUSE) (CHEERING)

Later, he added: 'All that I am saying is we cannot continue to be one-sided. There are two sides to the issue.' Taken as a whole, the above comments – plus the applause, cheers, and even an interjection from the audience – suggest something significant is happening within the Democratic party. As a report in the *New York Times* put it, Sanders' comments, while 'measured', were nonetheless 'striking' enough that they 'worried more traditionally pro-Israel Jewish Democrats and Jewish organizations trying desperately to maintain bipartisan support for the Israeli government but watching it slowly being chipped away'.[7] In the same piece, 'a prominent Brooklyn progressive rabbi' said the applause that greeted Sanders' criticism of Israel 'spoke to this growing rift in the Democratic Party', and 'was proof of a major crisis in the Jewish community that no major Jewish organization has resolved or figured out how to handle'.

A month later, Sanders placed public intellectual Dr Cornel West, Rep. Keith Ellison (D-Minn.), and Arab American Institute-founder James Zogby on the Democratic Party's Platform Drafting Committee, three individuals who all, in different ways, have voiced criticism of Israel and support for the Palestinians. Malcolm Hoenlein, executive vice chair of the Conference of Presidents of Major American Jewish Organizations, called the presence of such individuals on the committee 'disturbing', adding: 'For us, the concern is that it legitimizes and potentially puts into a major party platform' a point of view 'that undermines the principles of the Israeli-U.S. relationship that have been bipartisan for decades'.[8] Weeks later, the committee considered – but ultimately rejected – proposed language on the Israeli-Palestinian conflict that urged 'an end to occupation and illegal settlements' in the West Bank.[9] But the existence of the debate at all is what is instructive here. BBC correspondent Kim Ghattas, writing in *Foreign Policy*, noted how Sanders had 'clearly identified the Israel-Palestine conflict as another issue on which he could draw a sharp contrast with the Democratic Party establishment and excite its progressive base' – he 'had little to lose and everything to gain by speaking up for the Palestinians'.[10]

These divisions have been bubbling to the surface for some years now; at the 2012 Democratic National Convention, there was booing from delegates when a reference to Jerusalem as the capital of Israel, after having initially been dropped, was reinstated.[11] In a report on the 2016 convention, the *Jewish Telegraphic Agency* reported that 'delegates for Bernie Sanders, many of them young, would like to see America's sympathies shift from robust support of Israel to outspoken opposition to the oppression of Palestinians', adding: 'These delegates see opposing Israel's occupation of the West Bank as of a piece with other human rights issues they champion'.[12] For some experts, the trajectory is clear: 'The Democratic leadership will change on Israel and Palestine when they start to perceive that it's going to hurt them electorally and I do believe that's going to happen', political activist and pollster Peter Feld told the *Forward* in February 2017.[13] 'It's not going to be politically possible by 2020 for any Democrat to run for president with the type of pro-Israel platform that Hillary ran on in 2016.'

Friedman and Sanders are important parts of the story, but there are other recent examples. In 2015, US-Israeli relations were marred by an extraordinarily public dispute over negotiations, and the eventual deal, with Iran. The story was perhaps best typified by Benjamin Netanyahu's speech in Congress in March of that year, conducted without a formal invitation from the White House, urging US politicians to block Obama's nuclear deal with Tehran. The sight of a foreign leader allying with Republicans on Capitol Hill to undermine a Democratic president led, unsurprisingly, to considerable disquiet amongst Democrats, more than 50 of whom boycotted Netanyahu's speech entirely.[14] Six months later, Senate Democrats prevented the passing of legislation intended to kill the Iran nuclear deal, with only four of 46 Democrats siding with Republican senators in opposition to the deal.[15] The next day, only 25 of 187 Democrats voted against the deal in the House of Representatives.[16] As the dust started to settle, the *New York Times* said the debate in Washington over the deal had 'exposed the diminishing power of the Israeli lobbying force that spent tens of millions of dollars to prevent the accord'.[17] As Israeli journalist Chemi Shalev put it, 'the head to head clash between AIPAC (The American Israel Public Affairs Committee, which lobbied hard against the deal), the Jewish establishment and the Obama administration increases the already significant distance between Israeli policies and Democrats and the left'.[18] The fact is, he added, that 'an overwhelming majority of Democrats voted against Israel on a matter that it described as existential'.

The shift amongst Democrats is not restricted to a reluctance to sign up to anything that Israel and its lobby groups demand; there is also a growing awareness of, and opposition to, human rights violations experienced by Palestinians under occupation. In March

2016, Sen. Patrick Leahy (D-Vt.) and 10 other House members – all Democrats – signed a letter to the Obama administration demanding an investigation into claims that Egyptian *and Israeli* armed forces had committed 'gross violations of human rights'.[19] Three months later, 20 members of Congress (all Democrats) asked Obama to establish a Special Envoy for Palestinian Youth, in light of the abuses faced by children in Israeli detention and military courts.[20] At the end of the year, when the House of Representatives voted to condemn UN Security Council Resolution 2443 (which reaffirmed the illegality of Israeli settlements), 76 Democrats – and four Republicans – voted *against* the resolution, a development which some saw as 'a sign ... that the discussion around Israel is changing'.[21] Democrats who voted 'No' included House Minority Leader Nancy Pelosi and Keith Ellison, while another dissenting Democrat, Luis Gutierrez, explained that he objected to the idea that 'this Congress has allowed our chamber to be used as an Israeli campaign rally'. In June 2017, meanwhile, 32 Democratic members of Congress raised with Secretary of State Rex Tillerson the Israeli military trial of Palestinian human rights defender Issa Amro, asking him to use his influence with the Israeli authorities.[22]

The end of the bipartisan era has been driven by a shift over a number of years amongst Democrats' rank and file. In 2011, for example, a poll on Americans' views towards their government's recognition of a Palestinian state found that support for such a move among Democrats was precisely double that found among Republicans (54 versus 27 percent).[23] Another telling sign was a CNN poll taken in 2014 during 'Operation Protective Edge', when 51 per cent of Democrats thought Israel was using 'too much' force, a view shared by only 24 per cent of Republicans.[24] Indeed, 42 per cent of Democrats believed the Israeli assault to be unjustified entirely, a view held by only 19 per cent of Republicans. In a separate Pew Research Centre poll conducted during the war, while 60 per cent of Republicans saw Hamas as most responsible for the violence, Democrats were divided: 29 per cent fingered Hamas as more responsible, but 26 per cent said Israel.[25] The Pew survey included other findings that point to a related, but different and broader, problem for Israel, with Americans aged 18–29 more likely to blame Israel (29 percent) than Hamas (21 percent), a remarkable finding considering how both actors are portrayed in US media.

A poll in 2015 – the year that Israel sought to torpedo the Iran nuclear deal – conducted on behalf of the Brookings Institution showed that Democrats were twice as likely as Republicans to blame 'continued Israeli occupation and settlement expansion' for the lack of progress in peace talks, and 49 per cent of Democrats surveyed backed 'economic sanctions or … more serious action' by the US in response to Israeli settlement expansion (that figure rose to 56 per cent in 2017).[26] That same year, a survey carried out by Frank Luntz, a Republican, pro-Israel pollster, found that 47 per cent of Democrats believe Israel to be a 'racist country', as opposed to 13 per cent of Republicans.[27] Interestingly, in terms of longer-term implications for policy and a bipartisan divide, only 18 per cent of Democrats said they would be more likely to vote for a local politician who supports Israel, but 32 per cent said they would be *less* likely to support a local politician who backs Israel (for Republicans, the figures were 76 and 7 per cent respectively). Criticism of Israeli occupation by a local politician, meanwhile, was a turn-off for 75 per cent of Republicans – but only 23 per cent of Democrats. Summing up his findings, Luntz said 'Israel can no longer claim to have the bipartisan support of America.'

The divide is here to stay – and it is growing. In 2016, a survey carried out by the Brand Israel Group found that the demographic groups 'with relatively high levels of favourability toward Israel… included men, Republicans and older Americans'.[28] By contrast, 'the groups that like Israel less are … women, Democrats and millennials, along with African-Americans and Latinos'. Compared to an earlier survey in 2010, favourability among Democrats had dropped 13 points, from 73 per cent to 60 per cent, the group found. In January 2017, the 'difference between the proportion of Republicans and Democrats who sympathize with Israel over the

Palestinians' was the largest it had ever been in surveys going back to 1978.[29] The aforementioned Pew poll's findings also represented the first time that Democrats 'were about as likely to sympathize with the Palestinians as with Israel'. Among 'liberal Democrats' specifically (i.e. left-leaning, as opposed to 'centrist' Democrats) 38 per cent sympathised more with the Palestinians, compared to 26 per cent sympathising more with Israel.[30] That same month, a YouGov poll asked Americans to rate countries as an ally or enemy of the US.[31] While Israel dropped to 16th place from 6th in 2014, even more striking was the vast disparity between Republicans and Democrats, who placed Israel 5th and 28th respectively.

These shifts are not going to produce immediate change at the level of policy, and there will be stubborn resistance to even modest changes that reflect the opinion evidenced by polls. In the spring of 2017, efforts by some members of the Massachusetts Democratic Party to alter the platform so as to describe Israeli settlements as 'obstacles to peace' ran aground, after 'state party leaders and Jewish communal organizational leaders vehemently opposed the resolution'.[32] This was a timely reminder that even mild criticism of Israeli policies – even criticism in line with numerous past US administrations – can face strong opposition in a milieu where unquestioning support for Israel has been de rigueur for so long. Or take Bernie Sanders, for example, a lightning rod for many in the party who wish to see stronger support for Palestinian rights, but someone who still, when asked, denounced the Palestinian-led Boycott, Divestment, Sanctions (BDS) campaign.[33] Steve Cohen, a Hebrew Union College-based academic, I believe got it right when he argued in February 2017 that the Democratic Party would remain officially, and explicitly, 'pro-Israel' for the time being. 'Pro-Israel will mean to oppose expansionist policies of the Israeli government to save Israel from itself', he said.[34] But the processes underway, whose trajectory is from the bottom up, are not going to stop. And at some point, their impact will be felt at the level of national decision-makers.

Israel's deteriorating image amongst the liberal-left, or progressives, is a phenomenon not confined to the US – in fact, in other Western countries, it is arguably at a far more advanced stage. Westminster-based lobby group Labour Friends of Israel (LFI), for example, felt obliged to 'reinvent itself' in 2011, in order to 'develop the "progressive case" for Israel', a development prompted by what *The Jewish Chronicle* called 'a growing anti-Zionist sentiment in the Labour movement and the wider British left'.[35] At a conference held in March 2017 by UK-based Israel advocacy group, the Britain Israel Communications and Research Centre (BICOM), a senior official from polling firm Populus had some sobering words for the audience during a panel on Israel and public opinion. Analysing various polls in the UK, Western Europe and North America, Populus managing director Rick Nye explained how 'support for Israel has increasingly become ... the preserve of older, more male, more conservative parts of Western electorates, and in the US, evangelical, religious parts of the electorate'.[36] At the same time, 'supporting Israel becomes less attractive for people who aren't older, more conservative and more male', he added. 'And it impacts disproportionately on college-educated younger people, people on campus'. The challenge for Israel advocates, Nye said, is 'can you construct a contemporary narrative that's attractive to a millennial audience?'

That is a tall order, and the more perceptive Israel advocates are well aware of the challenge they face. As Alan Johnson, an academic turned BICOM staffer, admitted in a 2015 piece on Jews and the left, for many, 'one brute fact remains ... the Palestinians do not have a state or a vote and pretty soon it will be 50 years since 1967'.[37] For 'most people', moreover, 'it's the only fact that matters'. In other words, it's the occupation, stupid. Israel's 'problem', as Jewish American commentator Peter Beinart put it in February 2016, is its 'almost half-century-long control over millions of West Bank Palestinians who lack citizenship and the right to vote in the country that controls their lives, and live under a different legal system than their Jewish neighbours'.[38] Such a state of affairs, Beinart says, undermines what has legitimised Israel for many on the left: the perception that it is a democracy. 'Israel is now associated not with the higher goal of being a light onto the nations and the liberal ideal once part of socialist Zionism,' Samuel Heilman, a sociology professor at Queens College, told the *Forward* in early 2017, 'but increasingly associated with right-wing regimes and right-wing politics'.[39]

That dramatic change in association for progressives and leftists, from land of the kibbutz to belligerent occupier, is not, however, just about Israel – it's also about the left itself. In his book 'The British left and Zionism: History of a Divorce', the University of Manchester's Paul Kelemen makes the important point that while 'the disillusionment with Israel has been most pronounced on the left ... in retrospect, *it is the left's previous and longstanding commitment to the Zionist project that stands out*' (my emphasis).[40] By way of illustration, consider the following. In 1922, James Ramsay MacDonald, who became Labour's first ever prime minister, rejected Palestinian Arabs' claim to self-determination on the basis that 'the Arab population do not and cannot use or develop the resources of Palestine', echoing the same discourse that accompanied the displacement and genocide of indigenous populations in Australia, North America, and elsewhere.[41] Or recall how, at its 1944 annual conference, the Labour party adopted a resolution on Palestine which stated: 'Let the Arabs be encouraged to move out, as the Jews move in.'[42] Such views would be considered anathema to any self-identifying progressives or left-wingers today. Thus, while Israel's own trajectory and history – particularly post-1967 – has had a vital role to play in alienating the left from Israel, equally as important is how 'anti-racism and human rights have assumed greater prominence in the left's political outlook'.[43] To put it plainly, Israel has always been wedded to settler colonialism; the left (or at least a significant portion of it) has embraced decolonisation.

Far-right embrace

While liberals and the left have grown disillusioned with, or even hostile towards Israel, a parallel process in the opposite direction has taken place among important sections of the European and North American far right. Many Israeli politicians, including at the highest levels of government, have embraced these newfound friends, despite the disquiet among many – including in Jewish communities – at such alliances. According to Israeli writer and blogger Edo Konrad, '[the] logic that undergirds the thinking of Israeli politicians who back far-right European politicians such as [French National Front leader] Marine Le Pen, [Netherlands' Party for Freedom leader] Geert Wilders, and [Austrian Freedom Party leader] Heinz-Christian Strache' is straightforward: 'we will politely ignore their Nazi pasts, pesky anti-Semitic cartoons, and outright incitement – as long as they continue to back the Jewish state'.[44] Konrad added: 'This is what a deal with the devil looks like'.

In the summer of 2017, these developments came under an uncomfortable, though instructive, spotlight, in Hungary. At the time, Prime Minister Viktor Orban was busy 'courting radical right-wing voters ahead of 2018 elections', using language of 'ethnic homogeneity' that analysts saw as 'fashioned to occupy territory on the far right'.[45] In a June speech, Orban praised the role of Miklos Horthy, a Hungarian leader who collaborated with the Nazis during the Holocaust.[46] The remarks, however, came just two weeks before Netanyahu's scheduled participation in a diplomatic summit in Budapest, and, 'according to a senior Israeli official', Netanyahu's government 'agreed to accept a weak clarification by the Hungarian foreign minister in order to avoid damaging the upcoming summit'.[47] But there was more. Orban was also spearheading a nasty campaign against Hungarian-American investor and philanthropist George Soros, a campaign with clear anti-Semitic undertones (and which prompted explicit anti-Semitism Orban declined to condemn). After an appeal by Hungarian Jews, the Israeli embassy in Budapest published a condemnation – only for Netanyahu to instruct the Foreign Ministry to retract its statement, and to issue a 'clarification' which said Soros was a legitimate target for criticism.[48] With the path smoothed, Netanyahu proceeded to Budapest where he 'hailed Viktor Orban's government as one of Israel's foremost defenders'.[49]

In Austria, meanwhile, the far-right Freedom Party has also sought to build ties with Israeli politicians, a party whose first leader was a former Nazi party member and SS officer, and whose participation in a 2000 coalition government prompted international outrage. In January 2016, officials from Israel's ruling Likud party hosted Freedom Party leader Heinz-Christian Strache, an invitation they defended on the basis that 'Strache and his party had become more and more pro-Israel in recent years', and could 'soon come to power in Austria' (as indeed they did in December 2017, as part of a coalition agreement).[50] In June 2017, Likud parliamentarian Yehuda Glick met with Strache in Vienna, where the Freedom Party leader called for Jerusalem to be recognised as Israel's capital.[51] Earlier that same year, Nicolas Bay, secretary-general of the French National Front visited Israel and met with 'military, government and political officials', including the Israeli Health Ministry's deputy director general and Likud party members.[52] In Switzerland, meanwhile, the right-wing, anti-immigrant Swiss People's Party sponsored a bill in 2017 that sought to ban state funding for any groups 'implicated in racism, antisemitism, incitement to hatred or BDS campaigns'.[53] According to the *Jewish Telegraphic Agency*, the legislation was introduced following lobbying by the Israeli organisation NGO Monitor, a group dedicated to attacking Palestinian, Israeli and international human rights groups who speak out about the occupation.[54] In a blow to NGO Monitor, reference to BDS was stripped from the final version – but the political alliance between an Israel advocacy organisation and the People's Party was striking.[55]

Contemporary far-right support for Israel is based on three, main elements. First, it is part of attempts by far-right parties to sanitise the historic (and even current) anti-Semitism of their movements and traditions. A particularly crude illustration of this phenomenon occurred in October 2009, when British National Party (BNP) head Nick Griffin appeared on BBC current affairs show Question Time and claimed that he had transformed the BNP from an anti-Semitic organisation to 'the only party which … supported Israel's right to deal with Hamas terrorists' (a reference to 'Operation Cast Lead').[56] Coincidentally, just three weeks earlier right-wing Polish politician Michal Kaminski appeared at Conservative Party conference, a man who had previously declared 'we want Poland for the Poles', and opposed a public apology by the Polish president for a 1941 massacre of Jews.[57] According to *Jewish Chronicle* reporter Miriam Shaviv, Kaminski was 'in Britain as the special guest of the Conservative Friends of Israel', who had also taken him to Israel, 'where he was pictured smiling by the Western Wall and was welcomed by [then] deputy foreign minister Danny Ayalon'.[58] Well-known Israel apologists, like journalist Stephen Pollard, defended Kaminski from accusations of anti-Semitism on the basis of his defence of Israel.[59] Commenting on the Griffin and Kaminski controversies, Shaviv wrote how supporting Israel, for both men, 'is a strategic move'.

> Supporting Israel allows them to claim that they are not really racists or anti-Semites, and gives them cover for other objectionable views. It also allows them to portray themselves, to their supporters, as opponents of the Muslims – a position that carries far more electoral benefit in today's Europe than being anti-Semitic.[60]

Almost a decade on, and numerous far-right nationalist groups, from France, to the Netherlands and Sweden 'are pledging Israel their full support'.[61] At a conference in Brussels in January 2017, Holly R. Huffnagle, policy adviser on anti-Semitism at the US State Department, warned of European far-right groups attempting to legitimise themselves by posing as 'friends of Israel'.[62] Highlighting 'a very real concern today of the rise of the far right historically anti-Semitic parties in Europe', Huffnagle described such groups as campaigning on 'ethno-nationalist, anti-migrant and anti-Muslim platforms'. She added: 'They now proclaim that they are "pro-Israel" and therefore they are no longer antisemitic, [that] they can't be antisemitic.'

Huffnagle's remarks point towards the second element of the far right's embrace of Israel: the perception of a common enemy in the form of 'Islamic terrorism' (or just Muslims in general). Israel is seen to be fighting the good fight against 'radical Islam', including with methods that the far right would like to see adopted by Western governments. Dutch far-right populist Geert Wilders, for example, notorious for his explicitly Islamophobic views, has urged Israel to build 'more and more settlements' in the Occupied West Bank, and described Israel as 'the West's first line of defence'.[63] In 2011, a group of far-right European politicians visited Israel, where they 'signed a "Jerusalem Declaration" guaranteeing Israel's right to defend itself against terror', as reported by *Newsweek*.[64]

'We stand at the vanguard in the fight for the Western, democratic community' against the 'totalitarian threat' of 'fundamentalist Islam', says the document, which was signed by members of the group that included Heinz-Christian Strache, head of the Austrian Freedom Party; Filip Dewinter, head of Belgium's ultranationalist Vlaams Belang; René Stadtkewitz, founder of the German Freedom Party; and Kent Ekeroth, the international secretary for the Sweden Democrats, a populist anti-immigration party.

For many in Israel, this is music to their ears. In 2008, Israeli parliamentarian Arieh Eldad screened a film by Geert Wilders and declared that 'the spread of Islam threatens the foundations of Western civilization'.[65] He continued: 'Muslim immigrants in Europe ... have not necessarily come there to be assimilated into society, but rather to resist it from the inside. The feeling in Europe is that the time has come to stop jihadist Islam, and this may be the last opportunity'. In an echo of the type of aforementioned language used by Wilders himself, Eldad said: 'If Jerusalem capitulates, Europe will follow in its footsteps and fall.'

The third key element of the contemporary far-right support for Israel is an identification with Israel on the grounds that it is a demographics-obsessed, ethno-national state. 'White nationalists', a 2016 piece by the US' National Public Radio (NPR) noted, 'point admiringly to Israel's character as a Jewish state and argue that it shows how the country is organized along ethnic and religious lines'.[66] American white nationalist activist Richard Spencer, for example, who popularised the term 'alt-right', has described his vision as a 'sort of white Zionism'.[67] According to Spencer, in a 2013 speech, the 'White Ethno-State' he dreams of 'would be, to borrow the title of a novel by Theodor Herzl (one of the founding fathers of Zionism), an Altneuland – an old, new country'.[68] In December 2016, a rabbi at Texas A&M University asked Spencer to join him in Torah study. 'My tradition teaches a message of radical inclusion and love,' the rabbi said. Spencer declined the invitation, responding: 'Do you really want radical inclusion into the State of Israel? And by that I mean radical inclusion. Maybe all of the Middle East could go move in to Tel Aviv or Jerusalem. Would you really want that?' The rabbi didn't answer.[69] As an Anti-Defamation League (ADL) official summarised: 'there are some white nationalists who support Israel, and they support it for very specific reasons: Because they see it as a nationalist state, and they compare it to a white ethno-state that they want in this country'.[70]

At the aforementioned June 2017 summit in Budapest, Netanyahu slammed the European Union in comments captured in a hot-mic moment.[71] Sounding very much like the continent's populist far right, the Israeli premier told his hosts: 'I think Europe has to decide if it wants to live and thrive or if it wants to shrivel and disappear. I am not very politically correct ... But the truth is the truth. Both about Europe's security and Europe's economic future. Both of these concerns mandate a different policy toward Israel'. He added: 'We are part of the European culture. Europe ends in Israel. East of Israel, there is no more Europe.' Commenting on the remarks, Israeli journalist Chemi Shalev said Netanyahu had 'appealed to the nationalistic and xenophobic side of his ... hosts from Hungary, Poland, Slovakia and the Czech Republic', playing to their 'ethnocentric nationalism and their fear of a Muslim "mongrelization" of Europe'.[72] Hungarian PM Orban, meanwhile, as reported by the *Financial Times*, 'defended his hardline refugee policies ... [by] liken[ing] the stance to Israel's right to self-defence', stating: 'We do not want to have a mixed population and we do not wish to change the ethnic mix of this country due to any outside pressure.'[73]

While the left, liberals, and even moderate conservatives, in Europe and North America have been appalled by the far right's nationalist, Islamophobic, and demography-focused rhetoric, it is important to remember how, in the Israeli context, the idea of the country as an 'an outpost of civilization as opposed to barbarism' (the words of Theodor Herzl), or a 'villa in the middle of the jungle' (the words of former Labor premier Ehud Barak) is very much a mainstream one.[74] Indeed, it is often Israel's so-called centrists who are responsible for demographic scare-mongering and advocates of a politics of ethnic separation to 'save the Jewish state' (as we saw in Chapter 2). Israel's Separation Wall, initially justified in the name of 'security' by then Prime Minister Ariel Sharon, has become a demographics-based border-in-waiting for the likes of the Labor party and Yesh Atid. Likewise, the fence along Israel's border with Egypt was constructed in the first instance not as a 'security' measure, but in response to concern over (non-Jewish) African 'infiltrators', who, Netanyahu said, posed an existential threat to Israel as a 'Jewish state'.[75] No wonder then, that Israeli defence companies are hoping that Europe's 'migration crisis and security fears' will 'create big opportunities'.[76]

The Trump factor

The alienation of progressives and the left from Israel, and the embrace of Israel by the far right, were both already well underway when Donald J. Trump was elected 45th president of the USA. But the Trump presidency is set to expose both processes to an unprecedented level of exposure, and, crucially, act as a catalyst for them – including an acceleration of the bipartisan split. Part of this has to do with the way in which Trump built a political base amongst the far right and white nationalists, even appointing a figure like Steve Bannon as White House Chief Strategist (albeit a short-lived role). It was 'under Bannon's leadership', as NPR described, that alt-right news site Breitbart 'published anti-feminist, anti-Muslim, and anti-immigrant articles and won a reputation as being allied with nationalists who explicitly favour white European values'.[77] Yet it is also, as the *Forward* put it, 'brazenly Zionist, albeit peddling an exclusively right-wing perspective on Israel'.[78] This is not just a problem for 'brand Israel' – it is an indication that Israel will not be immune from the wider political polarisation characteristic of the Trump era.

The Trump administration's approach to Israel and the Palestinians has also been a further catalysing factor, in that it has animated right-wing opponents of the two-state solution and Palestinian statehood, at the same time as prompting centrists to despair. Trump's high-profile decision to recognise Jerusalem as Israel's capital in December 2017 – a move hailed by Netanyahu and opposed by major US allies – was approved of by 76 per cent of Republicans, compared to just 12 per cent of Democrats.[79] By way of another example, consider how the Congressional Israel Victory Caucus was established in the first few months of the Trump presidency, chaired by two Republicans. Its launch event on Capitol Hill was not attended by a single Democrat, but did receive support from the Zionist Organisation of America and Christians United for Israel (CUFI).[80] The Caucus, which has a sister group in the Israeli Knesset, was also backed by Middle East Forum, a hard-right group led by well-known anti-Muslim activist Daniel Pipes.[81] According to critics, who included senior Democrats and Israel Allies Caucus co-chairs Brad Sherman and Eliot Engel, the caucus is 'a purely partisan effort that further erodes the longtime bipartisan support for Israel while achieving little or nothing of value'.[82] Such developments have wider implications, beyond purely an acceleration of the bipartisan shift, as noted by Peter Beinart. Commenting on a speech by Bernie Sanders at a J-Street conference, Beinart suggested that 'the more Trump and his advisers question long-standing taboos by shifting right, the more Democrats will do the same by shifting left'.[83] In other words, ambivalence or hostility towards the two-state framework from the Trump and Republican right (and indeed, from the European and North American far right more generally), will, in the words of Beinart 'liberate Democratic politicians [in the years to come] to think beyond two states, too'.

Meanwhile, the Trump era is also birthing a politics of resistance characterised by intersectional solidarity across various groups opposed to racism, Islamophobia, militarisation, police brutality, imperialism, border walls, and so on. In this context, many will make the comparison – if they have not already done so – between Trump's brand of ethno-nationalist, security-state politics and what has long been the mainstream in Israel. In a 2016 article, Eastern Mennonite University-based Timothy Seidel wrote: 'Whether it is the construction of walls, militarisation of borders, the confiscation of land, or the brutalisation and incarceration of bodies, activists and academics are identifying commonalities across experiences that transcend national boundaries and identities', highlighting 'the situation in Palestine–Israel' in particular as having 'played an increasingly significant role in mobilising transnational solidarities that cross such boundaries'.[84] In summer 2017, Adalah, a legal rights and advocacy centre based in Israel, with the support of the transnational Cultures of Resistance Network, launched 'Freedom, Bound', described as 'an artistic and historical account of the shared struggle for collective liberation', and 'inspired by and rooted in the rich legacy of Black-Palestinian solidarity'.[85] The online, multi-media resource showcased the work of artists, who were invited to respond 'to the legacy of Black-Palestinian solidarity'. In a post for Mondoweiss, Purdue University professors Tithi Bhattacharya and Bill V. Mullen noted how the alt-right and Israel advocates were deploying similar tactics in seeking to blacklist academics and students seen as progressive and supportive of Palestinian rights respectively.[86] They urged students and faculty to 'show their own solidarity' by joining up 'with campus groups like Students for Justice in Palestine' or taking up 'with the new national campus anti-fascism network'.

Conclusion

At this juncture, an important point needs to be acknowledged. It is my contention that the end of Israel as a bipartisan issue of concern in US politics, along with the wider left's alienation from and the far right's embrace of Israel, are developments of profound long-term concern for the State of Israel, and its ability to maintain the apartheid status quo. These are, in other words, cracks in the wall, like the fragmentation of, and growing dissent among, Jewish communities with respect to Israel. However, it might be countered, with the far right on the ascendency in Europe and North America, might Israel's alliance with the right be an asset? Or as Trump would put it, if liberals and progressives look increasingly like 'losers', who cares if Israel can no longer depend on them? Here is why I do not believe this argument holds water. First, liberal opinion-formers and cultural elites remain highly influential in the West, in the media, in NGOs and human rights work, and in politics too. As an Israel lobby professional put it in 2015, 'Israel has lost the intellectual high ground [in the West], certainly in those places where the liberal left is dominant', adding: 'Today, the young idealist ... sees BDS as a reasonable political response. Tomorrow, the centre ground itself will be threatened'.[87] Second, putting Israel's eggs in a right-wing, or even far-right, basket, is short-sighted; in the US, the Democrats will at some point return to power, while across Europe and North America, an energised, radical left-wing politics is also on the rise – it's not just about *right-wing* populism. Finally, Israel remains highly dependent – practically, morally – on the support of Jewish communities worldwide, especially in the US and Europe. Yet the divisions and dissent described in Chapter 3 will only deepen if the emerging future is an apartheid Israel reliant on far-right friends.

In February 2017, Israel's Justice Minister Ayelet Shaked expressed her worry about the loss of support for Israel amongst Democrats in no uncertain terms. Speaking at the Conference of Presidents of Major American Jewish Organisations, Shaked said she 'almost didn't sleep at night' after seeing a recent poll, and called the drop 'a strategic issue for Israel'.[88] Other Israelis are similarly troubled. Shalom Lipner, who from 1990 to 2016 worked for seven Israeli premiers in the Prime Minister's Office, reminded readers in a June 2017 article that 'the literal ABCs of Israel's national security doctrine' is 'Jerusalem's airtight bond with the United States': 'America. Bipartisanship. Compulsory', he wrote.[89] Yet, he went on, 'the incontrovertible fact today is that Republican sympathies for Israel far outstrip Democratic ones, thus posing a challenge from which friends of this bilateral relationship dare not shirk; capitulation is an unaffordable luxury for them'. Not long after, an article with the title 'How Long Could Israel Survive Without America?' was published in *Newsweek* by Chuck Freilich, a Harvard University based, former Israeli deputy national security advisor.[90] After noting various aspects of 'Israel's dependence on the US' – such as the fact that, in recent years, US aid 'has accounted for some 3 percent of Israel's total national budget' and '40 percent of the Israel Defense Forces (IDF) budget' – Freilich cautioned that while 'there is nothing wrong with rising support for Israel on the right … the loss of support on the left, and the identification of Israel as a partisan issue, should be of deep concern'.

According to the Pew Research Centre, sympathy for Palestinians among US Millennials (Americans born after 1980) rose from 9 per cent in 2006 to 27 per cent in 2016.[91] In a Gallup poll conducted in early 2017, the two demographic subgroups with the most unfavourable attitudes towards Israel were Democrats (36 per cent of whom viewed Israel 'mostly or very unfavourably'), followed by the under-30s (33 per cent of whom viewed Israel unfavourably).[92] In a 'special report' by the Council on Foreign Relations published in November 2016 on 'Repairing the U.S.-Israel Relationship', co-authors Robert D. Blackwill and Philip H. Gordon pointed out that the trend amongst Millennials 'cannot be attributed to a perspective expected to change as this younger group ages, given that in the past a similar age gap did not exist'.[93] Summarising trends in the US they describe as 'troubling', Blackwill and Gordon write: 'the issues include a youth population less sympathetic to Israel than their older counterparts, demographic trends likely to give more political power to groups less traditionally supportive of Israel, an increasingly divided U.S. Jewish community, and – perhaps most troublingly – a growing and unprecedented partisan gap over Israel'. While none of these trends 'will necessarily lead to divorce between the United States and Israel', the authors add, 'to ignore their existence would be irresponsible'. Yet in an era of apartheid in Palestine, these trends will only continue to head in one direction.

5

BDS and the backlash

B.D.S. doesn't pose an existential threat to Israel; it poses a serious challenge to Israel's system of oppression of the Palestinian people.

– Omar Barghouti, April 2016[1]

[BDS] is but the newest weapon in a decades-old effort to eliminate Israel, and deny the Jewish people their right to self-determination.

– Israeli minister Gila Gamliel, February 2017[2]

In 2005, a group of Palestinian activists launched the Boycott, Divestment, Sanctions (BDS) Movement, a global campaign aimed at pressuring Israel to end human rights violations. At its launch, the BDS Call was backed by some 170 various trade unions, political groups, women's organisations, popular committees, and other Palestinian civil society bodies. As is clear from the BDS Movement's website, at the heart of the boycott campaign is a desire to end the impunity enjoyed by the State of Israel for human rights violations that, in other cases, have prompted international censure and sanction.[3] 'For nearly seventy years, Israel has denied Palestinians their fundamental rights and has refused to comply with international law', the BDS Movement writes. Israel's 'regime of settler colonialism, apartheid and occupation over the Palestinian people … is only possible because of international support', it continues.

Governments fail to hold Israel to account, while corporations and institutions across the world help Israel to oppress Palestinians. Because those in power refuse to act to stop this injustice, Palestinian civil society has called for a global citizens' response of solidarity with the Palestinian struggle for freedom, justice and equality.

Explicitly referencing the South African Anti-Apartheid Movement as a source of inspiration, the BDS campaign urges 'nonviolent pressure on Israel' until it 'meets its obligation to recognize the Palestinian people's inalienable right to self-determination and fully complies with the precepts of international law'.[4] Three, specific demands are cited: first, 'ending its occupation and colonization of all Arab lands and dismantling the Wall'; second, 'recognizing the fundamental rights of the Arab-Palestinian citizens of Israel to full equality'; and third, 'respecting, protecting and promoting the rights of Palestinian refugees to return to their homes and properties as stipulated in UN resolution 194'. Those three demands, crucially, do not refer to, or stipulate, political frameworks for the realisation of those rights – for example, two-states, or a single, democratic state – but rather affirms their inalienability and centrality in any final settlement.

The BDS Call has generated much controversy, largely as a result of being misrepresented and disingenuously smeared by the Israeli authorities and Israel advocacy groups. Yet the case for a boycott of Israel – of which I am proud to be a supporter – is straightforward, and based on three main elements. The first is the reality of Israel's policies of colonialism and apartheid, which we have already considered at some length in this book (though by no means comprehensively), and in Chapters 1 and 2 in particular. Second, the case for boycott is based on the appeals for solidarity from Palestinians – from trade unions, agricultural workers, students, professors, political activists, prisoners, and human rights defenders. Third and finally, the BDS campaign is an effective and empowering tactic. As Nelson Mandela wrote in 1958, boycott 'is in no way a matter of principle but a tactical weapon whose application should, like all other political weapons of the struggle, be related to the concrete conditions prevailing at the given time'.[5] Israel is vulnerable to pressure and isolation – economically, diplomatically, and culturally. Israel's crimes, the appeal for solidarity from Palestinians, and the utility of boycott as a tactic – these are the foundations of the case for BDS.

In recent years, the BDS campaign has grown considerably, across continents and in various sectors.[6] French multinational Veolia sold its Israeli subsidiaries and abandoned Israel as a market altogether in 2015, after a global campaign targeting its links to occupation and settlements.[7] Irish construction giant CRH withdrew from the Israeli market in 2016, while British security company G4S is also set to ditch its Israeli interests after a BDS campaign focused on its role in Israeli prisons and other occupation infrastructure.[8] These companies and others have lost contracts as a result of BDS campaigning, as well as suffering reputational damage.[9] BDS has been backed by numerous trade unions, while divestment campaigns have gained traction amongst a variety of financial institutions, investors, and pension funds, including in the Netherlands, Scandinavia, and amongst mainline Protestant church denominations in North America.[10] In March 2016 – in what the BDS Movement described as a sign that 'the logic of appeasing Israel's regime of oppression has started giving way to the logic of sustained international pressure' – the UN Human Rights Council adopted a motion that established a database of international businesses 'involved in activities' in the oPt.[11] That same month, a report in Israeli newspaper *Haaretz* claimed that 'a growing number of Israeli companies operating in the West Bank are moving their facilities to locations within [pre-1967 territory]', as a response to 'international boycott pressures and other constraints'.[12]

The BDS Movement has also seen considerable take-up amongst university students in Western Europe – the UK in particular – and North America. The website of National Students for Justice in Palestine, for example, an umbrella group for American campus-based solidarity groups, cites more than 50 'victories' in students' councils across the US since 2012.[13] In 2015, the

British National Union of Students (NUS) voted to endorse BDS, mandating the confederation of some 600 student unions to support the boycott campaign in various ways.[14] In 2016, graduate students at New York University voted to boycott Israel in what a pro-BDS Israeli activist and doctoral student said was indicative of how justice in Palestine had become 'one of the defining political issues of our time'.[15] That same year, the largest student union in Britain – the University of Manchester – voted to endorse BDS.[16] Academic unions have also fiercely debated, and in some notable cases endorsed, BDS. In the US, the Association for Asian American Studies, the American Studies Association, the Native American and Indigenous Studies Association, and National Women's Studies Association, have all endorsed a boycott of Israeli academic institutions, while in the UK, hundreds of academics have publicly declared their backing for the academic boycott.[17] 'As a global boycott movement against Israeli universities gains steam', Associated Press reported in February 2016, 'Israeli professors say they are feeling the pressure from their colleagues overseas'.[18]

Recent years have also seen growing support for the cultural boycott of Israel, with hundreds of artists and cultural figures from around the world heeding the call, including Alice Walker, Henning Mankell, Roger Waters, Naomi Klein, Ken Loach, Judith Butler, Elvis Costello, and Mira Nair.[19] In February 2015, almost a thousand UK artists signed a pledge in support of the cultural boycott (including this author).[20] Already in spring 2014, New York-based, Israeli writer Reuven Namdar wrote of how 'the international boycott ... is slowly solidifying around Israel's cultural life'.[21] In 2015, curators held a meeting in Tel Aviv on 'The Cultural Boycott of Israel and What It Means for Israeli Contemporary Art'. According to a report on the gathering, the boycott 'is practiced overtly as well as covertly, officially and unofficially, and by a variety of groups within the art world'.[22] When well-known public figures engage with the boycott, BDS has attracted mainstream attention; a good example of this was the refusal in February 2017 of American football star Michael Bennett to participate in an Israeli government-organised 'good will' tour.[23]

Israel and friends go on the offensive

As the BDS campaign started to gather momentum, Israeli officials were initially slow to respond to what Israel advocates had already labelled as early as 2012 a 'real threat'.[24] But by 2014, and even before the international outrage prompted by the unprecedented assault on the Gaza Strip which took place that summer, Israeli politicians were taking notice.[25] In February 2014, Netanyahu slammed the boycott movement as 'classical antisemites in modern garb', remarks said by the *Guardian* to be a reflection of 'anger and anxiety in Jerusalem about BDS'.[26] The following month, then Labor leader and Zionist Camp opposition head Isaac Herzog bemoaned that 'the boycott movement against Israel … is [unfortunately] turning into a strategic threat'.[27] By 2015, the Israeli government commissioned an internal report on the potential future damage of a boycott, with the worst case scenario seen as 'devastating' for the economy.[28] In June 2015, the *Guardian* noted how 'Israel and key international supporters have sharply ratcheted up their campaign against the Palestinian-led Boycott Divestment and Sanctions (BDS) movement, with senior Israeli officials declaring it a strategic threat', language that the government 'usually reserves for the likes of Hamas or Iran's nuclear programme'.[29] In September 2016, Israeli justice minister Ayelet Shaked said BDS is 'a new extension of terrorism', comparing the campaign to 'underground tunnels into Israel [from the Gaza Strip]'.[30] In early 2017, strategic affairs minister Gilad Erdan told Bloomberg: 'Israel is in the midst of a cognitive war, which is part of a new strategic challenge,' identifying adversaries such as 'non-violent campaigns like Boycott, Divestment, Sanctions'.[31]

The unprecedented Israeli offensive on Gaza in 2014, which killed some 2,200 Palestinians, gave a boost to the BDS Movement, and prompted even long-time friends of Israel to express public criticism of the ongoing occupation. Thus, if Israeli officials were initially inclined to ignore, or mock, the BDS campaign, they soon started to take it very seriously indeed; in one small, but instructive, illustration of this, an Israeli diplomat based out of the embassy in London in 2016 had a map of Britain on his wall which, according to *Haaretz*, 'show[ed] the front – the main [university] campuses, the deployment of pro-Israel activists and the location of the "enemy forces".[32] The reporter compared it to 'the war room of a brigade on the Lebanese border'. Israel's embassy in London would hit the headlines in early 2017, when an undercover Al Jazeera investigations team exposed some of the efforts being exerted by Israeli diplomats to undermine the BDS campaign and Palestine solidarity activism more broadly.[33] In February 2016, an Israeli Foreign Ministry spokesperson told the *Financial Times*: 'We have stepped up our efforts directly and indirectly, dealing with friends of Israel in a variety of countries in which we have the BDS movement, fighting it with legal instruments.'[34] That year, NIS (New Israeli Shekel) 10 million ($26 million) was allocated by the government to fighting BDS, with officials also revealing – in remarkably candid remarks to an Associated Press journalist – that they would use cyber technology to fight BDS campaigners, including through 'actions [that] will not be publicly identified with the government'.[35]

Over the years, one of the main forums for Israel and its advocates to discuss and strategise how to tackle BDS and Palestine solidarity activism has been the Ministry of Foreign Affairs-convened, Global Forum for Combatting Antisemitism (GFCA). At the 2009 conference, an anti-BDS working group proposed 'hav[ing] in place legislative prohibitions vs. BDS which can then be applied in different communities, acknowledging the different legal traditions'.[36] Four years later, an 'action plan' produced by the Forum's 'BDS and Delegitimization Task Force' included: 'Identify laws that can be used in different countries or states to fight discriminatory practices such as BDS.'[37] At the 2015 Forum, the BDS-focused working group – under the title 'Lawfare'

– stated: 'Pursue legislation at the local, state and federal level to constrain BDS.'[38] This was not idle talk. In February 2016, an Israeli spokesperson admitted to the *Financial Times* that Netanyahu's government had 'stepped up' its efforts, 'directly and indirectly, dealing with friends of Israel in a variety of countries in which we have the BDS movement, fighting it with legal instruments'.[39] As an AFP report put it a couple of months later, despairing of ever winning 'the battle for public support' in many countries, 'Israel has instead increasingly focused on measures limiting BDS legally.'[40] In November 2016, Israel's envoy to the UN, Danny Danon, boasted: 'We're advancing legislation in many countries ... so that it will simply be illegal to boycott Israel.'[41]

Such efforts have seen some fruit. In March 2017, a bill was tabled in the US Congress that would prohibit American citizens and companies from participating in or supporting boycotts of Israel organised by 'international governmental organizations like the United Nations or the European Union'.[42] The Israel Anti-Boycott Act, which amends pre-existing legislation concerning international trade and foreign government-sponsored boycotts, would impose 'severe civil and criminal punishment' on violators. The bill was originally co-sponsored by 32 Republicans and 15 Democrats, though, in an unusual development, Kirsten Gillibrand (D-NY) was the first senator to officially withdraw sponsorship.[43] The bill attracted considerable criticism from civil rights groups on the grounds that it constituted an infringement on First Amendment rights to free expression, including, notably, from the American Civil Liberties Union (ACLU), who wrote to all the bill's co-sponsors in defence of the right to boycott.[44] Interestingly, the bill itself specifically references the aforementioned UN database of companies complicit in Israeli occupation, an indication of just how much of a threat – or potential threat – such a step was perceived to be by Israel and its supporters.

This anti-BDS push on Capitol Hill followed a wave of anti-boycott bills at state level. In early 2016, Israeli newspaper Yediot Ahranoth reported how, 'in cooperation with Jewish and pro-

Israeli organisations', the Israeli government had 'convinced several American states to pass legislation against the boycott of Israel'.[45] The article explained that 'the need for this arose after several American pension funds divested from Israel following capitulation to the boycott movement', adding: 'such legislation, it became apparent, is the most effective weapon against boycott'. According to legal rights and civil liberties group Palestine Legal, 'since 2014, dozens of anti-BDS measures have been introduced in state legislatures across the country', with a total of 21 states enacting anti-BDS laws as of July 2017.[46] The legislation forbids authorities 'from contracting with individuals or companies who are unable to prove that they are not boycotting Israel or businesses in Israeli-controlled territories'.[47] That last reference is significant, 'extending the law's protection from boycott to products manufactured in Israel's illegal settlements in the West Bank' – Georgia, South Carolina, Florida, and Illinois, have all enacted laws with such protection for settlements.[48] The Illinois legislation 'prompted the drafting of a blacklist of companies "engaging in actions that are politically motivated and are intended to penalize, inflict economic harm on, or otherwise limit commercial relations with the State of Israel or companies based in the State of Israel or in territories controlled by the State of Israel"', an extraordinarily explicit – and broad – attack on Palestine solidarity activism.[49] The ACLU, referring to this 'wave after wave of legislation seeking to stamp out boycotts and divestment campaigns aimed at Israel', noted: 'None of them comport with the First Amendment.'[50]

In the UK, the approach has been one of intimidation, rather than criminalisation. In October 2015, the ruling Conservative Party announced it would be introducing 'new rules to stop politically-motivated boycott and divestment campaigns by town halls against U.K. defense companies and against Israel'.[51] These 'new rules' would, it was claimed, 'affect procurement policy for publicly-funded bodies, and local authorities' pension fund legislation'.[52] Yet when, in February 2016, the government duly published a procurement guidance note, there was no new legislation.

Commenting at the time, the Palestinian BDS National Committee (BNC) said the Conservative government's actions were 'an attempt to intimidate', and emphasised how 'it remains perfectly legal for councils and universities to take ethical stances that reflect the views of their communities and exclude companies that violate human rights or commit other forms of gross misconduct from tender exercises'.[53] The promised changes in pension investment regulations did materialise, despite overwhelming opposition during a public consultation exercise (98 per cent of respondents rejected the proposals).[54] However, just eight months after the new regulations came into force, key elements were struck down in the High Court, after legal action brought by the Palestine Solidarity Campaign and other activists.[55] The ruling came almost exactly a year after Jewish Human Rights Watch, a pro-Israel advocacy group focused on lawfare, lost – again in the High Court – its legal action against three local authorities who had passed resolutions in support of Palestinian rights.[56]

There have been more successes for Israel in France, the only country – outside of Israel – where those who merely advocate for BDS can be penalised. Interestingly, this is not a result of new laws, but rather thanks to the exploitation of long-standing legislation (from 1972 and 2003) designed, ironically, to combat racism.[57] The protection from discrimination and hatred offered in French legislation to 'national groups' (as well as ethnic groups, races and religions), gave pro-Israel groups a chance to prosecute BDS activists that they have eagerly pursued.[58] Indeed, the legislation has been described as 'among the world's most potent legislative tools to fight the growing [BDS Movement]', with attendees at the aforementioned GFCA in 2015 (optimistically) urging France's laws to be 'replicated where possible elsewhere in Europe'. For French BDS activists, this has had real consequences, with a number already convicted based on their participation in pro-boycott demonstrations.[59] The political atmosphere in France has only encouraged such prosecutions; in 2010, Justice Minister Michèle Alliot-Marie urged French prosecutors to go after those who advocate a boycott of Israel, on the grounds of incitement to hatred.[60] In January 2016, Prime Minister Manuel Valls told umbrella Jewish body CRIF (which has backed the prosecutions): 'We have passed from criticism of Israel to anti-Zionism and from anti-Zionism to anti-Semitism,' adding, 'We will be taking measures that will demonstrate that enough is enough and we cannot allow everything in our country.'[61]

Elsewhere in Europe, there have been mixed results for Israel's anti-BDS offensive. In Spain, pro-Israel activists have pursued lawsuits targeting local municipalities that have declared themselves 'free from Israeli apartheid'.[62] In Italy, 'a draft law to stifle the BDS movement has been deposited for examination at the Senate', again on so-called anti-discrimination grounds.[63] However, lawfare initiatives have also proved just as likely to prompt government-level affirmations of the right to boycott; in 2016, for example, the Dutch government affirmed that 'endorsing BDS falls under freedom of expression', while in June 2017, Spain's lower house unanimously backed a resolution affirming 'the right to promote boycott, divestment and sanctions (BDS) campaigns'.[64] In December 2016, some 200 legal scholars and practicing lawyers from 15 European states issued a statement affirming the BDS campaign as 'a lawful exercise of freedom of expression', joining the European Union, as well as the Swedish and Irish governments in supporting the right to boycott.[65]

Israel's pushback against the growing momentum of the BDS campaign has not just constituted lawfare. Another key element of Israel's global propaganda drive is 'rebranding', namely efforts to associate Israel with things like hi-tech, tourism, Tel Aviv nightlife, fine cuisine, and so on. This strategy actually predates the launch of the BDS Movement in 2005, as a response to the growth in the Palestine solidarity movement that took place in the context of the Second Intifada.[66] In 2009, not long after the 'Operation Cast Lead' assault on the Gaza Strip, a senior Israeli official told the *New York Times*: 'We will send well-known novelists and writers overseas, theatre companies, exhibits. This way, you show Israel's prettier face, so we are not thought of purely in the context of war.'[67] In 2011, a well-known Israeli chef told Australian media how 'the government decided, through culture, to start improving Israel's image. They started sending artists, singers, painters, filmmakers and then the idea came of sending chefs.'[68] Another part of the fight against BDS, as outlined in an influential report by Israeli think tank the Reut Institute, is to 'drive a wedge' between so-called 'moderates' and 'extremists'; put plainly, this means Israel lobbyists targeting 'problematic' mainstream NGOs (such as Amnesty International) through private engagement and public attack, in an effort to scare them off from partnering with or having any links to Palestine solidarity and human rights groups.[69]

Israel's efforts to combat BDS have also focused on the 'home front', where legislation and state-level intimidation has sought to undermine the political activism of international visitors *and* of Israeli citizens themselves. In July 2011, the Knesset approved the Bill for Prevention of Damage to the State of Israel Through Boycott, which, 'as a result of amendments that changed the provisions originally intended to create a criminal offence, sanctioned the promotion of boycott as a civil offence'.[70] The law 'imposes sanctions on any individual or entity that calls for an economic, cultural or academic boycott of Israel's West Bank settlements or of Israel itself', and it was subsequently upheld almost in its entirety by the Israeli Supreme Court.[71] In March 2016, Intelligence Minister Yisrael Katz advocated engaging in 'targeted civil eliminations' of BDS leaders with the help of Israeli intelligence, 'using language that deliberately evoked the Hebrew term for "targeted assassinations"'.[72] Omar Barghouti, one of the founders of the BDS Movement who has permanent residency status in Israel, has been subjected at various times to a de facto travel ban, threats to revoke his residency, and legal harassment.[73] In 2017, it emerged that Strategic Affairs Minister Gilad Erdan was seeking to 'expand the surveillance activities of his ministry to include Israeli citizens'.[74] In addition, at the time of writing, a new bill is being advanced in the Knesset that seeks to exempt the government's anti-BDS efforts from the country's Freedom of Information Law.[75] Meanwhile, in early 2017, the Knesset passed a new law, which 'forbids granting entry visas or residency rights to foreign nationals who call for economic, cultural or academic boycotts of either Israel or the settlements'.[76] Soon after, members of an interfaith group from the US was barred from catching a flight *before they even boarded*, after Israeli authorities had informed Lufthansa the individuals would not be allowed to enter – one was a rabbi.[77]

The 'new antisemitism'

As the overview of Israel's anti-BDS efforts suggests, a key part of the counter-boycott offensive is the accusation that BDS is 'anti-Semitic'. This deserves some unpacking, particularly because the ideas at play here go much broader than the specific focus on, or targeting of, the boycott campaign. According to Oxford University senior research fellow and international expert Brian Klug, 'a good, simple working definition of antisemitism, according to a broad consensus of scholars, is this: hostility towards Jews as Jews'.[78] He continues: 'It would be more accurate (if cumbersome) to define the word along these lines: a form of hostility towards Jews as Jews, in which Jews are perceived as something other than what they are. Or more succinctly: hostility towards Jews as not Jews.' When Antony Lerman, Senior Fellow at the Bruno Kreisky Forum for International Dialogue in Vienna, first started studying anti-Semitism 40 years ago, there was, he told me for a 2016 article, 'broadly speaking, a shared understanding of what antisemitism was. And Israel was hardly ever mentioned'.[79] Today, however, 'Israel is promoted as the central recipient of antisemitic hate'; for Lerman, this constitutes nothing less than 'a fundamental redefinition of antisemitism'.

It is easy to find examples of where this idea of a 'new anti-semitism' – one that targets Israel – is propagated. The British former chief rabbi Jonathan Sacks, writing in Newsweek, summarised the view thus: 'In the Middle Ages, Jews were hated because of their religion. In the 19th and 20th centuries they were hated because of their race. Today they are hated because of their nation state, Israel. Anti-Zionism is the new anti-Semitism.'[80] Much earlier, Jewish Agency head Natan Sharansky claimed to have developed a 'simple test' for 'exposing the new anti-Semitism', calling it the '3D' test: Demonisation, Double Standards and Delegitimisation.[81] For Sharansky – and many others – this was a fool proof way of 'distinguish[ing] legitimate criticism of Israel from anti-Semitism' – despite the obvious subjectivity of the 'test'. Israeli politicians, unsurprisingly, have not held back from pushing the concept of a 'new antisemitism'. 'In the past, we saw European leaders speaking against the Jews,' said Israeli justice minister Ayelet Shaked in a May 2016 interview with the *Washington Post*.[82] 'Now, we see them speaking against Israel. It is the same anti-Semitism of blood libels, spreading lies, distorting reality and brainwashing people into hating Israel and the Jews.' Israel's international friends have also got the message; French president Emmanuel Macron used a meeting with Netanyahu to assert: 'We will never surrender to the messages of hate; we will not surrender to anti-Zionism because it is a reinvention of anti-Semitism.'[83]

The concept of a 'new antisemitism' is not new, having emerged, as Lerman has explained, 'from serious discussions about the relationship between antisemitism and anti-Zionism'.[84] However, he continued, 'its ubiquity by the mid-2000s was a direct result of a concerted campaign to get individual governments, parliamentary bodies, the Organisation for Security and Cooperation in Europe, the Council of Europe and others to accept the validity of the notion'. This campaign was the result of 'a much closer nexus between Jewish communal leaderships, national and international Jewish organisations, pro-Israel advocacy groups, institutional arms of the Israeli government and academics and researchers promoting the idea of the "new antisemitism"'. The concept was the subject of a searing critique by Klug as far back as 2004, in an important intervention published by *The Nation*.[85] 'To argue that hostility to Israel and hostility to Jews are one and the same thing,' Klug wrote,

> is to conflate the Jewish state with the Jewish people. In fact, Israel is one thing, Jewry another. Accordingly, anti-Zionism is one thing, anti-Semitism another. They are separate. To say they are separate is not to say that they are never connected. But they are independent variables that can be connected in different ways.

In a follow-up response, the Oxford academic was categorical: 'It is time to reclaim the word "anti-Semitism" from the political misuses to which it is being put.' Steven Beller, Visiting Scholar at George Washington University and author of Oxford University Press's 'Antisemitism: A Very Short Introduction', has been similarly blunt: 'attempts to thus call this hostility to Israel "the new antisemitism" are, to my mind, misplaced and illegitimate'.[86]

So, while the discourse of a 'new anti-Semitism' has been around for some time, and acknowledging how, in the words of Israeli journalist Zvi Bar'el, 'successive Israeli governments have worked to blur the boundary between anti-Semitism and anti-Zionism', there is nonetheless a contemporary impetus to efforts at equating Palestine solidarity activism and BDS with antisemitism.[87] In her introduction to Jewish Voice for Peace's collection 'On Antisemitism', the group's director Rebecca Vilkomerson makes a connection between 'the growing strength of the movement for Palestinian rights', and the 'increasing efforts by those that unconditionally defend Israel to include criticism of Israel as part of the definition of antisemitism'.[88] She continues:

> Dubbed the 'new antisemitism', it defines Israel as the 'Jew among nations' in order to shield it from criticism, and has gained broad acceptance in the intervening years, leading to a dangerous blurring of lines that equates criticizing the actions of a state, Israel, with hatred of Jewish people.

In December 2016, Jewish American commentator Peter Beinart – who, unlike Vilkomerson, identifies as a Zionist – came to a similar conclusion.

> With every passing year, Israeli control of the West Bank grows more permanent. And so, with every passing year, more American progressives question Zionism … And the more those Americans voice this discomfort, the more establishment American Jewish organizations work to classify anti-Zionism as anti-Semitism, punishable by law.[89]

These arguments can be paraphrased with respect to the shape of this book thus: in response to the apartheid status quo on the ground (Chapters 1 and 2), opposition towards Israeli policies and solidarity with the Palestinians has grown in Jewish communities (Chapter 3), as well as among progressives and the left (Chapter 4). In response to such developments, and the growth of the BDS Movement, Israel is seeking to delegitimise efforts at holding it to account.

Redefining 'anti-Semitism'

As a central part of such efforts, the Israeli government and its allies are promoting a definition of anti-Semitism that incorporates the concepts of a 'new anti-Semitism'. In 2005, a draft, working definition of anti-Semitism was circulated by the European Union's Monitoring Centre on Racism and Xenophobia (EUMC).[90] The text, drafted with the help of pro-Israel groups, proved highly divisive for its muddled conflation of genuine anti-Semitism (e.g. Holocaust denial) with criticism of or opposition to Israel and Zionism (e.g. claiming the State of Israel 'is a racist endeavour').[91] By 2013, the EUMC's successor body, the European Union Agency for Fundamental Rights (FRA), had abandoned the politicised definition as unfit for purpose and removed it from its website, clarifying on numerous occasions that the document did not have any official status and had never been 'adopted' by the body.[92] Nevertheless, pro-Israel groups persisted in misrepresenting the status of the document as *the* 'European' or 'European Union' definition of anti-Semitism, and found some success in securing its adoption by, among others, the US State Department. However, it was clear to others that a fresh impetus was needed to salvage the 'definition' from the controversy – and obscurity – of its EUMC/FRA origins. At the Israeli-government convened GFCA in Jerusalem in 2015, a working group recommended 'that the Working Definition of Antisemitism should be reintroduced into the international arena with the aim of giving it legal status'.[93]

Step forward Mark Weitzman, a long-time senior official at the Los Angeles-based Simon Wiesenthal Centre, an institution which has embraced the idea of a 'new anti-Semitism' to the extent that it does not even pretend to separate fighting anti-Semitic hate and defending Israel. A prime illustration of this is the Centre's annual 'Top Ten Worst Anti-Semitic/Anti-Israel Incidents', which in 2015 listed the EU's decision to correctly label the origin of products made in Israeli settlements right after the activities of so-called Islamic State.[94] In 2016's 'Top Ten', the Centre ranked white nationalist Richard Spencer at number five, while at number *one* was UN Security Council Resolution 2334 on the illegality of Israeli settlements.[95] Crucially for this story, Weitzman also served as chair of the Committee on Antisemitism and Holocaust Denial for the International Holocaust Remembrance Alliance (IHRA), a 31-member body founded in 1998 by former Swedish Prime Minister Göran Persson. It was under Weitzman's chairmanship that the IHRA committee proposed, in 2015, a definition of anti-Semitism which almost exactly replicated the discredited EUMC 'working definition'.[96] In May 2016, the IHRA duly adopted it.

Celebrating the achievement, Weitzman told a right-wing news site: 'We decided a couple of years ago that IHRA was the right venue to bring up the definition for adoption. The idea was proposed to my committee, who recommended it to IHRA's Plenary and it took two years to get the definition through, which is remarkably fast in

IHRA terms' (he later claimed that the IHRA definition was 'taken from the EUMC definition as there was not enough time to invent a new one').[97] According to The Louis D. Brandeis Centre, which has often led attacks on Palestine solidarity activism and BDS on US campuses, while the IHRA definition was 'essentially the same text' as the EUMC working definition, 'because the IHRA has adopted it, the definition has now officially been given the international status that it was previously lacking'.[98] As a 2016 Israeli government report described, ever since the FRA ditched the draft working definition, 'Israeli representatives, individuals and organizations, Jews and non-Jews ... [had] been endeavouring to restore awareness of the definition as well as its use'.[99] Through Weitzman, and the IHRA, they had achieved their goal.

The birth of an 'IHRA definition' was celebrated at the time by a number of pro-Israel groups, who specifically highlighted – and praised – its recognition of the 'new antisemitism'.[100] The American Jewish Committee, for example, whose officials had played a key role in the drafting of the ill-fated EUMC document, said the IHRA definition 'offers a clear and comprehensive description of anti-Semitism in its various forms', but 'of particular note, anti-Semitism as it relates to Israel'.[101] The intended use of the definition soon became clear. In February 2017, pro-Israel groups in the UK – where the Conservative government had symbolically 'adopted' the IHRA definition – sought to have Israeli Apartheid Week events cancelled on the basis they were 'anti-Semitic'.[102] After one university cancelled a panel event on such grounds, the Simon Wiesenthal Centre, and Mark Weitzman, were delighted (the Centre had previously unsuccessfully sought to persuade the French government to outright ban Israeli Apartheid Week as 'a clear violation' of the EUMC working definition).[103] In a press release, the Centre proudly noted how Weitzman had 'spearheaded the IHRA's adoption of the definition', and quoted him as saying the university's decision to cancel the event – which sparked considerable outrage on freedom of speech grounds – was 'evidence that this internationally accepted definition can play a vital role in the fight against antisemitism'.[104]

In the UK, the definition was published on a government website some months before its so-called 'adoption', under the supervision of Eric Pickles, Special Envoy for Post-Holocaust issues and chair of Conservative Friends of Israel.[105] Days before it went online, Pickles had been a speaker at a conference on anti-Semitism, where he explicitly compared the BDS campaign to the Nazi boycott of Jewish goods. 'There's nothing complicated to it,' he told the audience. 'It's the same thing happening 70 years later. It's the same ideology, it's the same language, it's the same threats.'[106] Its use in the UK has generated a good deal of pushback; David Feldman, head of the Pears Institute for the Study of Antisemitism, criticised the text as 'bewilderingly imprecise', and highlighted 'a danger that the overall effect will place the onus on Israel's critics to demonstrate they are not antisemitic'.[107] The Jewish Socialists' Group, meanwhile, said the definition is 'being used to muzzle free speech on Israel/Palestine and on Zionism as a political ideology, which like any other political ideology can be supported or rejected and should be open to question'.[108] In fact, on that point, supporters and opponents of the definition are in agreement: an Israeli government document noted *approvingly* that 'the main innovation in the working definition is that it also includes expressions of Antisemitism directed against the State of Israel, when it is perceived as a Jewish collective'.[109] In other words, 'the definition also refers to anti-Zionism ... as a form of Antisemitism'.

In the US, meanwhile, a bill introduced on Capitol Hill in late 2016 sought to instruct the Department of Education to consider the contested definition of anti-Semitism when assessing federal discrimination claims brought by students and faculty. As the *Forward* reported, the background was years of 'efforts [by Jewish groups] into boosting the spread of State Department's definition of anti-Semitism', some of whom had also 'filed multiple civil rights claims' on the basis that certain campuses had become 'hostile environments' for Jewish students.[110] The head of one such group,

Morton Klein of the Zionist Organisation of America, said he hoped the law would 'help us in our efforts to minimize and more successfully fight against the increasing and dangerous scourge of campus anti-Semitism, led primarily by Muslim student members of Students for Justice in Palestine, and increasingly by antisemites affiliated with Black Lives Matter'.[111] The Anti-Defamation League was also clear about the bill's aim, tweeting: 'Worried about anti-#Israel activity on campus? We drafted a law that will help show when it's gone too far'.[112] The bill attracted heavy criticism, including from the ACLU and hundreds of Jewish students and scholars.[113] Though the 'Anti-Semitism Awareness Act' was passed in the Senate, the Congress session ended before there was time for the House to pass it (at the time of writing, it is unclear if it will be reintroduced).

The attempt to pass nationwide legislation followed on from a battle at the University of California, where pro-Israel groups had sought to persuade university authorities to adopt a statement on antisemitism that 'equated[d] anti-Zionism with religious bigotry'.[114] Thanks to the efforts of Palestine solidarity and civil liberty groups, the final statement was somewhat watered down, referring instead to 'antisemitic forms of anti-Zionism', but, as Dima Khalidi, the director of Palestine Legal, noted, pro-Israeli groups had 'succeeded in convincing the regents that Palestine advocacy is inherently antisemitic, and should be condemned'.[115] The Louis D. Brandeis Centre, meanwhile, who saw the University of California statement as a springboard for future action, has said that 'the next step is getting the University of California, and other universities nationwide, to follow the IHRA's good example, and adopt an official definition [of antisemitism]'.[116] Revealingly, in the context of these debates, one of the main authors of the original EUMC document – Ken Stern – came out *against* its 'official adoption' in California, arguing that to do so 'would do more harm than good'.[117] Stern had made his concerns explicit as early as 2010, when he regretted that some groups were using the EUMC working definition 'in an inappropriate way', citing attempts by

'American Jewish organizations from the right side of the political spectrum' to change campus policy.[118] According to Stern – who to be clear, is a firm believer in the new antisemitism – such groups were 'using the definition in a way it was never intended, and with the subtlety of a mallet'.

Drawing the red line

So why exactly is BDS such a target of attack by Israel? Put simply, BDS puts the focus on Israel's criminal policies, contextualises them with a framework of apartheid and colonialism, and demands accountability by way of response. These three elements, combined with its growth, and momentum, are at the heart of Israel's opposition to the boycott. But it is important to break down just why Israel and its allies allege that BDS is actually 'antisemitic' – and front and centre of such claims is the fact that the BDS Call demands the realisation of Palestinian refugees' rights to return. The return of expelled and denationalised Palestinians would significantly undermine, or end, Israel's Jewish majority of citizens (a majority achieved, of course, by those refugees' historic removal and ongoing exclusion). Such a scenario is anathema to the State of Israel, its political leadership, and the overwhelming majority of Zionists worldwide; in the words of an ADL official in May 2015: 'the unqualified right of return of all Palestinian refugees [to Israel] … would lead to the demise of Israel as a Jewish state. People who advocate that promote an idea that at its core is antisemitic'.[119] This opposition, and the implications and significance of the refugees' return, are the subject of the book's final chapter. Thus, at this point, it is sufficient to note how the BDS Movement's support for Palestinian refugees' right of return is enough to render it beyond the pale for Israel and its supporters.

Perhaps one of the most commonly advanced arguments in support of BDS being antisemitic is that it supposedly 'singles out' Israel as a unique evil in the world, or uniquely deserving of isolation and boycott. As the Board of Deputies of British Jews put it, 'we regard as antisemitic any exceptional treatment of Israel, where Israel is uniquely subjected, among all the countries in the world, to hostile behaviours such as denial of its right to exist and boycotts'.[120] Yet in reality, the BDS campaign is merely one of dozens of active consumer boycott campaigns (in the West alone), with a host of state and non-state targets.[121] At an inter-governmental and governmental level, the likes of the UN and EU, as well as the UK and US to name just two, currently impose sanctions and embargoes on a number of countries and other actors. Thus, in reality, it is Israel who is 'singled out' – but for diplomatic protection and impunity, military partnerships and aid, preferential trade deals, and institutional and governmental cooperation.

Those alleging that BDS is 'antisemitic' for singling out Israel often invoke examples of human rights and international law violations around the world. 'What about Turkey's occupation of Northern Cyprus, or China's occupation of Tibet?' they will say. Why is the BDS campaign not targeting *these* states? While offering some superficial, rhetorical satisfaction, this is not a serious argument. By their very nature, single-issue campaigns and movements concentrate on a specific issue; human trafficking activists 'single out' human trafficking (and are not accused of ignoring, say, climate change). No one accuses Tibetan solidarity campaigners of 'singling out' China. Only the Palestinians, it seems, are required to justify their right to resistance and solidarity. Palestinians 'single out' Israel because it is Israel who has expelled, dispossessed, colonised and occupied them. Are Palestinians uniquely prohibited from appealing for and receiving solidarity? In addition, and as discussed earlier in this chapter, boycott – and in this case, the BDS Movement – is a tactic, not a principle. What works in one situation, may not work in another. Furthermore, the BDS campaign has broad support amongst Palestinian activists *in Palestine* and beyond.

As the activists behind 'Artists for Palestine UK' pointed out:

Boycotts are selective, but this does not mean that they are morally tarnished ... If the demands of 'consistency' lead to the claim that nothing can be done unless and until everything is done, then passivity is bound to be the result. This, in relation to Israel, is surely what the critics intend.[122]

For a perfect illustration of how the inability, or refusal, to engage with BDS as a specific tactic in a specific situation leads to passivity, and complicity, consider British author Ian McEwan's defence of his decision to accept the Jerusalem Prize for literature in 2011. 'If I only went to countries that I approve of', he said, 'I probably would never get out of bed.'[123]

Those arguing that BDS is antisemitic for 'singling out' Israel not only have to prove that Israel is indeed being subjected to 'exceptional treatment' (it is not), but also that such 'exceptional treatment' is motivated by antisemitism, as opposed to any other kind of motivation. Instead, the fact that Israel is targeted for boycott is considered, ipso facto, antisemitic. In understanding this, one has to remember that such critics, nine times out of ten, do not accept that Israel is maintaining an apartheid regime; if you consider Israel to be 'the only democracy in the Middle East', no wonder you are mystified by – and look for sinister explanations for – the fact it is targeted for boycott.

There is a related, but subtler, objection to the BDS campaign. In the words of former Harvard University president Lawrence Summers, who is on the record as saying that he 'support[s] and feel[s] affinity with the State of Israel', the BDS Movement is 'antisemitic in effect if not intent'.[124] Why? Because BDS targets Israel, and the vast majority of Jews support Israel and identify as Zionists. As expressed by Jane Eisner, editor of the *Forward*:

Most American Jews feel some attachment to Israel, and that attachment has become a central part of Jewish identity ... So it is understandable that any Jew, particularly a susceptible college student, would be offended by an attack on Zionism that felt like an attack on his or her Jewish identity.[125]

In Britain, the chair of Labour Friends of Israel, Joan Ryan, put it like this: 'Some believe that antisemitism and anti-Zionism are separable. I do not agree, not least because the vast majority of British Jews have a strong attachment to Israel, the world's only Jewish state.'[126] In 2016, the chair of the Jewish Leadership Council (JLC) in Britain, Mick Davis, wrote in the *Telegraph*: 'More than 90 per cent of British Jews see Israel as part of their Jewish identity. Attacks on her legitimacy are an affront to our consciousness, an assault on our religious, cultural and moral heritage.'[127] In fact, surveys offer a more complicated picture than Ryan and Davis let on: 28 per cent of British Jews declined to identify themselves as 'Zionists' in a major 2010 survey, while in a 2015 survey, two-thirds of British Jews said they would 'support some sanctions against Israel if I thought they would encourage the Israeli government to engage in the peace process'.[128]

Nevertheless, it is undeniable that an overwhelming majority of Jews in Britain, the US, France and elsewhere, identify as proud Zionists and believe Israel should be a 'Jewish state' (even *if* Jewish opposition to Zionism and Israel, past and present, is too often neglected). It is here that the more intelligent opponents of BDS blur the boundaries between, on the one hand, *antisemitism*, and on the other hand, *offence* provoked by legitimate political expression or activism. As The Institute for Race Relations stressed, in a critical response to the UK government's endorsement of the IHRA definition of antisemitism, 'the conceptual flaw underlying ... [the] definition is to equate racism with anything that gives offence. For while racism is offensive, not everything which gives offence is per se racist.'[129] Yet the distinction between the two is often lost, unintentionally or disingenuously, in attacks on BDS. Furthermore, the positions expressed above by the likes of Davis and Ryan effectively place a veto on an essential tactic of solidarity with Palestinian rights, on the basis of what is, in reality, a momentary snapshot of a fluid, and ever-shifting relationship between Jews and Israel; remember that when Zionism emerged, the vast majority of Jews opposed it.

The Community Security Trust (CST) is the pre-eminent UK charity for recording and combating antisemitism. In 2014, during Israel's assault on the Gaza Strip, one of its senior officials, Mark Gardner, told an audience in a synagogue meeting that while the Jewish community would 'get through' a spike in antisemitic incidents, 'the boycott stuff is really, really serious'.[130] He added:

> Israel has, I think, come right up to that red line, to that tipping point, where it becomes in danger of really seriously being the new South Africa, the new South Africa that everybody should boycott, that Israel is equivalent to apartheid South Africa, and that therefore, if you support Israel well you're just like the Afrikaners of old.

Instructively, Gardner does not explicitly state that BDS is 'antisemitic'; rather, his concern is what an isolated, apartheid Israel will mean for Jews who continue to back the state. These candid comments help us understand part of the reason *why* BDS is attacked as 'antisemitic' – but it also demonstrates the weak foundations on which such an argument rests. In addition, by accusing BDS of being 'antisemitic' on the grounds that Israel is integral to Jewish identity, it is not just the civil society boycott campaign in the crosshairs – the very legitimacy of solidarity with the Palestinians' anti-apartheid struggle is at stake.

Dehumanising Palestinians, delegitimising solidarity

In March 2016, in an article on allegations of antisemitism within the Jeremy Corbyn-led Labour Party, the Board of Deputies of British Jews president Jonathan Arkush told the *Daily Mail* that 'this is not about criticism of Israel – every country can be subject to criticism'.[131] Some version of this point is made by most proponents of the 'new antisemitism', to the extent that it has become a cliché: mere *criticism* of Israel, we are assured, is not antisemitic. Yet just a few weeks earlier, Arkush had admonished then PM, David

Cameron, for having issued a very mild rebuke to Israel over illegal settlement construction, claiming that it had made 'many' in Britain's Jewish community 'concerned and uncomfortable'.[132] Arkush, speaking as president of the largest Jewish communal body, was telling the prime minister that to speak out about an issue on which there is international consensus – the illegality of the settlements and their role in obstructing a two-state solution – would make British Jews 'uncomfortable'.

In 2014, during a surge in solidarity with Palestinians as Israel devastated the Gaza Strip, some local councils decided to fly Palestinian flags; in response, the Board of Deputies said that such steps damaged 'community cohesion' and had 'the potential to intimidate and divide our communities'.[133] Or consider what happened to a Methodist church in London in 2016, when one of its members, having spent time in Palestine, organised an exhibition featuring a very simple 'mock checkpoint'. The church, as reported in the *Times*, was accused by a local rabbi of holding an exhibition that would 'fan the flames of antisemitism', while pro-Israel lobby group Jewish Human Rights Watch said the event caused 'significant distress'.[134] In other words, this is a much broader assault on political freedoms and the right of Palestinians and their allies to campaign against Israeli violations of international law. 'Of course, mere criticism of Israeli policies isn't antisemitic', say those who never actually criticise Israel, 'but – why are you singling out Israel?'

The same kinds of stories are repeated everywhere and anywhere that churches, trade unions, student councils, local authorities, cultural workers or elected officials express solidarity with the Palestinians' anti-apartheid struggle, or back initiatives to hold Israel and others to account for violations of international law and human rights. As Brian Klug wrote in *The Nation* in 2004,

when I say that 'anti-Zionism' puts the 'new' into 'new antisemitism', I am referring not only to anti-Zionism in the narrow sense; I am using the word broadly to include any position that lies on the far side of the line separating 'fair' from 'foul'. Now, if crossing the line is antisemitic, and if 'most of the current attacks on Israel and Zionism' cross the line, it follows that most current attacks on Israel and Zionism are antisemitic.[135]

All of the various efforts to undermine the BDS campaign, or ring-fence certain discussions about Israel as a 'Jewish state', share two characteristics in common: reliance on a reductionist definition or defence of Zionism, and the disappearing or dehumanising of Palestinians and their experience. To maintain that anti-Zionism is antisemitism is to deny the historical and contemporary reality of what Zionism has meant for Palestinians, and to dehumanise them as a people. For the Palestinians, Zionism has meant violent displacement, colonisation, and discrimination – are they 'antisemitic' for refusing to cheer their own dispossession? By extension, as orthodox Jewish studies and philosophy professor Charles H. Manekin put it, labelling Palestine solidarity activists as antisemitic is to imply that 'the Palestinians have little justified claim to sympathy'.[136] A handful of self-identifying Zionists acknowledge this; as Peter Beinart wrote in *Haaretz* in April 2016: 'Palestinians didn't become anti-Zionists because they needed a rationale for hating Jews and found the old ones outdated. They become anti-Zionists because their experience with Zionism was extremely rough.[137]

The offensive against the BDS Movement is a response to growing, global solidarity, an expanding BDS campaign, and, cracks in the consensus regarding Zionism and Israel as a 'Jewish state'; in other words, the backlash is a sign of certain kinds of weaknesses, not strength. Some have sought to diminish, or downplay, the significance of BDS, suggesting that Israeli politicians like Netanyahu, as well as right-wing lobby groups, benefit politically and financially respectively from playing up the BDS danger. But BDS critics almost always miss the point. Over the last decade, the BDS movement has done exactly what one would expect a dynamic grassroots campaign to do; attract support from numerous kinds of trade unions, church groups, political advocacy groups, human rights bodies, student associations, and so on. The BDS campaign is, ultimately, a tactic of solidarity; it is not a political programme, it cannot 'free Palestine', and it can only ever be complementary to, rather than a substitute for, a Palestinian national movement.

A campaign that began on the margins now has an impact on public debate and discussion; it is influential in ways that only a decentralised, grassroots campaign – in contrast to government propaganda initiatives – can be. BDS has even persuaded some Jewish Israelis that, in the words of writer Gideon Levy, 'boycott, divestment [and] sanctions is [the] only game in town, the last hope for ... change'.[138] In July 2016, Netanyahu – somewhat bizarrely – claimed to have 'defeated' the BDS Movement.[139] Not only was this untrue, it is also not possible, at least not in the way that Netanyahu, Israeli officials and pro-Israel groups imagine. Its growth, and the nature of its successes do indeed depend on various factors – but ironically, developments like Netanyahu's government of right-wing nationalists have proved to be a particularly potent accelerant.

6

Palestinian green shoots and signposts

From the refugees separated by a few miles from their expropriated lands, to the students in the Gaza Strip banned from studying in the West Bank, Israel has fragmented and divided the Palestinian people over the decades with physical obstructions (walls, fences, checkpoints), laws and bureaucracy (different ID cards and travel permits), and 'divide and conquer' style propaganda. Overcoming that fragmentation has been further complicated on account of the moribund state of representative bodies like the Palestine Liberation Organisation, as well as the long-running split between Fatah and Hamas. In recent years, however, there have been a number of developments emerging from Palestinian grassroots activists and intellectuals that offer signposts on the way to a post-apartheid Palestine/Israel – green shoots that are a stark contrast to the stagnation in the principal political organisations. One of the most striking threads running through such phenomena is the way in which Palestinians, especially youth, are forging new links across the various divisions imposed by Israeli colonisation. Ironically, one of the contributing factors here has been Israel's creation of a de facto, single state in all of historic Palestine; as the territory on both sides of the 1967 lines has been bound together, this has created different kinds of spaces and opportunities for Palestinian resistance and co-solidarity, for all those living under direct Israeli rule. The tools provided by social media platforms are part of the story, but it is also about a generation which rejects the fragmentation of the past. It is a reflection of a political consciousness that is both old and new: it harks back to before the time when the Palestinian issue was reduced to that of 'state-building', and is shaped by the realities and priorities of the present.

Hunger strikes and solidarity

On 17 April 2012, Palestinian prisoners in Israeli jails launched a mass hunger strike, beginning on the annually marked Prisoners' Day. The background to the strike included a number of hunger strikes by individual prisoners, including Khader Adnan's 66-day hunger strike from mid-December 2011 to late February 2012, in protest at detention without charge or trial (so-called administrative detention).[1] There had also been a three-week hunger strike and 'campaign of disobedience' in September–October 2011, prompting support actions such as solidarity hunger strikes by Palestinian youth in Haifa.[2] The April 2012 mass hunger strike, which 'sparked widespread sympathy protests and demonstrations across the West Bank and Gaza', saw participation by some 2,500 Palestinian prisoners, and only concluded on 14 May after a deal was struck with the Israeli authorities to secure 'an easing of their conditions'.[3] According to Palestinian activist and journalist Budour Hasan, the strike was 'accompanied by popular protests and escalated mobilization on the ground, not seen in Palestine since the early days of the second intifada more than a decade earlier', with participating prisoners coming from 'all political factions'.[4] Five years later, on 17 April, 2017, another mass hunger strike was launched, this time led by Fatah leader Marwan Barghouti. Around 1,500 prisoners launched the action, with more than 800 inmates sticking with the hunger strike until its negotiated end on 27 May.[5] Protests in support of the prisoners saw clashes with Israeli forces in the West Bank and Gaza Strip, while a general strike on 22 May was observed in communities across the occupied Palestinian territory (oPt), and, in a number of Palestinian communities inside the Green Line.[6]

Palestinian political prisoners have 'long used hunger strikes as a form of protest in response to violations of their rights by Israeli authorities', with a timeline dating the first use of the tactic to 1968.[7] As Palestinian academic Basil Farraj described, 'through hunger strikes, Palestinian prisoners have been able to continuously force their struggles onto the Palestinian and often the international political stage'.[8] He adds: 'given that there are currently no alternatives through which prisoners can secure their freedom or a change in Israeli policies, the importance of mobilizing communities and political bodies around prisoners' rights cannot be underestimated'. As in the cases mentioned above, 'grassroots, human rights organizations and official bodies both within and outside Palestine have mobilized during hunger strikes by Palestinian prisoners'. This support has included 'daily gatherings, protests outside the offices of international organizations, calls on the Israeli government to heed the prisoners' demands, and demonstrations outside prisons and hospitals'. Hunger strikes are thus a crucial way that Palestinians 'assert their political existence and demand their rights', and, as has been demonstrated in recent years, in particular, highlight forms of Palestinian solidarity and resistance that cross Israeli-imposed borders. As one former prisoner told a journalist in 2012, the tradition of hunger strikes are stories that 'give you power and hope'.[9]

Resisting dispossession in the Negev

In 2013, an unprecedented surge in activism by Palestinian citizens of Israel, that spilled over into the occupied West Bank and Gaza Strip and whose ripples went international, emerged to challenge a plan by the Israeli authorities to forcibly displace tens of thousands of Bedouin Palestinians in the Negev. The so-called 'Prawer Plan', named after the official who oversaw the relevant committee, envisaged the expulsion of dozens of entire communities in the Negev, in order to concentrate their residents into a smaller number of government-approved shanty towns (in the name of 'development'). On 15 July, a day of protests coordinated and publicised on social media with the hashtags #AngerStrike and #StopPrawerPlan saw demonstrations across historic Palestine – by Palestinians with Israeli citizenship from the Negev to Nazareth, and by Palestinians under military rule from Ramallah to the Gaza Strip. The day of action, which included a general strike inside the Green Line, and even saw Palestinian prisoners expressing their support, was hailed as an 'extraordinary show of solidarity', by Palestinians 'from the river to the sea'.[10] Even more strikingly, as Palestinian organiser and academic Abir Kopty pointed out, 'Palestinians in the West Bank and Gaza joined their brothers' and sisters' struggle within 48 hours, when it is usually the opposite'.[11] Palestinian journalist and activist Linah Alsaafin described the day as a demonstration that, 'despite political division, non-representative and collaborative leadership, Palestine remains from the river to the sea, with the Bedouins in the Naqab an integral component of the Palestinian population'.[12]

Later that year, on 30 November, an internationally observed 'Day of Rage' upped the ante even further, in what was the third such day that year.[13] Dozens of protests took place in Palestinian communities on both sides of the Green Line (Hura, Haifa, Jerusalem, Ramallah, Gaza), as well as in many cities around the world.[14] The following month, it was revealed that the Israeli government had halted the legislative process of the Prawer Plan. Though activists were under 'no illusion that the freeze would reverse the Israeli government's overall displacement policy', the fact that the Prawer Plan was 'stalled' signified 'a tremendous achievement'; the government's response 'demonstrated the combined strength of a community-led popular struggle, creative advocacy, and strategic legal and international interventions to disrupt the status quo'.[15] That 'popular struggle' was characterised by not just a 'new wave of Palestinian youth activism', but the 'unprecedented leadership of young people'.[16] The perspectives of this new generation – non-factional, open, and creative – spoke 'to new coalitions that might change things to come drastically'.

Battle of the Gates: Jerusalem in 2017

Jerusalem was never really the same after 16-year-old Muhammad Abu Khdeir was kidnapped and killed by three Jewish Israelis in July 2014. That summer, which also saw the Israeli military pound the Gaza Strip and launch an unusually brutal crackdown across the West Bank, Palestinian neighbourhoods in occupied East Jerusalem saw a marked uptick in activism and confrontations against Israeli forces and settlers. Since then, Israel's apartheid 'capital' has been on a permanent war footing, with Israeli authorities meting out collective punishment, mass arrests and police brutality against the city's rebellious Palestinian youth. By the summer of 2017, a perfect storm had been brewing, against the backdrop of this simmering revolt and Israel's crackdown, and in the absence of either the Palestinian Authority or a strong local leadership. On 14 July, three Palestinian citizens of Israel carried out a shooting attack on Israeli police officers posted at one of the entrances to the Al-Aqsa Mosque compound.[17] Israeli authorities responded by closing the compound for two days, then installing metal detectors and security cameras. In a spontaneous act of civil disobedience that gathered remarkable momentum, Palestinians refused to enter the compound until Israeli authorities removed the newly installed surveillance measures and obstacles to freedom of movement. Prayers were held in the streets of East Jerusalem, and protesters clashed with Israeli forces; over twelve days, more than 1,000 Palestinians were wounded, while on a 'Day of Rage' on Friday 21 July, three Palestinians were killed in demonstrations.[18] Eventually, on Thursday 27 July, the Israeli government removed the security cameras and metal detectors.

As Linah Alsaafin and Budour Hassan described in a subsequent analysis piece for Al Jazeera, 'the mass protests were characterised by their largely peaceful nature, which involved tens of thousands participating in sit-ins and prayers outside the entrances to the compound.[19] These sit-ins 'were often preceded and followed by chants that called for the liberation of Jerusalem and al-Aqsa

Mosque, in addition to chants that condemned Israeli occupation and the perceived complicity of Arab governments with the occupation'. The nature of the protests, meanwhile, made them 'open to Palestinians from all walks of life and from all ages, including children, families and the elderly'. There was also an outpouring of community support; 'people instinctively came out to support the protests and sustaining them by offering food, water, and a warm embrace to the protesters', said one participant quoted by Alsaafin and Hassan. Old City residents cooked meals, distributed 'food and fruits from their own homes', in addition to 'donations and prepared meals from Palestinian individuals and charities alike'. Strikingly, the protests were characterised by an absence of political leadership, something that some believed was 'one of the reasons why the sit-ins were so successful'. One activist said that while 'usually the leadership should be the advanced guard', in this case 'the leadership were running behind the masses'.[20] Dr Inas Abad, a political science researcher and lecturer and a political activist from East Jerusalem, hailed the events at Al-Aqsa as 'an important turning point in our struggle as one people, away from the factionalism that has divided our movement'.[21] Tellingly, the 'Israeli defense establishment' was said to be 'troubled by the Palestinian sense of victory' following the removal of the 'security measures'.[22]

Representation and strategy

One of the responses to an uptick in protests and attacks in the oPt in autumn 2015 was a heightened discussion amongst Palestinians about issues of representation, leadership and strategy. 'This popular uprising is spontaneous and who's leading it is the new generation – mostly university and school students', Ramallah-based lawyer Lema Nazeeh told Al Jazeera.[23] 'This time we are taking action in the streets and doubling the resistance everywhere, starting in Jerusalem, to the West Bank and Gaza. Palestinians living in the 1948 territories [i.e. citizens of Israel] are also participating in it'. Others believed that Palestinians would need to 'organize and expand their networks of communal solidarity and horizontal support to become a social movement' in order 'to overcome Israel's massive repression' and the 'complicity' of the Palestinian Authority.[24] 'The absence of authentic Palestinian national leadership is particularly acute at this time of crisis', wrote the Al-Shabaka think-tank, asking: 'what can other political parties and forces do to provide a framework for national leadership, whether within or outside the Palestine Liberation Organization?'[25] Those questions were explored in an Al-Shabaka convened roundtable, a forum typical of the work being done by the transnational network on the major issues facing Palestinians, whether it's questions of leadership, 'political disintegration', reform of PLO institutions, or what frame of analysis should shape the Palestinian struggle for self-determination.[26]

Al-Shabaka are not the only ones; there is also the Palestine Strategy Group (PSG), comprising Palestinians from across the social and political spectrum, which issued its first report in 2008.[27] The PSG 'subsequently embarked on a new initiative with the aim of crystallising a national Palestinian agenda', culminating in a report called 'Towards New Strategies for Palestinian National Liberation'.[28] In 2017, PSG published a report on 'Relations Between Palestinians Across the Green Line', the product of two years of work by 'Palestinian analysts, activists, intellectuals and politicians', and exploring the relationship between – and prospect of coordinated political action by – the Palestinians with Israeli citizenship, and Palestinians living under occupation in East Jerusalem, the West Bank, and Gaza Strip.[29] The debate about the ways forward is not just taking place in the context of think-tanks – there are also public discussions hosted by sites like *Jadaliyya*, on issues of crucial importance like 'Palestinian Diaspora and Representation'.[30] As Hani Al-Masri, Director General of Masarat, a Palestinian centre for policy research and strategic studies, has put it, Israel's opposition to a two-state solution, along with the Palestinians' rejection of either the status quo or a state with limited sovereignty, means that a 'new strategic space' has been 'opened'.[31]

7

Self-determination, not segregation

If the day comes when the two-state solution collapses, and we face a South African-style struggle for equal voting rights, then, as soon as that happens, the State of Israel is finished.

– Israeli Prime Minister Ehud Olmert, 2007[1]

Freedom means being able to do what formerly was unjustly forbidden.

– Albie Sachs, Justice of South Africa's
Constitutional Court, 1994–2009[2]

In October 2017, Israeli parliamentarian Miki Zohar explained in a newspaper interview why he was opposed to the creation of a Palestinian state.[3] 'In my opinion', the Likud MK said, 'he [the Palestinian] doesn't have the right to national identity, because he does not own the land of this country'. Zohar, who advocates the annexation of the West Bank but without giving citizenship to its Palestinian inhabitants, clarified that Palestinians could stay 'by virtue of my own sense of fairness', on the basis that they were born and live in the West Bank. Then he added: 'I'm sorry to say this, but they [the Palestinians] have one conspicuous liability: They weren't born Jews'. These are crudely offensive remarks – and note that at the time, Zohar was serving as chair of the Knesset's Special Committee for Distributive Justice and Social Equality. Yet Zohar's core assumptions – such as the belief in a defiantly and explicitly discriminatory political system – are what have shaped Israeli state policy for the past seventy years, are the organising principles of today's apartheid status quo, and guide the future visions being offered by Zionist political parties in Israel today.

This book began with, and is grounded in, the reality on the ground today in Palestine/Israel – that of a de facto, single apartheid state. We have also considered what I described as 'cracks in the wall', those widening pockets of resistance and growing possibilities for dissent in Israel's long-standing pillars of support internationally, and especially in the US. Now, we conclude with a vision of an alternative reality, one which, in fact, should not be too hard to imagine: a single *democratic* state. Efforts at dividing Palestine, an attempt to resolve the Zionist movement's aspirations for a 'Jewish state' at the expense of and in the face of opposition from Palestine's majority non-Jewish population, have been an abject failure, not least in terms of their human cost. Put simply, discrimination and segregation cannot be a blueprint for the future. Partition and privilege must be rejected; decolonisation and transformation must be embraced.

If not partition ... then what?

There are, of course, many versions of a 'one-state solution', including some very bad ones. The present reality may 'only' be a *de facto*, apartheid state, but there are some in Israel – like Zohar – who seek to formalise such arrangements into something permanent. Others, meanwhile – as we saw in Chapter 2 – are happy to maintain the status quo indefinitely; as Moshe Ya'alon, the former Israeli defense minister, put it while in office: 'I am not looking for a solution, I am looking for a way to manage the conflict.'[4] At the time of writing, there is nothing to suggest that Donald Trump's administration is prepared to pressure Israel to make much more than tokenistic economic gestures. But these are not the de facto or de jure types of 'one-state' that we are interested in examining at this point. Looking beyond a single, apartheid state we see that there are variations of a one-state solution premised on democratic values, and some of these differences are significant: binationalism, for example, or a federation of self-governing cantons. This book – this chapter – is not an attempt at a comprehensive review and assessment of the different practical options, let alone a detailed plan for how to achieve one in particular. Nevertheless, as a contribution to a vital discussion, and as a way of dealing with relevant arguments in this discussion, I am going to propose one particular model as optimal: a single democratic state in Palestine/Israel.

One democratic state has significant advantages and benefits for both Palestinians and Jewish Israelis. For Palestinians, it offers a framework that is the most promising and obviously capable of realising all of their rights, including self-determination, but also the refugees' right to return, the right of Palestinians who currently have Israeli citizenship to live without systematic discrimination, and the right of Palestinians in the occupied Palestinian territory (oPt) to be free of military rule. In a single democratic state, Palestinians can live anywhere in their homeland – Nablus and Haifa alike. As for Jewish Israelis, a democratic state where the Palestinian people's rights have been realised would constitute a genuine 'end of claims', and significantly reduce a major source of insecurity. As Palestinian intellectual and former MK Azmi Bishara has written: 'By rejecting a legitimate solution, Israel has chosen to remain a heavily fortified citadel, surviving by dint of its power of deterrence and inter-Arab squabbles'.[5] This is not sustainable, and it is certainly not desirable – including for Jewish Israelis. A single democratic state also means that Jewish Israelis can live anywhere in 'Eretz Israel', as equal citizens. 'Israelis and Palestinians alike feel that neither the physical nor the spiritual landscape is divisible', wrote former deputy mayor of Jerusalem Meron Benvenisti.[6] In one state, the unity of this dual landscape is preserved.

There are also significant practical benefits to a single democratic state, for the geography and natural resources of Palestine/Israel do not lend themselves to division. The Mountain Aquifer, for example, 'is the only source of water for Palestinians in the West Bank and the main provider of freshwater to Israelis, with 'the majority of its natural recharge area' lying within the West Bank and 'two of its three basins flowing naturally toward Israel'.[7] As Virginia Tilley wrote in her important book 'The One-State Solution', 'more than any other factor, water graphically demonstrates the indivisibility of this delicately balanced, ecologically sensitive territory'.[8] A single democratic state offers the possibility of solutions to the deadlocked problems of partition: 'freed from the imperative of maintaining an exclusivist ethno-religious state, issues like water rights or the status of Jerusalem are transformed from the stumbling blocks of tortuous negotiations into opportunities for celebratory affirmations of a common homeland and the mutual protection of both communities' rights'.[9] But what about the details? As I mentioned, while this chapter is not intended as a blueprint, I will mention two specific issues – starting with the Palestinian refugees.

The Palestinian refugees: return and restoration

When I went to Palestine for the first time in 2003, I broadly understood the Palestinian question in terms of a struggle against military occupation and for statehood. One day, I was speaking with my students after an English class in Bethlehem, and a resident of Dheishe refugee camp asked rhetorically: 'Why can't I go home?' And what I realised then, and my understanding of this truth has only deepened since, is that this question remains in the air – a stark, unanswered challenge – no matter how many efforts are made to smother it. For the State of Israel, and the Zionist movement, the return of Palestinian refugees constitutes the undoing of the 'miracle' of the Nakba, an end to the Jewish majority created through displacement and discrimination. Seen outside the lens of this demographic anxiety, however, the power of the Palestinians' return is transformative, rather than destructive. The imperative of return is four-fold. First, it is an individual right, belonging to each and every Palestinian refugee. Second, it is a right grounded in international law and conventions. Third, for Palestinians, 'the right of return is inextricably linked with the right to self-determination, since neither one can be realized fully in the absence of the other'.[10] And finally, return is at the heart of a wider decolonisation process: it seeks not to wind back the clock, but rather 'its potential is for a much more radical kind of transformation'.[11]

Before we think about practicalities, it is important to adjust our framework slightly. Though the majority of Palestinian refugees are excluded from their homeland, many are in fact present within historic Palestine. Of the approximately 5.8 million UN-registered Palestinian refugees, just over 40 per cent – two in five – live under direct Israeli (military) rule in the West Bank and Gaza Strip.[12] When you add some 300,000 'present absentees' within Israel's pre-1967 lines, for whom the Nakba entailed 'internal displacement' within what became the State of Israel, that makes some 2.7 million Palestinian refugees (excluding those who are not UN-registered) who currently live within Palestine/Israel.[13] They are, in other words, present within today's single apartheid state reality, but alienated from their lands and properties by law and by force. There are another 3 million refugees across Israel's walls and fences in Jordan, Lebanon and Syria. Thus, the majority of Palestinian refugees, even those in neighbouring states, 'live within tens of kilometres of their historic sites of dispossession'.[14] Seen from this point of view, we understand that 'return' is not just a physical question but one of transforming discriminatory structures.

But how can it be done? The issue of the practicalities of return is often linked to the number of Palestinian refugees who would actually want to return on a permanent basis, but, at this juncture, a figure is not the primary concern. It is hard to have a reliable overall picture, since Palestinian refugees are found in dozens of different locations (camps and outside of camps), and efforts at comprehensive polling come up against substantial logistical and political obstacles. It can also be expected that there would be some degree of variation in Palestinian refugees' answers based on their present circumstances. But crucially, the numbers involved are not as significant as Israel's ideological, political objections to their return; note how even internally displaced Palestinian *citizens* of Israel are denied restitution because, from the state's point of view, this would have 'far-reaching and strategic implications'.[15]

Though certainly complicated, the practicalities of return can draw on a number of precedents: as Palestinian refugees rights group BADIL has tirelessly documented, 'provision for restitution has taken a major role in resolving conflicts including long-term conflicts in Cyprus (40 years) and South Africa (90 years)'.[16] Some, like Palestinian scholar Salman Abu Sitta, point to 'dozens of similar cases' that can help provide a 'legal framework' for return and a 'reconstituted Palestine', noting that 'the real question that remains is whether or not the great powers that created the problem in the first place have the political will to enforce outstanding international resolutions'.[17] In 2013, a conference at Boston University examined 'the political, legal, humanitarian, and practical aspects of return', including precedents in East Timor, Bosnia, and South Africa.[18] Israeli NGO Zochrot, which has partnered with BADIL in seriously examining the implementation of the refugees' return, has conducted workshops to ask questions like 'How many new housing units will be built?' and 'How will industrial and agricultural regions be allocated?'[19] One of Zochrot's main aims in studying the issue is to show that 'refugee return, as well as being legal and just, can also be achieved in a manner which also takes into account the rights of the existing receiving communities; thereby moving the focus from prejudiced assumptions to a reasonable discussion on the practical aspects of refugee return'.[20]

In 2017, a competition was held for the best architectural design of a reconstructed, formerly destroyed, Palestinian village (the winner was a student from Birzeit University in the West Bank).[21] The initiative recalls words written in 2011 as part of two Palestinian architects' 'Arena of Speculation' project. In the move 'from a nostalgic imaginary to something both tangible and realisable', they wrote, 'we are forced to engage in new ways with the spatial, political and social landscapes of Israel-Palestine. Instead of asking "can we return?" or "when will we return?", Palestinians are suddenly allowed to ask "what kind of return do we want to create for ourselves?".[22]

A democratic constitution

In 2007, Adalah – full name 'The Legal Centre for Arab Minority Rights in Israel' – published a significant document, which it called 'The Democratic Constitution'.[23] It was, the organisation declared, 'a constitutional proposal for the state of Israel, based on the concept of a democratic, bilingual, multicultural state', drawing on 'universal principles and international conventions on human rights, the experiences of nations and the constitutions of various democratic states'. The constitution provides for a state 'that is based on full equality between all of its residents and between all of the different groups within it', where 'Jewish and Arab citizens shall respect each other's rights to live in peace, dignity and equality, and will be united in recognizing and respecting the differences between them, as well as the differences that exist between all the groups in a democratic, bilingual and multicultural state.' The 'liberties and rights' in Adalah's constitutional proposal are based 'on the constitutions and legal experience of many democratic states', as well as 'international human rights covenants and declarations', such as the Universal Declaration of Human Rights, the International Covenant on Civil and Political Rights, and the UN Declaration on the Rights of Persons Belonging to National or Ethnic, Religious and Linguistic Minorities (1992).

Reading this document, one is struck by how, though primarily crafted as a response to the needs of Israel's Palestinian citizens, in the context of a single democratic state, it offers a guide for how to protect Jewish and Palestinian rights. As Palestinian-American scholar Saree Makdisi commented, 'although Adalah's proposal is explicitly intended as a constitution for the State of Israel within its pre-1967 borders, if all of its principles of equality and justice were to be applied, Israel would no longer be, or claim to be, a Jewish state'.[24] Thus, he added, Adalah's 'Democratic Constitution' 'serves implicitly as a draft constitution' for one 'bilingual and multicultural' democratic state, 'in all of historic Palestine, a state in which Jews and Palestinian Arabs could live together as equal citizens'.[25] By itself, it is important to stress, a liberal constitution is ill-equipped to unsettle settler colonialism – it must be accompanied by, *inter alia*, mechanisms for land redistribution and restorative justice. But it can play a vital role in the transformation.

Adalah's document provides a fascinating glimpse of what might be, but there are many other sources of insights and inspirations. Indeed, a forensic analysis of how the State of Israel systematically discriminates against non-Jewish citizens offers not just a grim account of the current state of affairs but, by implication, suggests how things could be different. This was the conclusion of Palestinian legal scholar Mazen Masri, in his recent book 'The Dynamics of Exclusionary Constitutionalism: Israel as a Jewish and Democratic State', who noted that his analysis can also be 'useful in a prospective way. By identifying how the definition is used in each discrete area to produce the dynamics of exclusionary constitutionalism, one can discern what has to be changed. A roadmap for democratisation starts to come into view'.[26] Others, like Palestinian-American author and activist Ali Abunimah writing in his 2006 book *One Country*, have highlighted sets of 'principles for the one-state solution', in Abunimah's case, 'rooted in the Universal Declaration of Human Rights and informed by such worthy models as the Belfast Agreement signed by parties to the conflict in Northern Ireland'.[27] The 'One State Declaration' of 2007, meanwhile, similarly offers a set of 'principles' on which to base one, democratic state.[28]

There are also some largely – or completely – forgotten historical resources to draw on – such as the Anglo-American Committee of Inquiry into Palestine of 1946, which recommended that the constitutional future of Palestine should be based on three principles, including 'that Jew shall not dominate Arab and Arab shall not dominate Jew', and that 'Palestine shall be neither a Jewish

State nor an Arab State.'[29] In 1947, a senior US State Department official drafted a secret memorandum titled 'A Plan for the Future Government of Palestine', which recommended that 'Palestine should become neither an Arab State nor a Jewish State but a single independent Palestine State in which all its people, of whatever religion or blood, may dwell together in concord.'[30] Palestine, it continued, 'should continue to provide a Jewish National Home in its spiritual and cultural aspects, as well as a home for the Arabs and all others who live there', in the context of 'all the inhabitants of Palestine' accepting the responsibilities and sharing 'the rights and privileges of a common Palestinian citizenship'. The government of Palestine would 'represent all Palestinian citizens and should protect their human rights and fundamental freedoms'. As American author and campaigner Josh Ruebner commented, 'in laying down principles and a suggested form of government for a non-confessional, multi-religious democracy premised on equality, the memorandum still offers substantial concrete guidance for a one-state resolution today'.[31]

Self-determination without domination

One of the objections to a single democratic state as a solution is the claim that neither Jewish Israelis nor Palestinians actually want one or, more accurately that a *majority* of both peoples are opposed to this scenario. It is true that only a minority of Jewish Israelis express support for such a model; 18.7 per cent, according to a February 2017 poll (with 78.1 per cent opposing).[32] Of course, this is to be expected given the current de jure and de facto privileges afforded to Jews under the status quo (if anything, the support of almost 1 in 5 Jewish Israelis is encouragingly high). But it is unreasonable to allow the privileged group to set or limit the parameters of what is possible. Responding to and dealing with the fact that most Jewish Israelis oppose a single democratic state – including through both pressure, and dealing with their concerns – is distinct from accommodating such opposition. But what about the Palestinians? In the same poll as previously cited, 36.2 per cent of Palestinians in the West Bank and Gaza Strip backed one, democratic state, and 61.2 per cent opposed. Again, given the situation of Palestinians in the oPt and the length of time that a 'two-state solution' paradigm has dominated, even this level of support is perhaps surprisingly high.

But – and too often this is not taken into account – Palestinians in the oPt represent one third of the Palestinian people; one in seven are citizens of Israel, of whom 55.6 per cent already back a single democratic state. With respect to the Palestinian refugees outside of Palestine/Israel, meanwhile, one can expect that a sizeable proportion, probably a majority, would be in favour of a single state framework and its facilitation of the realisation of their right to return. That being said, as University of Oxford-based academic Karma Nabulsi has cautioned,

> none of the current assertions, claims, or arguments in favour of either a one-state or a two-state strategy by political groups, intellectuals, and rights-based organisations can have any real meaning until there is a method to incorporate these claims within a deliberative discussion that is understood and agreed upon by all sectors of society – inside and outside Palestine. At the moment there is no collective process to ensure that all voices are heard.[33]

There is another related objection raised to the one-state solution, namely: Israelis and Palestinians have failed to agree even a two-state solution, so how do you expect them to agree to and live together in one? A variation of this criticism argues that since the situation facing Palestinians in the oPt is so dire, the priority must be to end military occupation and establish a Palestinian state in the West Bank and Gaza Strip, even if as an intermediary measure. But the logic of both objections is flawed. All of the Israeli political parties who could feasibly lead a government are opposed to the establishment of a genuinely sovereign state in the oPt (see Chapter 2). Maintaining the status quo, annexation, or 'separation' – these are the possible offers on the table with respect to the current Israeli government or any that might plausibly follow it. All are variations of managing, rather than solving, the so-called conflict – and none of them allow for the creation of a sovereign Palestinian state (and note that only 32 per cent of Jewish Israelis back a two-state peace package – even with a 'demilitarised' Palestinian state).[34] In other words, if we allow what Israel is prepared to accept to define the parameters of the possible, then both a Palestinian state in the oPt, *and* a single democratic state are off the table. Attempts to create a genuine two-state solution are dealing with symptoms; a transformative decolonisation of Palestine/Israel in its entirety addresses the root cause.

A different kind of objection to a single democratic state concerns what for many people is the ultimate justification for a 'Jewish state' in Palestine – the need for a sanctuary, or 'lifeboat state', for the Jewish people in light of historic atrocities and ongoing antisemitism. In 1967, Israeli novelist Amos Oz claimed that 'the Zionist enterprise has no other objective justification than the right of a drowning man to grasp the only plank that can save him'.[35] Oz repeated the same metaphor in his book *In the Land of Israel*, with some small additions. '[Zionism's] justification in terms of the Arabs who dwell in this land is the justness of the drowning man who clings to the only plank he can,' he wrote.[36] He continued: 'And the drowning man clinging to this plank is allowed, by all the rules of natural, objective, universal justice, to make room for himself on the plank, even if in doing so he must push the others aside a little. Even if the others sitting on that plank leave him no alternative but force'. Except, of course, the Palestinians were not asked to 'share a plank'; they were expelled en masse and remain excluded from their homeland simply because they are not Jewish. Moreover, what actual cost is there to simply sharing a plank? None. And who, other than a monster, would refuse a drowning man room on the driftwood? Thus, Oz's metaphor both whitewashes the reality of the Nakba, *and* blames the Palestinians themselves, portraying them as callous brutes who had to be 'forced' to share their plank.[37]

There is a further dimension to the 'lifeboat state' argument. As Adam Shatz wrote in 2004,

> leaving aside the question as to why this sanctuary should come at the expense of the Palestinians, who played no role in the Holocaust, it is by no means clear today that the existence of a Jewish ethno-state in the Middle East makes Jews safer today, or whether it actually exposes them to greater dangers.[38]

As Charles H. Manekin put it: this 'argument seems to say that unless there is a Jewish state of refuge, some Jews may die or suffer antisemitism. But with a Jewish state some Jews may die or suffer antisemitism'.[39] The 'real question', he added, 'is or should be, "Can Judaism and the Jewish people survive without a Jewish state". And the answer is, so far, yes. In fact several thousand years of Jewish survival teaches us that'.

A final objection to a single democratic state – as opposed to the existence of a 'Jewish state' in Palestine – is that it would be a denial of the Jewish people's right to self-determination (and, some add, is thus an antisemitic proposal). In fact, self-determination 'doesn't necessarily mean that every national or ethnic group must have its own state, but rather that the government should represent all the different groups'.[40] As legal scholar Michael Kearney told me, self-determination is 'less understood these days as a right to one's own exclusive state, and more as a right to non-discrimination and to democratic participation in society'.[41] In his famous 2003 essay in the *New York Review of Books*, the late Tony Judt described 'the very idea of a "Jewish state" – a state in which Jews and the Jewish religion have exclusive privileges from which non-Jewish citizens are forever excluded' as 'rooted in another time and place'.[42] Israel, he added, 'is an anachronism'. Israel's advocates do their best to confuse the issue by speaking of Israel as a Jewish state in the same way that France is French, a comparison which is unintentionally revealing. To quote Judt (responding to the critics of his 2003 essay), 'France is the state of all the French; all French persons are by definition citizens of France; and all citizens of France are ... French.'[43] Israel, 'by contrast', is 'by its own account the "state of all the Jews" (wherever they live and whether or not they seek the association), while containing non-Jewish (Arab) citizens who do not enjoy similar status and rights. There is no comparison.' Put simply, the right to self-determination does not equate to a right to an ethno-state, and it is certainly never a right to expel, colonise and discriminate.

Decoupling self-determination and ethnic statehood is not easy, especially when many Jewish Israelis fear the consequences of a loss of 'power and privilege'.[44] Haifa University professor Arnon Soffer told the *Guardian* in 2007: 'We have to do everything to keep Israel as a Jewish state ... They use words like "democracy", but if they are in power, it is the end of democracy. We have to stop being naïve.'[45] In Soffer's words, we see that nothing has changed since Revisionist Zionist leader Vladimir Jabotinsky declared that 'the name of the disease is minority' and 'the name of the cure is majority'.[46] Nor are such anxieties unique to the Israeli right – in fact, they are often best articulated by the self-described 'Zionist left'. In March 2015, Amos Oz wrote in the *Los Angeles Times*: 'Let's start with a matter of life and death. If there are not two states, there will be one. If there is one, it will be Arab. If Arab it is, there is no telling the fate of our children and theirs.'[47] But why? What is so terrible about this prospect? Tellingly, Oz never really explains, directly, why 'an Arab state' would be such a terrible prospect for his children and grandchildren – it is just assumed. The language used is revealing. A state with, say, a 60 per cent Arab (Palestinian) majority of citizens, is not the same thing as an 'Arab state'. Oz's shorthand betrays the majoritarian, ethnocratic ethos of the 'Jewish state' he seeks to preserve.

There are echoes here of white South Africans' fears right up to the final years of the apartheid regime. In one 1987 poll of white South Africans, 91.4 per cent of Afrikaners and 78.2 per cent of English speakers thought black majority rule would mean discrimination against whites, while 78.5 per cent of Afrikaners and 70.1

per cent of English speakers believed that 'the physical safety of whites would be threatened'.[48] In 1990, Albie Sachs – a lawyer and anti-apartheid activist who Nelson Mandela would later appoint to the country's Constitutional Court – acknowledged concerns 'that removing one tyranny might lead to its replacement by another'.[49] However, he continued, 'from a moral point of view, it seems most dubious to refrain from dealing with an actual and manifest evil because of anxiety that its elimination might lead to the appearance of another evil ... The best time for fighting for freedom is always now, and the best starting point is always here.'

As it was for many decades in Apartheid South Africa, for now, 'Israeli military and economic power insulates them from having to face reality,' as Edward Said put it in 2001.[50] 'Therefore, it is up to us [the Palestinians] to provide the answer that power and paranoia cannot.' He continued: 'If we are all to live ... we must capture the imagination not just of our people, but that of our oppressors.' Abunimah expressed a similar sentiment in a 2009 piece, writing: 'Without indulging Israeli racism or preserving undue privilege, the legitimate concerns of ordinary Israeli Jews' – such as 'personal and family dislocation, loss of socioeconomic status and community security' – can be 'addressed directly in any negotiated transition to ensure that the shift to democracy is orderly, and essential redistributive policies are carried out fairly'.[51] According to legal scholar (and Israeli citizen) Raef Zreik,

[the Palestinians'] main role is to show that a Jewish nationalism that is not colonial is a viable option. This means that while the Palestinians say 'No' to Jewish supremacy they can say 'Yes' to Jewish equality, while they say 'No' to Jewish privileges they can say 'Yes' to Jewish rights, 'No' to Jewish superiority but 'Yes' to Jewish safety.[52]

In a critical response to Tilley's *One Country*, Israeli academic Yoav Peled claimed that 'adherents of the one-state solution should have the courage to face the fact that *without Jewish domination* of whatever portion of Palestine/Israel, there will be no Jewish national home' (my italics).[53] In response, Tilley challenged the assumption that equality in immigration and land control (two 'resources' cited by Peled that must remain under 'Jewish control') would necessarily 'eradicate the Jewish national home'.[54] Would such processes of decolonisation and democratisation, she asked rhetorically, 'dissolve Jewish-national life for a Jewish-Israeli population ... that sustains a sophisticated national literature and media, vigorous arts and a sturdy political culture? It is hard to defend such a claim'. It is only by uncoupling 'domination' and self-determination, two concepts that the Zionist movement has fought hard to weld together, that Palestine/Israel can move from a single apartheid state to a democratic one. 'Decolonization should not be understood as a blunt and absolute reversal of colonization', Omar Barghouti wrote, 'putting us back under pre-colonial conditions and undoing whatever rights had been acquired to date. Instead, decolonization can be regarded as a negation of the aspects of colonialism that deny the rights of the colonized indigenous population and, as a byproduct, dehumanize the colonizers themselves'.[55]

Fertile soil – the Jewish alternative to an ethno-state

As we look forward beyond apartheid in Palestine/Israel, to a de-coupling of self-determination and domination, there is a wealth of Jewish traditions, intellectual history, and contemporary dissent, that forms fertile soil for developing an alternative to a majoritarian, ethno-state.[56] Writing on 'the inevitable impossible', South African academic Steven Friedman described how, under the historic Apartheid regime, 'the leadership of Afrikaner nationalism came to see a democratic state as a better guarantor of their interests than domination through separation'.[57] He added: 'This makes it significant that an alternative Jewish tradition does exist that could help to prepare Jews for a shared future not premised on ethnic nationalism' – traditions, he added, that 'may make both the advent of a shared state and its success more likely'.[58] In Chapter 3 we considered some of the historic and contemporary oppositions and alternatives to Zionism amongst Jews, grounded in widely divergent motivations. The point is, as Judith Butler put it, that 'there are forms of Judaism or Jewishness that would oppose all forms of domination of this kind'.[59]

In a 2013 blog post, Charles H. Manekin explained that, 'as a religious Jew', he believes that 'the Jew qua Jew has three homes: the state of which she is a citizen; the Jewish community of which she is a participant, and the land of Israel'.[60] But crucially, he added, 'Jews do not need political sovereignty in an exclusivist ethnic state in order to feel at home in that land [i.e. Palestine/Israel].' Some years previously, reflecting on the necessity of Israel as a state of all its citizens, rather than 'a Jewish state as constituted now', Manekin wrote: 'People say to me, "Why would any Jew be interested to live in a state like that?"'[61] He continued: 'The funny thing is that the Jews who ask me this question actually do live in a state like that – it is called the USA.' Once again, we see that the key issue here is decoupling elements that the Zionist movement has (often very successfully) sought to irrevocably bind together, namely: Jewish peoplehood, self-determination, and a 'Jewish state'/ethno-state in Palestine.

But it's not just a question of dusting off forgotten histories or reviving marginalised traditions – it's also about new visions, in Palestine/Israel and the Jewish world. Some of these are being forged, as you read this, in the context of a combined struggle against Donald Trump, white supremacy, and far-right nationalism at home, and apartheid in Palestine/Israel. 'Over the next few years', wrote Ben Lorber, Jewish Voice for Peace campus coordinator, in February 2017, 'the twin barbarisms of the Trump and Netanyahu regimes will continue to dovetail, and the rift between Israel and the bulk of American Jewry will continue to widen'.[62] He continued:

> While a few American Jews will cast their lot with Trump, Netanyahu and the rising global forces of fascism, hundreds of

thousands more will overcome the inertia of our mainstream institutions and take to the streets to defend our lives and communities against tyranny. Through this experience of struggle, American Jews will reconnect to the social movements from which, for too long, too many of us have been estranged. We will re-learn the muscles of tzedek (justice) and tikkun olam (healing the world) which, for too long, too many of us had failed to put to use.

According to Lorber, 'the old dream of a liberal Zionism will not survive to carry us through the 21st century'. But, he went on,

out of the fire of our reborn commitment to our principles, a new diaspora Jewish identity can be formed, founded on prophetic values of social justice, solidarity and love. We will again bear witness to 'mi-melech malche ha-melachim', to a 'king who rules over kings', a force of divine righteousness greater than earthly power. Let us cleave to this vision, and this work, without fear, with a clear head and a strong moral compass. It is our only hope.

In an important essay published by *The Nation* in 2007 ('The State of Zionism'), Brian Klug, Senior Research Fellow in Philosophy at St. Benet's Hall, Oxford, and renowned expert on antisemitism, wondered whether Zionism is 'caught in a time warp', writing: 'Could Israel, under its influence, be continually undermining itself, while millions of Jews who have no say in the matter are implicated in its policies? ... What, in short, if our "liberation" entraps us in an illusion?'[63] For Klug, 'Jewish ethnic nationalism is no solution to the problems we face today' – 'it is time to move on'. But the debate on how to 'reconfigure' Israel is being inhibited by the latter's 'fear of abandoning its Zionist script; fear of being a normal country, one that is home to all its citizens; fear of equality, of an inclusive and open-ended society that evolves into something that is and is not Jewish'.

But if Israel cannot give up this fear, what hope is there for the future? A state that does not believe in its own possibility, except as a perpetual interloper at odds with its neighbours, has no future.

Some Jewish Israelis are already giving up on the fear, and embracing that future vision. In a 2010 video made by Zochrot, Israelis in the streets, shops and cafes of Jaffa are asked what they will do on the day the city's Palestinian refugees return.[64] 'I'll be glad to meet them, that's all,' said one woman. 'I hope they'll invite me over for good food,' said another, smiling. 'I'll start believing there's a chance for the idea of a state of all its citizens,' said one young man, 'and things will actually begin to move in a natural, sensible direction, like in every proper, sensible state, not delusional, like this one.' Another young man commented: 'I hope I'll be around to see it.'

Conclusion

The memoirs of former US Secretary of State Condoleeza Rice may seem like an unlikely source of inspiration at this juncture, but they include a fascinating anecdote that tells us something important about the prospects for a Palestine/Israel beyond apartheid. Recounting a meeting with then Israeli minister Tzipi Livni in March 2004, Rice explains how the Israeli politician was categorical about the impossibility of Palestinian refugees returning, since this would 'change the nature' of the State of Israel (i.e. as a 'Jewish state').[65] Rice's reflections are unusually candid. 'I must admit that though I understood the argument intellectually', she wrote, 'it struck me as a harsh defence of the ethnic purity of the Israeli state when Tzipi said it.' She continued: 'It was one of those conversations that shocked my sensibilities as an American. After all, the very concept of 'American' rejects ethnic or religious definitions of citizenship. Moreover, there were Arab citizens of

Israel. Where did they fit in?' Though, by her own account, Rice was apparently convinced by Livni's apologia for Zionism, she nevertheless acknowledges that she supported the denial of the Palestinian refugees' right to return 'despite the dissonance that it stirred in me'.

Such 'dissonance' is only tolerable when Palestinian rights are subordinated to Israeli demands, and when the Zionist movement's insistence on an ethno-state in Palestine is accepted and unchallenged. Yet, as we have seen at various stages of this book, both of these positions are under growingly intolerable pressure, processes only accelerating in the Trump era. As the cracks widen, Israeli leaders are right to be worried about the long-term consequences – and likely shelf life of apartheid – should the paradigm of partition be definitively abandoned. According to an April 2017 poll by University of Maryland based academics examining 'American Attitudes to the Israeli-Palestinian Conflict', 31 per cent of Americans *already* support 'a single democratic state' in all of Palestine/Israel as the ideal future for Israel and the Palestinians that the US should be supporting.[66] Even more instructively, when the 37 per cent of respondents who currently back a two-state solution were asked what they prefer if this 'turns out over time to be impossible', an overwhelming majority – 63 per cent – supported a single democratic state.

Almost two decades ago, Edward Said, describing how the 'peace process' had 'become the only game in town', sounded a profound note of caution.[67] 'What if the "peace process" has in fact put off the real reconciliation that must occur if the hundred-year war between Zionism, Jewish nationalism, and the Palestinian people is to end?' For, as he had written many years earlier, 'to found a state in Asia and people it with a largely immigrant population drawn initially from Europe means depopulating the original territory'.[68] Yet, while 'for the native Arab Palestinian and for the immigrant Jew who took his place, the mere fact of substitution has never really varied', he continued, 'it is this fact with which the search for peace in the Middle East must begin, *and with which it has not yet even begun to deal*' (my emphasis). This is a reckoning, pregnant with liberatory potential, whose time has come. As Israeli journalist Gideon Levy wrote in 2015, 'out of the fire and despair, we must start talking about the last way out: equal rights for all'.[69]

Indeed, this one state is not so hard to imagine, especially when you travel around that land (as I have done, on and off, over the last 15 years). As this book has been at pains to describe, a de facto single state already exists, and has for some time. Only it is an apartheid one, defined by harsh boundaries of inclusion and exclusion, whose power structures are shaped by the politics and priorities of settler colonialism. It is a landscape of walls and watchtowers. Yet these visible and concrete divisions can, counter-intuitively but undeniably, speak to and evidence a kind of intimacy, albeit one that has, for decades now, been of a dark sort – the closeness of a coloniser and colonised, master and slave. And it is precisely in the acknowledgement of this bond, through an unflinching inventory of what Zionism and the State of Israel has meant for the Palestinians, that it is possible to imagine the transformation of the settler and native into citizens.

A book which moved me very much when I first read it is Mourid Barghouti's memoir 'I Saw Ramallah', based on the poet's return to Palestine after an enforced absence of some 30 years. 'When Palestine is no longer a chain worn with an evening dress, an ornament or a memory or a golden Qur'an', Barghouti recounts telling a friend, 'when we walk on Palestinian dust, and wipe it off our shirt collars and off our shoes, hurrying to conduct our daily affairs – our passing, normal, boring affairs – when we grumble about the heat in Palestine and the dullness of staying there too long, then we will really have come close to it.'[70] Later, he writes: 'the Palestinian has his joys too. He has his pleasures alongside his sorrows. He has the amazing contradictions of life, because he is a living creature before being the son of the eight o'clock news.'[71]

A single democratic state thus offers something extraordinarily ordinary; the prospect of Jewish Israelis and Palestinians escaping 'the iron circle of inhumanity' created by 'the radical Zionist distinction between privileged Jews in Palestine and unprivileged non-Jews', moving beyond apartheid, and instead, cooperating and arguing, loving and hating, praying and protesting, working and resting – *living*, in other words – as equal citizens of a shared home.[72]

Notes

Introduction

1. Protesters at the David Friedman Confirmation Hearing, 16 February 2017. www.youtube.com/watch?v=Je4KAJh906s (last accessed 13/3/17).
2. 'AMP staffers arrested protesting David Friedman's hearing at Senate Foreign Relations Committee', American Muslims for Palestine, 17 February, 2017, www.ampalestine.org/newsroom/amp-staffers-arrested-protesting-david-friedman%E2%80%99s-hearing-at-senate-foreign-relations (last accessed 13/3/17); 'BREAKING: FEDS DROP CHARGES AGAINST AMP STAFFERS', 22 April, 2017, www.ampalestine.org/newsroom/breaking-feds-drop-charges-against-amp-staffers (last accessed 3/5/17).
3. 'About Us', IfNotNow, https://ifnotnowmovement.org/about-us/ (last accessed 13/3/17).
4. 'Activists with IfNotNow Stand Against Friedman's Nomination as Ambassador to Israel', IfNotNow, 16 February 2017, https://ifnotnowmovement.org/press/ (last accessed 13/3/17).
5. David Friedman, 'Ambassador for Apartheid', Institute for Middle East Understanding, 8 March 2017, https://imeu.org/article/fact-sheet-david-friedman-ambassador-for-apartheid (last accessed 13/3/17).
6. 'David Friedman, Choice for Envoy to Israel, Is Hostile to Two-State Efforts', *New York Times*, 16 December 2016, www.nytimes.com/2016/12/16/world/middleeast/david-friedman-us-ambassador-israel.html (last accessed 13/3/17); 'Trump Israel ambassador pick bragged of removing two-state solution from GOP platform at November event', CNN, 23 February 2017, http://edition.cnn.com/2017/02/23/politics/kfile-david-friedman-november-speech/index.html (last accessed 13/3/17); Also see Friedman's own op-eds 'The Dreyfus Affair 2015', Arutz Sheva, August 20, 2015, www.israelnationalnews.com/Articles/Article.aspx/17419 (last accessed 13/3/17), and, 'Read Peter Beinart and you'll vote Donald Trump', Arutz Sheva, 5 June 2016, www.israelnationalnews.com/Articles/Article.aspx/18828 (last accessed 13/3/17).

7. 'Trump's Israel Envoy Pick Gave Funds to Settle Jews in Muslim Quarter of Jerusalem's Old City', *Haaretz*, 7 March 2017, www.haaretz.com/us-news/.premium-1.775611 (last accessed 13/3/17); see also 'Fund Headed by Trump's Israel Ambassador Pumped Tens of Millions Into West Bank Settlement', *Haaretz*, 16 December 2016, www.haaretz.com/israel-news/.premium-1.759484 (last accessed 13/3/17).

8. 'Mr. Friedman is completely unfit for ... any diplomatic office', US Campaign for Palestinian Rights, 27 February 2017, http://uscpr.org/mr-friedman-completely-unfit-diplomatic-office/ (last accessed 15/3/17).

9. 'Former U.S. Ambassadors Urge Senate Not to Confirm Friedman as Trump's Israel Envoy', *Haaretz*, 16 February 2017, www.haaretz.com/us-news/1.772048 (last accessed 15/3/17); 'Senate panel backs Trump nominee to be ambassador to Israel', Reuters, 9 March 2017, www.reuters.com/article/us-usa-israel-diplomacy-idUSKBN 16G2CA (last accessed 15/3/17).

10. 'Statement following SFRC vote on David Friedman: opposition shows support for equal rights', 9 March 2017, https://jewish voiceforpeace.org/statement-following-sfrc-vote-david-friedman-opposition-shows-support-equal-rights (last accessed 15/3/17); 'Statement of Senator Patrick Leahy On The Nomination of David Friedman to be U.S. Ambassador to Israel', 13 March 2017, www.leahy.senate.gov/press/statement-of-senator-patrick-leahy-on_the-nomination-of-david-friedman-to-be-us-ambassador-to-israel (last accessed 15/3/17).

11. 'Trump's pick for ambassador to Israel sparks hot debate', Associated Press, 26 December 2016, www.yahoo.com/news/trumps-pick-ambassador-israel-sides-edge-083406166--election.html (last accessed 16/3/17).

12. 'Jewish Storm Builds Over David Friedman's Appointment as Israel Ambassador', *The Forward*, 16 December 2016, http://forward.com/news/national/357426/jewish-storm-builds-over-david-friedmans-appointment as israel-ambassador/ (last accessed 16/3/17); 'Trump's Pick for Israel Envoy: Where Do Jewish Groups Stand?' *Haaretz*, 6 March 2017, www.haaretz.com/us-news/.premium-1.775394 (last accessed 16/3/17); Also see 'With Friedman's confirmation looming, US Jews range from despondent to exhilarated', *The Times of Israel*, 16 March 2017, www.timesofisrael.com/with-friedmans-confirmation-looming-us-jews-range-from-despondent-to-exhilarated/ (last accessed 16/3/17).

13. '40,000 Sign Petition Against Trump's Israel Envoy Pick David Friedman', *Haaretz*, 2 March 2017, www.haaretz.com/us-news/. premium-1.774582 (last accessed 16/3/17).

14. 'Activists with IfNotNow Stand Against Friedman's Nomination as Ambassador to Israel', IfNotNow, 16 February 2017, https://ifnotnowmovement.org/press (last accessed 16/3/17); 'Why We Protested David Friedman's Senate Hearing', *Haaretz*, 19 February 2017, www.haaretz.com/opinion/.premium-1.772512 (last accessed 16/3/17).

15. 'Friedman confirmed as U.S. ambassador to Israel', *Politico*, 23 March 2017, www.politico.com/story/2017/03/david-friedman-ambassador-to-israel-confirmed-236428 (last accessed 27/4/17).

16. C-SPAN, 16 February 2017, www.c-span.org/video/?424017-1/israeli-ambassador-nominee-david-friedman-testifies-confirmation-hearing (last accessed 27/4/17).

17. 'Americans Tepid on Palestinian Statehood', Gallup, 13 February 2017, www.gallup.com/poll/203900/americans-tepid-palestinian-statehood.aspx (last accessed 2/5/17).

18. 'Which Country Is America's Strongest Ally? For Republicans, It's Australia', *New York Times*, 3 February 2017, www.nytimes.com/interactive/2017/02/03/upshot/which-country-do-americans-like-most-for-republicans-its-australia.html (last accessed 2/5/17).

19. 'Demographics and Democrats: Brand Israel's big problems ahead', *Middle East Eye*, 16 April 2017, www.middleeasteye.net/columns/demographics-and-democrats-brand-israels-big-problems-ahead-158651491 (last accessed 2/5/17).

20. 'In Trump's America, can Israel remain bipartisan?', 25 April 2017, www.jpost.com/Israel-News/Post-election-divide-in-US-makes-it-harder-to-keep-Israel-bipartisan-488964 (last accessed 2/5/17).

21. 'Dani Dayan: Support for Israel must not become partisan', *Newsweek*, 21 April 2017, www.newsweek.com/dani-dayan-support-israel-must-not-become-partisan-586864 (last accessed 2/5/17).

22. 'For pro-Israel Americans, Trump's support may be less than welcome', 22 April 2017, www.dw.com/en/for-pro-israel-americans-trumps-support-may-be-less-than-welcome/a-38528174 (last accessed 2/5/17).

Chapter 1

1. 'A Temporary State of Permanence', *Haaretz*, 27 October 2015, www.haaretz.com/peace/.premium-1.682645 (last accessed 8/11/17).

2. 'Israeli lawmakers both praise and slam settlement law', *The Jerusalem Post*, 7 February 2017, www.jpost.com/printarticle. aspx?id=480770 (last accessed 9/5/17).

3. 'Israel: Halt Demolitions of Bedouin Homes in Negev', HRW, 1 August 2010, www.hrw.org/news/2010/08/01/israel-halt-demolitions-bedouin-homes-negev (last accessed 3/5/17).

4. Ibid.

5. 'A Test of Wills Over a Patch of Desert', *New York Times*, 25 August 2010, www.nytimes.com/2010/08/26/world/middleeast/26israel. html (last accessed 3/5/17); 'Police Destroy Dozens of Buildings in Unrecognized Bedouin Village in Negev', *Haaretz*, 28 July 2010, www.haaretz.com/police-destroy-dozens-of-buildings-in-unrecognized-bedouin-village-in-negev-1.304443 (last accessed 3/5/17).

6. 'Police Destroy Dozens of Buildings in Unrecognized Bedouin Village in Negev', *Haaretz*, 28 July 2010, www.haaretz.com/police-destroy-dozens-of-buildings-in-unrecognized-bedouin-village-in-negev-1.304443 (last accessed 3/5/17).

7. '1,300 policemen guard razing of Bedouin village', *Ynet*, 27 July 2010, www.ynetnews.com/articles/0,7340,L-3925793,00.html (last accessed 3/5/17).

8. 'Bedouins evicted from village in southern Israel', CNN, 27 July 2010, http://edition.cnn.com/2010/WORLD/meast/07/27/israel. bedouins.demolitions/ (last accessed 3/5/17).

9. 'Israel criticised over demolition of "unrecognised" Bedouin villages', *Guardian*, 3 August 2010, www.theguardian.com/world/2010/aug/03/israel-criticised-demolition-bedouin-villages (last accessed 9/5/17).

10. 'From Al-Araqib to Susiya: The forced displacement of Palestinians on Both Sides of the Green Line', *Adalah*, May 2013, www.adalah. org/uploads/oldfiles/Public/files/English/Publications/Position_Papers/Forced-Displacement-Position-Paper-05-13.pdf (last accessed 4/5/17).

11. Ibid.

12. 'Israel: Halt Demolitions of Bedouin Homes in Negev', HRW, 1 August 2010, www.hrw.org/news/2010/08/01/israel-halt-demolitions-bedouin-homes-negev (last accessed 3/5/17).

13. Ibid.

14. Ibid.

15. Ibid.

16. 'Oxfam calls for compensation from Israel', *Ma'an News Agency*, 24 July 2010, http://www.maannews.com/Content.aspx?id=302109 (last accessed 3/5/17).

17. 'ON THE BRINK: Israeli settlements and their impact on Palestinians in the Jordan Valley', www.oxfam.org/sites/www.oxfam.org/files/bp160-jordan-valley-settlements-050712-en_1.pdf (last accessed 3/5/17).

18. 'Oxfam calls for compensation from Israel', *Ma'an News Agency*, 24 July 2010, www.maannews.com/Content.aspx?id=302109 (last accessed 3/5/17).

19. '12 August 2010: Civil Administration demolishes Bedouin village of al-Farisiyah, in the Jordan Valley', *B'Tselem*, 12 August 2010, www.btselem.org/planning_and_building/20100812_whole_village_demolished_in_jordan_valley (last accessed 3/5/17).

20. For more on this issue, see 'The truth about West Bank demolitions', Al Jazeera, 9 February 2015, www.aljazeera.com/indepth/opinion/2015/02/truth-west-bank-demolitions-150209061227822.html (last accessed 11/5/17) and 'How home demolitions threaten Palestinian statehood', Al Jazeera, 20 April 2016, www.aljazeera.com/news/2016/04/home-demolitions-threaten-palestinian-statehood-160416103012972.html (last accessed 11/5/17).

21. 'UN: Israel 'systematically' emptying Area C of Palestinians', *Times of Israel*, 28 July 2016, www.timesofisrael.com/un-israel-systematically-emptying-area-c-of-palestinians/ (last accessed 11/5/17).

22. Report to the Ad Hoc Liaison Committee, Office of the UN Special Coordinator for the Middle East Peace Process (UNSCO), May 2017, http://reliefweb.int/sites/reliefweb.int/files/resources/UNSCO%20Report%20to%20AHLC%20-%201%20May%202017.pdf (last accessed 11/5/17).

23. Ibid.

24. Ibid.

25. 'Improving the Gazan Economy and Utilizing the Economic Potential of the Jordan Valley', The Aix Group, February 2017, http://aix-group.org/index.php/2017/02/07/two-further-studies-improving-the-gazan-economy-and-utilizing-the-economic-potential-of-the-jordan-valley-2/ (last accessed 11/5/17).

26. Ibid.

27. Ibid.

28. 'ON THE BRINK: Israeli settlements and their impact on Palestinians in the Jordan Valley', https://www.oxfam.org/sites/www.

oxfam.org/files/bp160-jordan-valley-settlements-050712-en_1.pdf (last accessed 3/5/17).

29. 'Fifty years of occupation: Where do we go from here?', ICRC, 2 June 2017, www.icrc.org/en/document/fifty-years-occupation-where-do-we-go-here (last accessed 6/6/17).

30. 'Land Expropriation and Settlements', B'Tselem, www.btselem.org/settlements (last accessed 16/6/17).

31. '1967 Meron Opinion', SOAS University of London, www.soas.ac.uk/lawpeacemideast/resources/ (last accessed 16/6/17).

32. The Yesha settler council said the West Bank settler population exceeded 421,000 in 2016 – see 'NGO: Israeli settlers in West Bank top 421,000', 10 February 2017, http://en.qantara.de/content/ngo-israeli-settlers-in-west-bank-top-421000 (last accessed 16/6/17); Haaretz cited a West Bank settler population of 382,000 in 2015, excluding outposts – see 'How Many Settlers Really Live in the West Bank? Haaretz Investigation Reveals', *Haaretz*, 15 June 2017, www.haaretz.com/israel-news/.premium-1.794730 (last accessed 16/6/17).

33. 'Israeli settlements in the Occupied Palestinian Territory, including East Jerusalem, and in the occupied Syrian Golan – Report of the Secretary-General', A/HRC/34/39, 16 March 2017, www.ohchr.org/EN/HRBodies/HRC/RegularSessions/Session34/Pages/ListReports.aspx (last accessed 20/6/17); 'Oslo Process 20 Years', PLO Negotiations Affairs Department, www.nad.ps/en/publication-resources/publication/oslo-process-20-years (last accessed 20/6/17), also see 'Statement by Lara Friedman, Americans for Peace Now Delivered at the United Nations Security Council – October 14, 2016', https://peacenow.org/WP/wp-content/uploads/UNSC-speech-by-Lara-Friedman-Oct-14-2016.pdf (last accessed 20/6/17).

34. 'A Defiant Israel Vows to Expand Its Settlements', *New York Times*, 26 December 2016, www.nytimes.com/2016/12/26/world/middleeast/israel-settlements-un-security-council-benjamin-netanyahu-obama.html?_r=0 (last accessed 20/6/17); 'Israeli settlements grew on Obama's watch. They may be poised for a boom on Trump's', *Washington Post*, 2 January 2017, www.washingtonpost.com/world/middle_east/israeli-settlements-grew-on-obamas-watch-they-may-be-poised-for-a-boom-on-trumps/2017/01/02/24feeae6-cd23-11e6-85cd-e66532e35a44_story.html (last accessed 20/6/17).

35. 'Sharp rise in Israeli settlement projects in 2016', AFP, 22 March 2017, www.yahoo.com/news/sharp-rise-israeli-settlement-projects-2016-164025511.html (last accessed 20/6/17).

36. '40% Increase in Construction Starts in West Bank Settlements in 2016', *Peace Now*, 22 March 2017, http://peacenow.org.il/en/40-increase-construction-starts-west-bank-settlements-2016 (last accessed 20/6/17).

37. 'Peace Now Settlement Watch: Jurisdiction of The New Settlement "Amihai" Approved', *Peace Now*, 30 May 2017, http://peacenow.org/entry.php?id=24126#.WUkqDk6GPIW (last accessed 20/6/17).

38. 'Israel: Reverse Illegal Plans for West Bank', Human Rights Watch, 3 September 2014, www.hrw.org/news/2014/09/03/israel-reverse-illegal-plans-west-bank (last accessed 20/6/17).

39. 'Sharp increase in ratification of declarations of "state land"', UN OCHA, 4 July 2016, www.ochaopt.org/content/sharp-increase-ratification-declarations-state-land (last accessed 20/6/17).

40. 'Israel Passes Contentious Palestinian Land-grab Bill in Late Night Vote', *Haaretz*, 7 February 2017, www.haaretz.com/israel-news/.premium-1.770099 (last accessed 20/6/17).

41. 'Explained: Israel's New Palestinian Land-grab Law and Why It Matters', *Haaretz*, 7 February 2017, www.haaretz.com/israel-news/1.770102 (last accessed 20/6/17); 'Israel passes bill retroactively legalising Jewish settlements', *Guardian*, 6 February 2017, www.theguardian.com/world/2017/feb/06/israel-likely-pass-bill-retroactively-legalising-jewish-settlements (last accessed 20/6/17).

42. 'The secret life of settlement outposts', Yesh Din, 1 April 2015, www.yesh-din.org/en/the-secret-life-of-settlement-outposts/ (last accessed 20/6/17).

43. 'Israel Markedly Increased Settlement Construction, Decisions in Last Three Months, Middle East Special Coordinator Tells Security Council', 24 March 2017, www.un.org/press/en/2017/sc12765.doc.htm (last accessed 20/6/17); 'Statement by the HRVP Federica Mogherini on the most recent announcement of 3,000 new settlement units in the West Bank', 1 February 2017, https://eeas.europa.eu/headquarters/headquarters-homepage/19698/statement-hrvp-federica-mogherini-most-recent-announcement-3000-new-settlements-west-bank_en (last accessed 20/6/17).

44. 'Occupation, Inc', Human Rights Watch, 19 January 2006, www.hrw.org/report/2016/01/19/occupation-inc/how-settlement-businesses-contribute-israels-violations-palestinian (last accessed 20/6/17).

45. 'Restricting Space: The Planning Regime Applied By Israel in Area C of the West Bank', UN OCHA, December 2009, www.ochaopt.org/sites/default/files/special_focus_area_c_demolitions_december_2009.pdf (last accessed 20/6/17); 'Land Expropriation and

Annexation and Local Government', B'Tselem, 1 January 2017, www.btselem.org/settlements/annexation (last accessed 20/6/17); 'Restricting Space', UN OCHA.

46. 'The humanitarian impact of de facto settlement expansion: common features, conclusions and the way forward', UN OCHA, 11 March 2017, https://www.ochaopt.org/content/humanitarian-impact-de-facto-settlement-expansion-common-features-conclusions-and-way (last accessed 20/6/17).

47. 'Israeli Lawmaker Miki Zohar Wants to Annex the West Bank, What on Earth Is People's Problem With Him?', *Haaretz*, 9 March 2017, www.haaretz.com/opinion/.premium-1.776053 (last accessed 20/6/17).

48. Ibid.

49. 'Separate and Unequal', Human Rights Watch, 19 December 2010, www.hrw.org/report/2010/12/19/separate-and-unequal/israels-discriminatory-treatment-palestinians-occupied (last accessed 20/6/17); 'Israel's settlement building and revenue freezing plan is 'unacceptable', Amnesty, 3 November 2011, www.amnesty.org.uk/press-releases/israels-settlement-building-and-revenue-freezing-plan-unacceptable (last accessed 20/6/17); 'Israel/OPT: Trump must oppose all Israeli settlements in meeting with Netanyahu', Amnesty, 14 February 2017, www.amnesty.org/en/documents/mde15/5693/2017/en/ (last accessed 20/6/17).

50. 'UN report: Occupation is the main cause of humanitarian needs in the occupied Palestinian territory', UN OCHA, 31 May 2017, www.ochaopt.org/content/un-report-occupation-main-cause-humanitarian-needs-occupied-palestinian-territory (last accessed 20/6/17).

51. 'Settlements Do Not Serve Israel's Security Needs, Say Former Generals', *Haaretz*, 5 June 2017, www.haaretz.com/israel-news/.premium-1.793609 (last accessed 20/6/17).

52. Amir S. Cheshin, Bill Hutman, Avi Melamed, *Separate and Unequal: The Inside Story of Israeli Rule in East Jerusalem* (Cambridge: Harvard University Press, 2001), p.56.

53. 'Legal Status of East Jerusalem and its Residents', B'Tselem, www.btselem.org/jerusalem/legal_status (last accessed 20/6/17).

54. Cheshin, Hutman, Melamed, *Separate and Unequal*, p.56.

55. Ibid.

56. 'Basic Law: Jerusalem, Capital of Israel', www.knesset.gov.il/laws/special/eng/basic10_eng.htm (last accessed 20/6/17).

57. 'The Real Reason Israel Annexed East Jerusalem', *Haaretz*, 25 May 2017, www.haaretz.com/israel-news/.premium-1.791568 (last accessed 20/6/17).

58. Ibid.

59. 'Wary Israel Tried to Conceal East Jerusalem's Annexation in 1967, Documents Reveal', *Haaretz*, 18 April 2017, www.haaretz.com/israel-news/1.783429 (last accessed 20/6/17).

60. UN General Assembly Resolution 2253, 4 July 1967, https://unispal.un.org/DPA/DPR/unispal.nsf/1ce874ab1832a53e852570bb006dfaf6/a39a906c89d3e98685256c29006d4014?OpenDocument (last accessed 20/6/17).

61. 'The settlers' goal is not the settlements', +972 *Magazine*, 8 June 2017, https://972mag.com/the-settlers-goal-is-not-the-settlements/127948/ (last accessed 20/6/17).

62. Eyal Weizman, *Hollow Land* (London: Verso, 2007), p. 92.

63. Ibid.

64. Ibid.

65. Ibid.

66. Ian Lustick, *The 'Irreversibility' of Israel's annexation of the West Bank and Gaza Strip: Critical Evaluation*, US Defense Intelligence Agency, October 1985.

67. 'Abroad at home; 5 Minutes to Midnight', *New York Times*, 1 November 1982, www.nytimes.com/1982/11/01/opinion/abroad-at-home-5-minutes-to-midnight.html (last accessed 20/6/17). Also see 'The West Bank in year 2010', *Christian Science Monitor*, 25 April 1984, www.csmonitor.com/1984/0425/042522.html (last accessed 20/6/17).

68. Ian Lustick, *Unsettled States, Disputed Lands* (Ithaca: Cornell University Press, 1993), p. 15.

69. Lustick, 1985.

70. 'How Long Can Israel Deny Its Civil War?', *New York Times*, 27 December 1987, www.nytimes.com/1987/12/27/weekinreview/how-long-can-israel-deny-its-civil-war.html (last accessed 20/6/17).

71. 'The Irrelevance of a Palestinian State', *New York Times*, 20 June 1999, www.nytimes.com/1999/06/20/magazine/the-irrelevance-of-a-palestinian-state.html (last accessed 20/6/17).

72. 'Israel has de facto annexed the Jordan Valley', *B'Tselem*, 13 February 2006, www.btselem.org/settlements/20060213_annexation_of_the_jordan_valley (last accessed 20/6/17).

73. 'Military effectively shutting down Palestinian quarries in Beit Fajjar to aid de facto annexation of area', *B'Tselem*, 21 April 2016, www.

btselem.org/planning_and_building/20160421_military_shuts_ down_palestinian_quarries (last accessed 20/6/17).

74. 'New UN map charts West Bank reality', *Financial Times*, 4 June 2007, www.ft.com/content/728a69d4-12b1-11dc-a475-000b5d f10621 (last accessed 20/6/17).

75. 'Israel-Palestine is already a de facto single state', *Guardian*, 29 April 2009, www.theguardian.com/commentisfree/2009/apr/29/israel- palestine-one-state-solution (last accessed 20/6/17).

76. 'Amona Live Updates: After Years of Delay, Israel Evacuates Illegal West Bank Outpost', *Haaretz*, 2 February 2017, www.haaretz.com/ israel-news/LIVE-1.768926/Amona-bennett (last accessed 20/6/17).

77. 'Netanyahu calls in US envoy in fallout over UN vote', AFP, 25 December 2016, www.yahoo.com/news/un-demands-end-israeli- settlements-us-abstains-193027638.html (last accessed 20/6/17).

78. 'Justice Minister Ayelet Shaked: "Annexing all of West Bank will be the end of Israel"', *Jerusalem Post*, 16 February 2017, www.jpost.com/ Breaking-News/Justice-Minister-Ayelet-Shaked-Annexing-all-of- West-Bank-will-be-the-end-of-Israel-481814 (last accessed 20/6/17).

79. 'Hotovely calls for gradual sovereignty', *Arutz Sheva*, 13 February 2017, www.israelnationalnews.com/News/News.aspx/224868 (last accessed 20/6/17).

80. 'The incremental annexation of Palestine', *+972 Magazine*, 4 May 2016, https://972mag.com/the-incremental-annexation-of- palestine/119042/ (last accessed 20/6/17).

81. 'An Israeli Guide to Annexation', 23 June 2016, http://nakbafiles. org/2016/06/23/israel-and-annexations-a-guide/ (last accessed 20/6/17).

82. Ibid.

83. 'Israel's parliament passes a controversial "regulation" bill on settlements', *Economist*, 7 February 2017, www.economist.com/ news/middle-east-and-africa/21716563-high-court-may-yet-strike- it-down-israels-parliament-passes-controversial (last accessed 20/6/17).

84. 'In step toward annexation, ministers demand new laws include settlements', *Times of Israel*, 6 June 2017, www.timesofisrael.com/ in-step-toward-annexation-ministers-demand-new-laws-include- settlements/ (last accessed 20/6/17).

85. 'Have two ministers annexed Area C of the West Bank?', *Jerusalem Post*, 7 June 2017, www.jpost.com/Israel-News/Have-two-ministers- annexed-Area-C-of-the-West-Bank-496188 (last accessed 20/6/17).

86. Lustick, 1985.

87. 'Comprehensive Settlement Population 1972-2011', *Foundation for Middle East Peace*, 13 January 2012, http://fmep.org/resource

88. Lustick, 1985.

89. 'Why more and more Israeli Jews think the settlements are in Israel', *Fathom*, Spring 2017, http://fathomjournal.org/1967-why-more-and-more-israeli-jews-think-the-settlements-are-in-israel/ (last accessed 20/6/17).

90. 'The Peace Index: May 2017', 4 June 2017, www.peaceindex.org/indexMonthEng.aspx?num=322 (last accessed 21/6/17).

91. 'The Peace Index: April 2016', 9 May 2016, www.peaceindex.org/indexMonthEng.aspx?num=304 (last accessed 21/6/17).

92. 'What Israelis Aren't Being Taught in School, and Why', *Haaretz*, 3 January 2016, www.haaretz.com/opinion/.premium-1.695164 (last accessed 21/6/17).

93. 'The Peace Index: May 2017'.

94. 'Country Reports on Human Rights Practices for 2016', US State Department, www.state.gov/j/drl/rls/hrrpt/humanrightsreport/index.htm?year=2016&dlid=265500#wrapper (last accessed 21/6/17).

95. For more on the 'de-development' of Gaza, see the work of Sara Roy e.g. *Failing Peace: Gaza and the Palestinian-Israeli Conflict* (London: Pluto Press, 2006).

96. 'State opposes final appeal against demolition of Umm al-Hiran; bulldozers set to move on Bedouin village tomorrow', *Adalah*, 21 November 2016, www.adalah.org/en/content/view/8956 (last accessed 21/6/17).

97. 'In Umm al-Hiran, it is 'a continuing Nakba'', Al Jazeera, 22 January 2017, www.aljazeera.com/indepth/features/2017/01/umm-al-hiran-continuing-nakba-170122085822718.html (last accessed 21/6/17), 'PHOTOS: Israel demolishes homes in Umm el-Hiran amid violence', *+972 Magazine*, 19 January 2017, https://972mag.com/photos-israel-demolishes-homes-in-umm-el-hiran-amid-violence/124583/ (last accessed 21/6/17), 'Reconstruction of Umm al-Hiran killings disproves car-ramming claims', *+972 Magazine*, 18 May 2017, https://972mag.com/reconstruction-of-umm-al-hiran-killings-proves-no-car-ramming-attack/127351/ (last accessed 21/6/17).

98. 'U.S.: Israeli Demolition of Palestinian Village Sussia Would Be "Very Troubling"', *Haaretz*, 10 August 2016, www.haaretz.com/israel-news/.premium-1.736266 (last accessed 21/6/17); see also 'Update on Susya Court Hearing', Rabbis for Human Rights, 18 August 2016,

http://rhr.org.il/eng/2016/08/update-susya-high-court-hearing/ (last accessed 21/6/17).

99. 'Israel: Court Permits Discriminatory Evictions', Human Rights Watch, 19 May 2015, www.hrw.org/news/2015/05/19/israel-court-permits-discriminatory-evictions (last accessed 21/6/17).

100. 'There is no Green Line when it comes to home demolitions', +972 *Magazine*, 17 August 2016, https://972mag.com/there-is-no-green-line-when-it-comes-to-home-demolitions/121206/ (last accessed 21/6/17).

101. 'UN: About 2,000 Palestinians Harmed by Israeli Demolitions in Jordan Valley So Far This Year', *Haaretz*, 31 October 2016, www.haaretz.com/israel-news/.premium-1.749977 (last accessed 21/6/17).

102. 'Israel Planning Three New Settlements in Jordan Valley', *Haaretz*, 20 December 2017, www.haaretz.com/israel-news/1.830114 (last accessed 3/1/18).

103. 'East Jerusalem: Palestinians at risk of eviction', UN OCHA, 3 November 2016, www.ochaopt.org/content/east-jerusalem-palestinians-risk-eviction (last accessed 21/16/17).

104. 'Settlement through Excavation', *London Review of Books*, 5 September 2014, www.lrb.co.uk/blog/2014/09/05/natasha-roth/settlement-through-excavation (last accessed 21/6/17).

105. Ben White, *The 2014 Gaza War: 21 Questions & Answers*, eBook, 2016, p. 11.

106. 'Is the Gaza Strip really under Israeli occupation?', *Medium*, 12 June 2017, https://medium.com/@benabyad/is-the-gaza-strip-really-under-israeli-occupation-f1e9ea7a5781 (last accessed 21/6/17).

107. 'Money, Media and Policy Consensus: The Washington Institute for Near East Policy', *Middle East Report*, Volume 23, (January/February 1993), www.merip.org/mer/mer180/money-media-policy-consensus (last accessed 21/6/17).

108. 'Creeping apartheid' in Israel/Palestine', *Middle East Report*, Volume 39, (Winter 2009), www.merip.org/mer/mer253/creeping-apartheid-israel-palestine (last accessed 21/6/17).

109. '50 Years – A State Without Borders', The Association for Civil Rights in Israel, www.acri.org.il/campaigns/50yearsen/ (last accessed 21/6/17).

110. 'Israel's unlawfully prolonged occupation: consequences under an integrated legal framework', European Council on Foreign Relations, 2 June 2017, www.ecfr.eu/publications/summary/israels_unlawfully_prolonged_occupation_7294 (last accessed 21/6/17).

111. 'Israel must face new international legal push to end illegal occupation of Palestine, UN expert says', UN Human Rights Office of the High Commissioner, 26 October 2017, www.ohchr.org/EN/NewsEvents/Pages/DisplayNews.aspx?NewsID=22315 (last accessed 22/12/17).

112. Aeyal Gross, *The Writing on the Wall: Rethinking the International Law of Occupation* (Cambridge: Cambridge University Press, 2017), p. 176-7.

113. Ibid.

114. V. Tilley, 'After Oslo, a Paradigm Shift? Redefining Sovereignty, Responsibility and Self-determination in Israel-Palestine', *Conflict, Security and Development*, 15, No. 5 (October 2015).

115. 'Should Abbas' Peace Talks Deadline Be the Last Chance for a Two-state Solution?', *Haaretz*, 3 September 2014, www.haaretz.com/blogs/west-of-eden/.premium-1.613977 (last accessed 21/6/17).

116. 'British FM: alternative to two-state solution is Israel apartheid', AFP, 9 March 2017, www.yahoo.com/news/british-fm-alternative-two-state-solution-israel-apartheid-085241861.html (last accessed 21/6/17).

117. 'Exclusive: Kerry Warns Israel Could Become "An Apartheid State"', *Daily Beast*, 27 April 2014, www.thedailybeast.com/exclusive-kerry-warns-israel-could-become-an-apartheid-state (last accessed 21/6/17).

118. 'Barak: make peace with Palestinians or face apartheid', *Guardian*, 3 February 2010, www.theguardian.com/world/2010/feb/03/barak-apartheid-palestine-peace (last accessed 21/6/17). Barak repeated a similar warning in June 2017, see 'Ehud Barak Warns: Israel Faces "Slippery Slope" Toward Apartheid', *Haaretz*, 21 June 2017, www.haaretz.com/israel-news/1.796949 (last accessed 21/6/17).

119. 'Netanyahu weakens Israel' *Ynet*, 23 September 2011, www.ynetnews.com/articles/0,7340,L-4126434,00.html (last accessed 21/6/17).

120. 'Annexation – What's in a name?' The Nakba Files, 21 June 2016, http://nakbafiles.org/2016/06/21/annexation-whats-in-a-name/ (last accessed 21/16/17).

121. The Eighth United Nations Seminar on the Question of Palestine, 9–13 May 1983, https://unispal.un.org/DPA/DPR/unispal.nsf/0/44ECF112F30E45C28525749800514AE8 (last accessed 21/6/17).

122. Justin McCarthy, *The Population of Palestine* (New York: Columbia University Press, 1990), p. 10.

123. Nur Masalha, *Expulsion of the Palestinians: The Concept of "Transfer" in Zionist Political Thought, 1882–1948* (Washington D.C.: Institute for Palestine Studies, 1992), p. 1.

124. Tom Segev, *One Palestine Complete* (London: Abacus, 2000), p. 405.

125. Charles D. Smith, *Palestine and the Arab-Israeli Conflict* (Boston, MA: Bedford/St Martin's, 2004), p. 200; Rosemary Sayigh, *The Palestinians: From Peasants to Revolutionaries* (London: Zed Books, 2007), p. 99.

126. Hussein Abu Hussein and Fiona McKay, *Access Denied* (London: Zed Books, 2003), p. 4.

127. Ze'ev Sternhell, *The Founding Myths of Israel* (Princeton, NJ: Princeton University Press, 1998), p. 14.

128. Edward W. Said, *The Question of Palestine* (London: Vintage, 1992), p. 82.

Chapter 2

1. 'A. B. Yehoshua at Haaretz Conference: Recognize a Palestinian State at the UN', *Haaretz*, 8 May 2017, www.haaretz.com/israel-news/1.787996 (last accessed 13/7/17).

2. 'Bennett: Apply Israeli sovereignty over Area C', *Jerusalem Post*, 17 June 2013, www.jpost.com/Diplomacy-and-Politics/LIVE-Settlers-conference-on-public-relations-316793 (last accessed 13/7/17).

3. 'Netanyahu: Left knows if Likud is in power, no concessions will be made', *Ynetnews*, 15 March 2015, www.ynetnews.com/articles/0,7340,L-4637305,00.html (last accessed 13/7/17).

4. 'Netanyahu says no Palestinian state as long as he's prime minister', Reuters, 16 March 2015, www.reuters.com/article/us-israel-election-idUSKBN0MC1I820150316 (last accessed 13/7/17).

5. 'Trump is just what Netanyahu needs to annex the West Bank', *+972mag*, 10 February 2017, https://972mag.com/trump-is-just-what-netanyahu-needs-to-annex-the-west-bank/125141/ (last accessed 13/7/17).

6. 'Is 2-State Solution Dead? In Israel, a Debate Over What's Next', *New York Times*, 16 February 2017, www.nytimes.com/2017/02/16/world/middleeast/israel-palestinians-two-state-solution.html (last accessed 13/7/17).

7. 'Donald Trump Playacts Peace in the Middle East', *Foreign Policy*, 23 May 2017, https://foreignpolicy.com/2017/05/23/donald-trump-playacts-peace-in-the-middle-east (last accessed 26/6/17).

8. 'PM Netanyahu on Fareed Zakaria GPS', CNN, 5 October 2014, http://cnnpressroom.blogs.cnn.com/2014/10/05/pm-netanyahu-on-fareed-zakaria-gps/ (last accessed 13/7/17).

9. Israeli PM Netanyahu's Bar-Ilan Speech – English (2009), http://ecf. org.il/media_items/1141 (last accessed 13/7/17).

10. Remarks by President Trump and Prime Minister Netanyahu of Israel in Joint Press Conference, 15 February 2017, www.whitehouse. gov/the-press-office/2017/02/15/remarks-president-trump-and-prime-minister-netanyahu-israel-joint-press (last accessed 13/7/17).

11. Excerpts from the 'Peace & Security' chapter of the Likud Party platform, https://web.archive.org/web/20070930181442/https:/www. knesset.gov.il/elections/knesset15/elikud_m.htm (last accessed 13/7/17).

12. Abridged excerpts correct as of 22 October 2016, www.likudanglos. org.il/2010/08/likud-party-constitution.html (last accessed 13/7/17).

13. 'Likud party calls for de-facto annexation of Israeli settlements', Reuters, 31 December 2017, www.reuters.com/article/us-israel-palestinians-likud/likud-party-calls-for-de-facto-annexation-of-israeli-settlements-idUSKBN1EP0M2 (last accessed 3/1/18).

14. 'West Bank Settlement-building Activity Quadrupled This Year, Monitoring Group Says', *Haaretz*, 7 October 2016, www.haaretz. com/israel-news/.premium-1.746087 (last accessed 13/7/17).

15. 'Israel set to approve 2,500 settlement housing units', Al Jazeera, 2 June 2017, www.aljazeera.com/news/2017/06/israel-set-approve-2500-settlement-housing-units-170602190241755.html (last accessed 13/7/17); 'APN's Stephanie Breitsman in the Washington Jewish Week: Netanyahu calls Trump's bluff on settlements', *Americans for Peace Now*, 16 June 2017, https://peacenow.org/entry. php?id=24274#.WWefapWGPIV (last accessed 13/7/17).

16. 'Erdan: No minister, including Netanyahu, wants a Palestinian state soon', *Times of Israel*, 13 June 2017, www.timesofisrael.com/erdan-no-minister-including-netanyahu-wants-a-palestinian-state-soon/ (last accessed 13/7/17).

17. 'Israeli Minister to Present Cabinet With Proposal to Annex Dozens of Jerusalem-area Settlements', *Haaretz*, 22 January 2017, www. haaretz.com/israel-news/.premium-1.766618 (last accessed 13/7/17).

18. 'Elkin: Declaring sovereignty now would be a mistake', *Arutz Sheva*, 7 March 2017, www.israelnationalnews.com/News/News. aspx/226254 (last accessed 13/7/17).

19. 'Likud Minister: 'Israel is whole, there is no Palestine'', *Arutz Sheva*, 26 December 2015, www.israelnationalnews.com/News/News. aspx/205491#.Vn7ULPmLTIV (last accessed 13/7/17).

20. 'Hotovely: Oslo Failed – Time to Move On', *Arutz Sheva*, 21 June 2013, www.israelnationalnews.com/News/News.aspx/169153#. UcQNJspQrt4 (last accessed 13/7/17).

21. "Netanyahu was right, transferring Jews is ethnic cleansing", *Jerusalem Post*, 23 November 2016, www.jpost.com/Arab-Israeli-Conflict/Netanyahu-was-right-transferring-Jews-is-ethnic-cleansing-473425 (last accessed 13/7/17); 'Celebrating 50 years since liberation of Judea and Samaria', Arutz Sheva, 28 March 2017, www. israelnationalnews.com/News/News.aspx/227418 (last accessed 13/7/17).

22. 'Naftali Bennett interview: 'There won't be a Palestinian state within Israel'', *Guardian*, 7 January 2013, www.theguardian.com/ world/2013/jan/07/naftali-bennett-interview-jewish-home (last accessed 13/7/17).

23. 'Give Palestinians autonomy but not state, Bennett says', *i24 News*, 5 June 2016, www.i24news.tv/en/news/israel/diplomacy-defense/115655-160605-give-palestinians-autonomy-but-not-state-bennett-says (last accessed 13/7/17).

24. 'Bennett: First Gush Etzion, Then All of Judea and Samaria', *Arutz Sheva*, 30 May 2014, www.israelnationalnews.com/News/News. aspx/181200#.U4gX7fldXs8 (last accessed 13/7/17).

25. 'Israeli minister: The Bible says West Bank is ours', Al Jazeera, 24 February 2017, www.aljazeera.com/programmes/upfront/2017/02/ israeli-minister-bible-west-bank-170224082827910.html (last accessed 13/7/17).

26. 'Jewish Home minister says PM's peace overtures will go nowhere', *Times of Israel*, 8 June 2016, www.timesofisrael.com/israeli-minister-remove-palestinians-from-west-bank-area-c-annex-territory/ (last accessed 13/7/17); 'Netanyahu slams French proposal for foreign observers in Jerusalem', i24 News, 18 October 2015, www.i24news. tv/en/news/israel/diplomacy-defense/89389-151018-israel-s-us-envoy-refutes-claim-that-settlements-linked-to-current-violence (last accessed 13/7/17).

27. 'Only Four of 20 Israeli Ministers Openly Declare Support of Two-state Solution', *Haaretz*, 27 June 2016, www.haaretz.com/israel-news/1.727431 (last accessed 13/7/17).

28. 'The Zionist Union's plan for a Palestinian Bantustan', *Middle East Monitor*, 10 March 2015, www.middleeastmonitor.com/20150310-

the-zionist-unions-plan-for-a-palestinian-bantustan/ (last accessed 13/7/17).

29. 'Zionist Union platform aims to set Israel's final borders', *Jerusalem Post*, 8 March 2015, www.jpost.com/Israel-Elections/Zionist-Union-platform-aims-to-set-Israels-final-borders-393308 (last accessed 13/7/17).

30. Isaac Herzog: I don't say the word 'peace' so I don't raise expectations', *Jerusalem Post*, 1 March 215, www.jpost.com/Israel-Elections/Herzog-I-dont-say-the-word-peace-so-I-dont-raise-expectations-392623 (last accessed 13/7/17).

31. 'Labor Adopts Herzog's Plan for Separation From Palestinians as Party Platform', *Haaretz*, 8 February 2016, www.haaretz.com/israel-news/.premium-1.702002 (last accessed 13/7/17).

32. 'Why Herzog's diplomatic plan looks an awful lot like apartheid', *+972mag*, 11 February 2016, https://972mag.com/why-herzogs-diplomatic-plan-looks-an-awful-lot-like-apartheid/116946/ (last accessed 13/7/17).

33. 'Isaac Herzog Details His 10-point Plan for Israeli-Palestinian Peace', *Haaretz*, 23 February 2017, www.haaretz.com/israel-news/.premium-1.773312 (last accessed 13/7/17).

34. 'Labor chief: Settlements represent the "beautiful face of Zionism"', *Times of Israel*, 19 October 2017, www.timesofisrael.com/labor-chief-settlements-represent-the-beautiful-face-of-zionism/ (last accessed 22/12/17); 'New Leader of Israeli Left: We Don't Need to Evacuate Settlements if There's a Peace Deal', *Haaretz*, 16 October 2017, www.haaretz.com/israel-news/1.817602 (last accessed 22/12/17).

35. 'Herzog: Jerusalem won't stay Jewish, safe without "dramatic" change', *Times of Israel*, 1 June 2016, www.timesofisrael.com/liveblog_entry/herzog-jerusalem-wont-stay-jewish-safe-without-dramatic-change/ (last accessed 13/7/17).

36. 'Lapid: 'I'm the only alternative to Netanyahu'', *Arutz Sheva*, 11 December 2016, www.israelnationalnews.com/News/News.aspx/221538 (last accessed 13/7/17); 'Lapid: We need to build a high wall and get the Palestinians out of our sight', *Times of Israel*, 10 December 2016, www.timesofisrael.com/lapid-israel-needs-to-separate-from-the-palestinians/ (last accessed 13/7/17).

37. 'Lapid: Israel's global standing has never been worse; I could change that', *Times of Israel*, 4 December 2015, www.timesofisrael.com/lapid-israels-global-standing-has-never-been-worse-i-could-change-that/ (last accessed 13/7/17).

38. 'Security and Foreign Relations Platform', *Yesh Atid*, www.yeshatid. org.il/defense?languagecode=en (last accessed 13/7/17).

39. 'Yair Lapid: The southern man and his cosmopolitan ghetto', Al Jazeera, 12 February 2013, www.aljazeera.com/indepth/opinion/201 3/02/2013211112856254494.html (last accessed 13/7/17).

40. 'Security and Foreign Relations Platform', *Yesh Atid*, www.yeshatid. org.il/defense?languagecode=en (last accessed 13/7/17).

41. "'Cut A Deal With The World' On Settlements'", *New York Jewish Week*, 11 October 2016, http://jewishweek.timesofisrael.com/cut-a-deal-with-the-world-on-settlements/ (last accessed 13/7/17); 'Lapid Drops Demand for Palestinian State', *Haaretz*, 26 March 2017, www. haaretz.com/israel-news/.premium-1.779437 (last accessed 13/7/17).

42. 'Israel's Lieberman insists land swaps key to two-state solution', AFP, 19 February 2017, www.yahoo.com/news/israels-lieberman-insists-land-swaps-key-two-state-114726421.html (last accessed 13/7/17).

43. 'Analysis: A dovish Avigdor Liberman sings sweetly of two-states', *Jerusalem Post*, 31 May 2016, www.jpost.com/Israel-News/Politics-And-Diplomacy/Analysis-A-dovish-Liberman-sings-sweetly-of-two-states-455501 (last accessed 13/7/17); 'Livni: National Aspirations of Israel's Arabs Can Be Met by Palestinian Homeland', *Haaretz*, 11 December 2008, www.haaretz.com/news/livni-national-aspirations-of-israel-s-arabs-can-be-met-by-palestinian-homeland-1.259321 (last accessed 13/7/17).

44. About BWF, http://bluewhitefuture.org/about-bwf/ (last accessed 13/7/17).

45. 'Don't believe the hype: the settlers have not made the two-state solution unachievable', *Fathom*, http://fathomjournal.org/dont-believe-the-hype-the-settlers-have-not-made-the-two-state-solution-unachievable/ (last accessed 13/7/17).

46. 'Don't Make Legalizing Settlements Israel's Grave', *Haaretz*, 18 July 2012, www.haaretz.com/opinion/don-t-make-legalizing-settlements-israel-s-grave-1.451970 (last accessed 13/7/17).

47. 'About Us', Commanders for Israel's Security, http://en.cis.org.il/about/ (last accessed 14/7/17).

48. 'Former Israeli officials launch "racist" pro-separation ad campaign', *Middle East Monitor*, 16 January 2017, www.middleeastmonitor. com/20170116-former-israeli-officials-launch-racist-pro-separation-ad-campaign/ (last accessed 14/7/17).

49. 'Advances for women, and other surprising Israeli election results', *JTA*, 19 March 2015, www.jta.org/2015/03/19/news-opinion/ politics/knesset-by-the-numbers (last accessed 17/7/17).

50. Eighteenth Knesset, https://knesset.gov.il/description/eng/eng_mimshal_res18.htm (last accessed 17/7/17).

51. Nineteenth Knesset, https://knesset.gov.il/description/eng/eng_mimshal_res19.htm (last accessed 17/7/17).

52. Twentieth Knesset, https://knesset.gov.il/description/eng/eng_mimshal_res20.htm (last accessed 17/7/17).

53. 'Olmert clinches majority coalition as Shas signs up', *Guardian*, 1 May 2006, www.theguardian.com/world/2006/may/01/israel (last accessed 17/7/17).

54. 'Shas: We will always support the right-wing candidate', *Arutz Sheva*, 14 July 2017, www.israelnationalnews.com/Generic/Generic/SendPrint?print=1&type=0&item=232471 (last accessed 17/7/17).

55. 'In Israel's elections, racism is the winning ballot', *Adalah*, 23 March 2015, www.adalah.org/en/content/view/8491 (last accessed 17/7/17).

56. 'Lapid: We won't join bloc to prevent Netanyahu premiership', *Jerusalem Post*, 23 January 2013, www.jpost.com/Diplomacy-and-Politics/Lapid-We-wont-join-bloc-to-prevent-Netanyahu-premiership (last accessed 17/7/17).

57. 'Kerry Places Blame on Israel for Crisis in Peace Talks', *Haaretz*, 8 April 2014, www.haaretz.com/israel-news/.premium-1.584518 (last accessed 17/7/17).

58. 'Israel and the Middle East: 50 Years Since the Six-Day War', *BICOM*, 16 March 2017, www.bicom.org.uk/analysis/watch-live-50-years-since-the-six-day-war/ (last accessed 17/7/17).

59. 'Knesset passes settlement regulation law', 7 February 2017, www.knesset.gov.il/spokesman/eng/PR_eng.asp?PRID=13341 (last accessed 17/7/17).

60. 'Israeli minister: The Bible says West Bank is ours', Al Jazeera, 24 February 2017, www.aljazeera.com/programmes/upfront/2017/02/israeli-minister-bible-west-bank-170224082827910.html (last accessed 17/7/17); 'The world respects countries that protect their land', *Arutz Sheva*, 13 February 2017, www.israelnationalnews.com/News/News.aspx/224906 (last accessed 17/7/17).

61. 'Celebrating 50 years since liberation of Judea and Samaria', *Arutz Sheva*, 28 March 2017, www.israelnationalnews.com/News/News.aspx/227418 (last accessed 17/7/17).

62. 'After UNESCO vote, Netanyahu reads from Bible to prove Jewish ties to Hebron', 9 July 2017, www.jta.org/2017/07/09/news-opinion/israel-middle-east/netanyahu-reads-ftom-genesis-to-illustrate-jewish-peoples-israels-claim-to-cave-of-patriarchs (last accessed 17/7/17).

63. 'Deri calls for long-term Palestinian peace deal', *Jerusalem Post*, 4 January 2013, www.jpost.com/Diplomacy-and-Politics/Deri-calls-for-long-term-Palestinian-peace-deal (last accessed 17/7/17).

64. 'Government Rifts Over Peace Process Revealed During Knesset Committee Meeting', *Haaretz*, 21 May 2013, www.haaretz.com/israel-news/government-rifts-over-peace-process-revealed-during-knesset-committee-meeting-1.525153 (last accessed 17/7/17); *Yesh Atid*, www.yeshatid.org.il/defense?languagecode=en (last accessed 17/7/17).

65. 'Who needs the Right when we have Isaac Herzog?', +972mag, 8 June 2015, https://972mag.com/who-needs-the-right-when-we-have-isaac-herzog/107550/ (last accessed 17/7/17); 'Livni: Outpost legalization bill will land IDF troops in ICC', *Times of Israel*, 4 February 2017, www.timesofisrael.com/livni-outpost-legalization-bill-will-land-idf-troops-in-icc (last accessed 17/7/17).

66. 'AP Analysis: Few alternatives to Palestinian state', AP, 15 February 2017, www.yahoo.com/news/few-good-alternatives-palestinian-state-131159269.html (last accessed 17/7/17).

67. 'Secret 1978 Talks Lay Bare the Hawk That Peacemaker Peres Once Was', *Haaretz*, 11 October 2016, www.haaretz.com/israel-news/.premium-1.747031 (last accessed 17/7/17).

68. 'PM Rabin in Knesset- Ratification of Interim Agreement', 5 October 1995, http://mfa.gov.il/MFA/MFA-Archive/1995/Pages/PM%20Rabin%20in%20Knesset-%20Ratification%20of%20Interim%20Agree.aspx (last accessed 17/7/17).

69. 'Trump may not pursue two-state solution for Israel and Palestinians', *Guardian*, 15 February 2017, www.theguardian.com/us-news/2017/feb/15/trump-may-not-pursue-two-state-solution-for-israel-and-palestinians-peace (last accessed 17/7/17); 'Trump open to one-state or two-state solution in Middle East', *The Hill*, 15 February 2017, http://thehill.com/policy/international/319673-trump-open-to-one-state-or-two-state-solution-in-middle-east (last accessed 17/7/17).

70. 'Is 2-State Solution Dead? In Israel, a Debate Over What's Next', *New York Times*, 16 February 2017, www.nytimes.com/2017/02/16/world/middleeast/israel-palestinians-two-state-solution.html (last accessed 26/6/17).

71. 'An Inside Look at Israeli National Security Strategy', The Washington Institute, 19 September 2016, www.washingtoninstitute.org/policy-analysis/view/an-inside-look-at-israeli-national-security-strategy (last accessed 17/7/17).

72. 'A Best-Selling Israeli Philosopher Examines His Country's Inner Conflict', *New York Times*, 9 June 2017, www.nytimes.com/2017/06/09/world/middleeast/a-best-selling-israeli-philosopher-examines-his-countrys-inner-conflict.html (last accessed 17/7/17); 'The peace process hasn't brought peace. The case for moving on', *Times of Israel*, 27 June 2017, www.timesofisrael.com/a-gentler-war/ (last accessed 17/7/17).

73. 'Donald Trump says US not committed to two-state Israel-Palestine solution', *Guardian*, 16 February 2017, www.theguardian.com/world/2017/feb/15/trump-says-us-not-committed-to-two-state-israel-palestine-solution (last accessed 17/7/17).

74. 'Decades of failed peace talks: How Israel negotiates with itself', *+972mag*, 28 June 2017, https://972mag.com/decades-of-failed-peace-talks-how-israel-negotiates-with-itself/128401/ (last accessed 17/7/17).

75. 'Israel's false narrative on land swaps', Al Jazeera, 26 March 2017, www.aljazeera.com/indepth/features/2017/03/israel-false-narrative-land-swaps-170312095110936.html (last accessed 26/6/17).

Chapter 3

1. Elmer Berger, 'Zionist Ideology: Obstacle to Peace', in Anti-Zionism: Analytical Reflections (Brattleboro, VT: Amana Books, 1989), p. 4.

2. Dov Waxman, *Trouble in the Tribe: The American Jewish Conflict Over Israel* (Princeton, NJ: Princeton University Press, 2016), p. 212.

3. Yakov M. Rabkin, *What Is Modern Israel?* (London: Pluto Press, 2016), p. 4; Laura Robson, States of Separation: Transfer, Partition, and the Making of the Modern Middle East (Oakland, CA: University of California Press, 2017), p. 3.

4. Maxime Rodinson, *Israel: A Colonial-Settler State?* (New York: Pathfinder, 2001), p. 38.

5. Ze'ev Sternhell, *The Founding Myths of Israel* (Princeton, NJ: Princeton University Press, 1998), p. 6.

6. Alain Dieckhoff, *The Invention of a Nation* (London: Hurst & Company, 2003), p. 248.

7. 'Fewer British Jews identifying as "Zionists", poll shows', *+972 Magazine*, 13 November 2015, https://972mag.com/fewer-british-jews-identifying-as-zionists-poll-shows/113858/ (last accessed 19/10/17).

8. 'Is the American Jewish pro-Israel Consensus Dying?' *Haaretz*, 12 April 2016, www.haaretz.com/jewish/books/.premium-1.713898 (last accessed 19/10/17).

9. Michael Stanislawski, *Zionism: A Very Short Introduction* (Oxford: Oxford University Press, 2017), p. 18.

10. Ze'ev Sternhell, *The Founding Myths of Israel* (Princeton, NJ: Princeton University Press, 1998), p. 13.

11. Shlomo Avineri, *The Making of Modern Zionism* (New York, NY: Basic Books, 2017), p. 148.

12. Antony Polonsky, 'The Bund in Polish Political Life, 1935-1939', in *Essential Papers on Jews and the Left*, ed. Ezra Mendelsohn (New York, NY: NYU Press, 1997), p. 172.

13. Ibid., p. 172.

14. 'Memorandum of Edwin Montagu on the Antisemitism of the Present (British) Government – Submitted to the British Cabinet, August 1917', www.jewishvirtuallibrary.org/montagu-memo-on-british-government-s-anti-semitism (last accessed 19/10/17).

15. Yosef Salmon, 'Zionism and Anti-Zionism in Traditional Judaism in Eastern Europe', in *Zionism and Religion*, ed. Shmuel Almog, Jehuda Reinharz, Anita Shapira (Brandeis University Press, Hanover, NH: Brandeis University Press, 1998), p. 25.

16. Stanislawski, p. 2.

17. Aaron J. Hahn Tapper, *Judaisms: A Twenty-First-Century Introduction to Jews and Jewish Identities* (Oakland, CA: University of California Press), p. 194.

18. Yakov M. Rabkin, 'Judaism: The Search for Peace in the Holy Land', in *Holy Land Studies*, 10.2 (2011), Edinburgh University Press.

19. Alain Dieckhoff, *The Invention of a Nation* (London: Hurst & Company, 2003), p. 141.

20. Rabkin, 'Judaism: The Search for Peace in the Holy Land'.

21. Yakov M. Rabkin, *What is Modern Israel?* (London: Pluto Press, 2016), p. 122.

22. Ibid., p. 122.

23. Roselle Tekiner, 'The 'Who is a Jew?' Controversy in Israel: A Product of Political Zionism', in *Anti-Zionism: Analytical Reflections*, ed. Roselle Tekiner, Samir Abed-Rabbo, Norton Mezvinsky (Brattleboro, VT: Amana Books, 1989), p. 67.

24. Waxman, p. 3.

25. Ibid., p. 3.

26. Ibid., p. 3; p. 15.

27. 'U.S. Jews Divided Over Whether to Celebrate or Mourn 50th Anniversary of Six-Day War', *Haaretz*, 14 May 2017, www.haaretz. com/us-news/.premium-1.788691 (last accessed 19/10/17); see also 'Truah letter calls on Israel to end occupation, create Palestinian state', Jewish Telegraphic Agency, 11 June 2017, www.jta.org/ 2017/06/11/news-opinion/united-states/truah-letter-calls-on-israel-to-end-occupation-create-palestinian-state (last accessed 19/10/17).

28. 'How Jews Across North America Will Mark the 50th Anniversary of the Six-Day War', *Haaretz*, 12 May 2017, www.haaretz.com/ us-news/.premium-1.788179 (last accessed 19/10/17).

29. Ibid.

30. 'Rabbi Sacks, Why Are You Cheerleading for anti-Palestinian Provocateurs?' *Haaretz*, 17 May 2017, www.haaretz.com/opinion/ 1.789728 (last accessed 19/10/17).

31. 'The Young Jewish Americans Coming to Israel to Fight the Occupation', *Haaretz*, 26 May 2017, www.haaretz.com/israel-news/. premium-1.792000 (last accessed 19/10/17).

32. Waxman, p. 80.

33. 'J Street in the age of Trump', Pittsburgh Jewish Chronicle, 2 March 2017, https://jewishchronicle.timesofisrael.com/j-street-in-the-age-of-trump/ (last accessed 19/10/17).

34. 'J Street, ADL Slam Controversial "Nation-state" Bill for Undermining "Israel's Diversity"', *Haaretz*, 10 May 2017, www. haaretz.com/israel-news/1.788288 (last accessed 19/10/17).

35. 'Bernie Sanders' Speech on Israel, Trump and antisemitism at J Street Conference', *Haaretz*, 28 February 2017, www.haaretz.com/us-news/ 1.774304 (last accessed 19/10/17).

36. 'Open Hillel calls on Hillel to reject funding by Naftali Bennett project', Jewish Telegraphic Agency, 3 November 2016, www.jta. org/2016/11/03/news-opinion/united-states/open-hillel-calls-on-hillel-to-reject-funding-by-naftali-bennett-project (last accessed 19/10/17), 'Open Hillel', Middle East Report, 280, Volume: 46, (Fall 2016), www.merip.org/mer/mer280/open-hillel (last accessed 19/10/17).

37. '"Devastating" survey shows huge loss of Israel support among Jewish college students', *Times of Israel*, 21 June 2017, www. timesofisrael.com/devastating-survey-shows-huge-loss-of-israel-support-among-jewish-college-students/ (last accessed 19/10/17).

38. Peter Beinart, *The Crisis of Zionism* (New York, NY: Times Books, 2012), p. 171.

39. 'Liberal Zionism After Gaza', *New York Review of Books*, 26 July 2014, www.nybooks.com/daily/2014/07/26/liberal-zionism-after-gaza/ (last accessed 22/12/17).

40. 'Mission', https://jewishvoiceforpeace.org/mission/ (last accessed 19/10/17).

41. *On Anti-Semitism*, ed. Jewish Voice for Peace (Chicago, IL: Haymarket Books, 2017), p. 2.

42. 'Israeli Government Is Petrified of the Boycott, Divestment and Sanctions Movement', *Truth Out*, 16 April 2017, www.truth-out.org/opinion/item/40224-israeli-government-is-petrified-of-boycott-divestment-and-sanctions-bds-movement (last accessed 19/10/17).

43. 'Mission', https://jewishvoiceforpeace.org/mission/ (last accessed 19/10/17).

44. 'About JVP', https://jewishvoiceforpeace.org/faq/ (last accessed 19/10/17).

45. 'Why Jews Shouldn't Be Scared of the Palestinian Right of Return', *Haaretz*, 17 September 2017, www.haaretz.com/opinion/.premium-1.812660 (last accessed 19/10/17).

46. Anti-Zionism Isn't a 'Form of Discrimination', and It's Not anti-Semitism', *Haaretz*, 18 March 2016, www.haaretz.com/opinion/.premium-1.709457 (last accessed 19/10/17).

47. 'Unlearning apartheid apologism: A Jewish response to Israeli Apartheid Week', *Columbia Spectator*, 5 March 2017, http://columbiaspectator.com/opinion/2017/03/06/unlearning-apartheid-apologism-a-jewish-response-to-israeli-apartheid-week/ (last accessed 19/10/17).

48. 'About', http://jfjfp.com/?page_id=2 (last accessed 19/10/17).

49. 'About', https://ijv.org.uk/about/ (last accessed 19/10/17).

50. 'About', https://jews4big.wordpress.com/about/ (last accessed 19/10/17).

51. 'About', http://www.jewishsocialist.org.uk/about/politics (last accessed 19/10/17).

52. Ibid.

53. 'BDS supporter seeks presidency of UK Jewish students union', *Electronic Intifada*, 2 December 2016, https://electronicintifada.net/blogs/asa-winstanley/bds-supporter-seeks-presidency-uk-jewish-students-union (last accessed 19/10/17).

54. 'Israel boycott activist is running as a candidate for the UJS presidency', *Jewish Chronicle*, 22 November 2016, www.thejc.com/news/uk-news/israel-boycott-activist-is-running-as-a-candidate-for-the-ujs-presidency-1.147851 (last accessed 19/10/17).

55. 'The Attitudes of British Jews Towards Israel', Department of Sociology, School of Arts and Social Sciences, City University London, 2015, http://yachad.org.uk/wp-content/uploads/2015/11/British-Jewish-Attitudes-Towards-Israel-Yachad-Ipsos-Mori-Nov-2015.pdf (last accessed 19/10/17).

56. 'I back Eran's campaign as I feel pushed out by the community', *Jewish News*, 2 December 2016, http://blogs.timesofisrael.com/eran-cohen-ujs/ (last accessed 19/10/17).

57. Tweet by North West Friends of Israel, 27 November 2016, https://twitter.com/NorthWestFOI/status/802932440536846336 (last accessed 19/10/17), 'Josh Holt wins UJS election – pro-BDS Eran Cohen in last place', *Jewish News*, 12 December 2016, http://jewishnews.timesofisrael.com/josh-holt-wins-ujs-election-pro-bds-eran-cohen-in-last-place/ (last accessed 19/10/17).

58. 'Every Jew who quietly backs boycotts must speak out', *Jewish News*, 10 March 2017, http://blogs.timesofisrael.com/jews-boycotts/ (last accessed 19/10/17).

59. 'I'm a former president of the Jewish Society. BDS is not anti-Semitic', *Student Newspaper*, 7 April 2016, www.studentnewspaper.org/i-was-president-of-the-jewish-society-bds-is-not-anti-semitic/ (last accessed 19/10/17).

60. 'Liberal Zionists, We Lost the Kids', *Haaretz*, 31 October 2016, www.haaretz.com/opinion/.premium-1.750081 (last accessed 19/10/17).

61. 'On Anti-Semitism', p. 1.

62. Ibid., p. 1.

63. 'The Israeli Right Wing Is Delighted by Trump's Win – and Why That's So Dangerous', *Forward*, 13 November 2016, http://forward.com/opinion/354320/the-israeli-right-wing-is-delighted-by-trumps-win-and-why-thats-so-dangerou/ (last accessed 19/10/17).

64. 'Outraged at Netanyahu Over Western Wall, Jewish Agency to Rethink Ties With Israeli Government', *Haaretz*, 26 June 2017, www.haaretz.com/israel-news/.premium-1.797842 (last accessed 19/10/17).

65. 'Israel Faces Uproar Abroad as Netanyahu Yields to Ultra-Orthodox Jews', *New York Times*, 3 July 2017, www.nytimes.com/2017/07/03/world/middleeast/israel-benjamin-netanyahu-ultra-orthodox-western-wall.html (last accessed 19/10/17).

66. 'Israel to American Jews: You Just Don't Matter', *New York Times*, 12 July 2017, www.nytimes.com/2017/07/12/opinion/israel-american-jews-benjamin-netanyahu.html (last accessed 19/10/17).

67. 'Holy War', *New York Review of Books*, 3 August 1967, www.nybooks. com/articles/1967/08/03/holy-war/ (last accessed 19/10/17).

68. Peter Beinart, 'Netanyahu's Real Victim? The American Jewish Establishment', *Haaretz*, February 2015, www.haaretz.com/opinion/. premium-1.641988 (last accessed 19/10/17).

69. 'Israel's Rash Embrace of Trump Accelerates the Jewish Schism', *Haaretz*, 21 August 2017, www.haaretz.com/us-news/1.807936 (last accessed 19/10/17).

70. 'Ties between US Jews and Israel could reach breaking point in 2017', *Jerusalem Post*, 27 March 2017, www.jpost.com/printarticle. aspx?id=485337 (last accessed 19/10/17), 'The Future of the Nation State of the Jewish People: Consolidation or Rupture?' Reut Institute, March 2017, https://reutgroup.org/wp-content/uploads/ sites/17/2017/04/20170331-Reut-Nation-State-English-FINAL.pdf (last accessed 19/10/17).

71. 'Trump, Israel, and the American Jewish Community', Institute for National Security Studies, 19 January 2017, www.inss.org.il/ publication/trump-israel-american-jewish-community/ (last accessed 19/10/17).

72. 'Israel vs. America: What Jewish Millennials Think About God and the Occupation', *Haaretz*, www.haaretz.com/jewish/news/.premium-1.780938 (last accessed 19/10/17).

73. 'Trump, Israel, and the American Jewish Community', The Institute for National Security Studies.

74. 'Relationship with American Jews is strategic', *Arutz Sheva*, 13 June 2017, www.israelnationalnews.com/News/News.aspx/230989 (last accessed 19/10/17).

75. 'A sledge-hammer blow to American Jewry', *Ynet*, 29 June 2017, www.ynetnews.com/articles/0,7340,L-4982617,00.html (last accessed 19/10/17).

Chapter 4

1. 'Losers of Iran-deal War Use Orwellian Newspeak to Claim Victory', *Haaretz*, 12 September 2015, www.haaretz.com/blogs/west-of-eden/. premium-1.675769 (last accessed 8/11/17).

2. 'Richard Spencer Is Simply the Latest Far-right Extremist to Laud Israel as a White "Ethno-state" Model', *Haaretz*, 21 October 2017, www.haaretz.com/us-news/1.818342 (last accessed 8/11/17).

3. 'Statement by the President on the Memorandum of Understanding Reached with Israel', 14 September 2016, https://obamawhitehouse.

archives.gov/the-press-office/2016/09/14/statement-president-memorandum-understanding-reached-israel (last accessed 6/8/17).

4. 'Friedman confirmed as U.S. ambassador to Israel', *Politico*, 23 March 2017, www.politico.com/story/2017/03/david-friedman-ambassador-to-israel-confirmed-236428 (last accessed 6/8/17).

5. 'U.S. Ambassador to Israel Confirmation Hearing', C-SPAN, 16 February 2017, www.c-span.org/video/?424017-1/israeli-ambassa dor-nominee-david-friedman-testifies-confirmation-hearing (last accessed 6/8/17).

6. 'The Brooklyn Democratic debate transcript, annotated', *Washington Post*, 14 April 2016, www.washingtonpost.com/news/the-fix/wp/2016/04/14/the-brooklyn-democratic-debate-transcript-annotated/ (last accessed 6/8/17).

7. 'Criticizing Israel, Bernie Sanders Highlights Split Among Jewish Democrats', *New York Times*, April 15 2016, www.nytimes.com/2016/04/16/us/politics/bernie-sanders-israel.html?_r=0 (last accessed 2/8/17).

8. 'A Split Over Israel Threatens the Democrats' Hopes for Unity', *New York Times*, 25 May 2016, www.nytimes.com/2016/05/26/us/politics/bernie-sanders-israel-democratic-convention.html (last accessed 2/8/17).

9. 'Democrats' draft platform excludes call to end occupation', *Times of Israel*, 25 June 2016, www.timesofisrael.com/democrats-approve-platform-with-sanders-mark-but-not-on-israel/ (last accessed 6/8/17).

10. 'The Democratic Party's Israel Crack-Up', *Foreign Policy*, 22 June 2016, http://foreignpolicy.com/2016/06/22/the-democratic-partys-israel-crack-up/

11. 'Democratic convention erupts over reinstatement of Jerusalem to policy', *Guardian*, 6 September 2012, www.theguardian.com/world/2012/sep/06/democratic-convention-reinstatement-jerusalem (last accessed 6/8/17).

12. 'Democrats seek unity on Israel, but cracks begin to show', *JTA*, 26 July 2016, www.jta.org/2016/07/26/news-opinion/politics/democrats-seek-unity-on-israel-but-cracks-begin-to-show (last accessed 6/8/17).

13. 'Unholy Land: Young Democrats Are Spurning Israel for Good Reason', *Forward*, 15 February 2017, http://forward.com/opinion/363253/unholy-land-young-democrats-are-spurning-israel-for-good-reason/ (last accessed 6/8/17).

14. 'Netanyahu's speech to Congress snubbed by prominent Democrats', *Guardian*, 3 March 2015, www.theguardian.com/world/2015/mar/03/netanyahu-speech-congress-democrats-snub (last accessed 6/8/17).

15. 'Last bid to kill Iran nuclear deal blocked in Senate', Reuters, 17 September 2015, www.reuters.com/article/us-iran-nuclear-congress-idUSKCN0RF2VX20150917 (last accessed 3/8/17).

16. http://clerk.house.gov/evs/2015/roll493.xml (last accessed 8/11/17).

17. 'Democrats Hand Victory to Obama on Iran Nuclear Deal', *New York Times*, 10 September 2015, www.nytimes.com/2015/09/11/us/politics/iran-nuclear-deal-senate.html (last accessed 3/8/17).

18. 'Losers of Iran-deal War Use Orwellian Newspeak to Claim Victory', *Haaretz*, 12 September 2015 www.haaretz.com/blogs/west-of-eden/.premium-1.675769

19. 'Leahy asked State Dept. to investigate Israeli human rights "violations"', *Politico*, 29 March 2016, www.politico.com/story/2016/03/patrick-leahy-senate-israel-egypt-state-221366 (last accessed 3/8/17).

20. 'FCNL Applauds Lawmakers' Call for Special Envoy for Palestinian Youth', Friends Committee on National Legislation, 20 June 2016, www.fcnl.org/updates/fcnl-applauds-lawmakers-call-for-special-envoy-for-palestinian-youth-140 (last accessed 6/8/17).

21. 'US House condemns UN resolution on Israeli settlements, Democrats split', *Middle East Monitor*, 6 January 2017, www.middleeastmonitor.com/20170106-us-house-condemns-un-resolution-on-israeli-settlements-democrats-split (last accessed 6/8/17).

22. 'US lawmakers urge secretary of state to help Palestinian activist going on trial in Israel', Jewish Telegraphic Agency, 29 June 2017, www.jta.org/2017/06/29/news-opinion/politics/us-lawmakers-urge-secretary-of-state-to-help-palestinian-activist-going-on-trial-in-israel (last accessed 6/8/17).

23. 'Poll: High ambivalence on Palestinian statehood', *Washington Post*, 20 September 2011, www.washingtonpost.com/blogs/behind-the-numbers/post/poll-high-ambivalence-on-palestinian-statehood/2011/09/07/gIQAtt10iK_blog.html (last accessed 6/8/17).

24. CNN poll, 21 July 2014, http://i2.cdn.turner.com/cnn/2014/images/07/21/rel7b.pdf (last accessed 6/8/17).

25. 'Hamas Seen as More to Blame Than Israel for Current Violence', Pew Research Centre, 28 July 2014, www.people-press.org/

2014/07/28/hamas-seen-as-more-to-blame-than-israel-for-current-violence/ (last accessed 6/8/17).

26. 'American Attitudes Toward the Middle East and Israel, Centre for Middle East Policy', Centre for Middle East Peace at Brookings, Fielded November 4–10, 2015, www.brookings.edu/wp-content/uploads/2016/07/2015-Poll-Key-Findings-Final.pdf (last accessed 15/3/17); 'American Attitudes on the Israeli-Palestinian Conflict', A survey sponsored by University of Maryland Critical Issues Poll, fielded by Nielsen Scarborough, conducted 12–17 April 2017, https://sadat.umd.edu/sites/sadat.umd.edu/files/american_attitudes_on_israel-palestine.pdf (last accessed 3/8/17).

27. 'Israel losing Democrats, 'can't claim bipartisan US support,' top pollster warns', *Times of Israel*, 5 July 2015, www.timesofisrael.com/israel-losing-democrats-cant-claim-bipartisan-us-support-top-pollster-warns/ (last accessed 6/8/17).

28. 'Israel is losing support among minorities and millennials, study finds', Jewish Telegraphic Agency, 30 June 2017, www.jta.org/2017/06/30/news-opinion/united-states/israel-is-losing-support-among-democrats-minorities-and-millennials-study-finds (last accessed 6/8/17).

29. '74% Republicans, 33% Democrats sympathize with Israel over Palestinians, survey finds', Jewish Telegraphic Agency, 12 January 2017, www.jta.org/2017/01/12/news-opinion/politics/74-republicans-33-democrats-sympathize-with-israel-over-palestinians-survey-finds (last accessed 6/8/17).

30. 'The World Facing Trump: Public Sees ISIS, Cyberattacks, North Korea as Top Threats', Pew Research Centre, 12 January 2017, www.people-press.org/2017/01/12/the-world-facing-trump-public-sees-isis-cyberattacks-north-korea-as-top-threats/9-10/ (last accessed 6/8/17).

31. 'Which Country Is America's Strongest Ally? For Republicans, It's Australia', *New York Times*, 3 February 2017, www.nytimes.com/interactive/2017/02/03/upshot/which-country-do-americans-like-most-for-republicans-its-australia.html

32. 'Massachusetts Democrats reject anti-settlements plank', Jewish Telegraphic Agency, 4 June 2017, www.jta.org/2017/06/04/news-opinion/united-states/massachusetts-democratic-party-fails-to-pass-resolution-calling-settlements-obstacles-to-peace (last accessed 7/8/17).

33. 'Bernie Sanders Says BDS Won't Solve Mideast Impasse', *Forward*, 4 May 2017, http://forward.com/fast-forward/370906/bernie-sanders-says-bds-wont-solve-mideast-impasse/ (last accessed 7/8/17).

34. 'Unholy Land: Young Democrats Are Spurning Israel for Good Reason', *Forward*, 15 February 2017, http://forward.com/opinion/363253/unholy-land-young-democrats-are-spurning-israel-for-good-reason (last accessed 7/8/17).

35. 'Israel friends change tack and relaunch', *Jewish Chronicle*, 13 January 2011, www.thejc.com/news/uk-news/israel-friends-change-tack-and-relaunch-1.20544 (last accessed 7/8/17).

36. 'Israel and the Middle East: 50 Years Since the Six-Day War', BICOM, 16 March 2017, www.bicom.org.uk/analysis/watch-live-50-years-since-the-six-day-war/ (last accessed 7/8/17).

37. 'The Left and the Jews: Time for a Rethink', *Fathom*, Autumn 2015, http://fathomjournal.org/the-left-and-the-jews-time-for-a-rethink/ (last accessed 7/8/17).

38. 'How to Stop Israel's "Delegitimization" Among American Progressives', *Haaretz*, 16 February 2016, www.haaretz.com/opinion/.premium-1.703644 (last accessed 7/8/17).

39. 'Unholy Land: Young Democrats Are Spurning Israel for Good Reason', *Forward*, 15 February 2017, http://forward.com/opinion/363253/unholy-land-young-democrats-are-spurning-israel-for-good-reason (last accessed 7/8/17).

40. Paul Kelemen, *The British left and Zionism: History of a divorce* (Manchester: Manchester University Press, 2012), p. 2.

41. James Ramsay MacDonald, *A Socialist in Palestine* (London: Jewish Socialist Labour Confederation Poale-Zion, 1922).

42. Rosemary Sayigh, *The Palestinians: From Peasants to Revolutionaries* (London: Zed Books, 2013).

43. Kelemen, p. 203.

44. 'Israel's biggest paper ignores anti-Semitism of senior Trump advisor', +972 *Magazine*, 14 November 2016, https://972mag.com/israels-biggest-paper-ignores-anti-semitism-of-senior-trump-advisor/123158/ (last accessed 7/8/17).

45. 'Hungary's Orban courts far-right voters ahead of 2018 vote', Reuters, 30 June 2017, www.reuters.com/article/us-hungary-orban-farright-analysis-idUSKBN19L244 (last accessed 7/8/17).

46. 'Hungary's prime minister praises a Hitler ally', Jewish Telegraphic Agency, 26 June 2017, www.jta.org/2017/06/26/news-opinion/world/hungarian-jews-slam-prime-ministers-praises-for-hitler-ally-horthy (last accessed 7/8/17).

47. 'Hungarian Premier Praises Hitler Ally, Israel Accepts Clarification to Avoid Marring Netanyahu Visit', *Haaretz*, 2 July 2017, www.haaretz.com/israel-news/.premium-1.798853 (last accessed 7/8/17).

48. 'In Netanyahu's World, George Soros' Politics Justify Throwing Him to Hungary's anti-Semitic Dogs', *Haaretz*, 12 July 2017, www.haaretz.com/opinion/1.800819 (last accessed 7/8/17); 'On Netanyahu's Orders: Israel's Foreign Ministry Retracts Criticism of anti-Semitism in Hungary and Slams George Soros', *Haaretz*, 10 July 2017, www.haaretz.com/israel-news/1.800437 (last accessed 7/8/17).

49. 'Netanyahu hails Orban's Hungary as an ally of Israel', *Financial Times*, 18 July 2017, www.ft.com/content/1652bef2-6bb4-11e7-bfeb-33fe0c5b7eaa (last accessed 7/8/17).

50. 'Likud unapologetic for inviting politician from far-right Austrian faction', *Jerusalem Post*, 25 January 2016, www.jpost.com/Israel-News/Politics-And-Diplomacy/Likud-unapologetic-for-inviting-politician-from-far-right-Austrian-faction-442737 (last accessed 4/8/17).

51. 'Austrian far-right leader: Jerusalem is capital of Israel', *Jerusalem Post*, 21 June 2017, www.jpost.com/International/Austrian-far-right-leader-calls-to-recognize-Jerusalem-as-capital-497537 (last accessed 7/8/17).

52. 'French far-right party official holds meetings in Israel', AP, 26 January 2017, www.yahoo.com/news/secretary-french-far-party-holds-meetings-israel-135642196.html (last accessed 4/8/17).

53. 'Switzerland's largest political party insists on depicting foreigners as black sheep', *Quartz*, 16 February 2016, https://qz.com/617050/switzerlands-largest-political-party-insists-on-depicting-foreigners-as-black-sheep/ (last accessed 7/8/17); 'Swiss parliament lower house votes to halt funds to groups promoting anti-Semitism', Jewish Telegraphic Agency, 9 March 2017, www.jta.org/2017/03/09/news-opinion/world/swiss-parliament-lower-house-votes-to-halt-funds-to-groups-promoting-anti-semitism (last accessed 7/8/17).

54. 'Swiss parliament lower house votes to halt funds to groups promoting anti-Semitism', Jewish Telegraphic Agency, 9 March 2017, www.jta.org/2017/03/09/news-opinion/world/swiss-parliament-lower-house-votes-to-halt-funds-to-groups-promoting-anti-semitism (last accessed 7/8/17).

55. 'Swiss lawmakers roll back anti-BDS law', *Electronic Intifada*, 14 April 2017, https://electronicintifada.net/blogs/adri-nieuwhof/swiss-lawmakers-roll-back-anti-bds-law (last accessed 7/8/17).

56. 'BNP on BBC's Question Time: key quotes', *Telegraph*, 23 October 2009, www.telegraph.co.uk/news/politics/6411261/BNP-on-BBCs-Question-Time-key-quotes.html (last accessed 7/8/17).

57. 'Digging up the truth about Michal Kaminiski', BBC, 23 November 2009, http://news.bbc.co.uk/1/hi/programmes/newsnight/8374686.stm (last accessed 7/8/17).

58. 'Israel does not need friends like these', *Sydney Morning Herald*, 28 October 2009, www.smh.com.au/federal-politics/political-opinion/israel-does-not-need-friends-like-these-20091027-hjb2 (last accessed 7/8/17).

59. 'Analysis: Kaminski is our friend – this is a smear campaign', Stephen Pollard, *Jewish Chronicle*, 8 October 2009, www.thejc.com/analysis-kaminski-is-our-friend-this-is-a-smear-campaign-1.11772, (last accessed 5/8/17).

60. 'Israel does not need friends like these', *Sydney Morning Herald*, 28 October 2009, www.smh.com.au/federal-politics/political-opinion/israel-does-not-need-friends-like-these-20091027-hjb2 (last accessed 7/8/17).

61. 'How the far right is trying to woo an unlikely ally – Jews', *Washington Post*, 29 November 2016, www.washingtonpost.com/world/europe/how-the-far-right-is-trying-to-woo-an-unlikely-ally--jews/2016/11/28/36002402-b187-11e6-bc2d-19b3d759cfe7_story.html (last accessed 7/8/17).

62. 'EU Jewish leaders warned against embrace by alt-right nationalists', EURACTIV, 24 January 2017, www.euractiv.com/section/justice-home-affairs/news/eu-jewish-leaders-warned-against-embrace-by-alt-right-white-nationalists/ (last accessed 7/8/17).

63. 'Dutch leader tells Israel to "ignore UN and continue building"', *Arutz Sheva*, 26 December 2016, www.israelnationalnews.com/News/News.aspx/222286 (last accessed 7/8/17).

64. 'Far-Right Politicians Find Common Cause In Israel', *Newsweek*, 27 February 2011, www.newsweek.com/far-right-politicians-find-common-cause-israel-68583 (last accessed 7/8/17).

65. 'MK Eldad forms anti-Islam coalition', *Ynet*, 3 September 2008, www.ynetnews.com/articles/0,7340,L-3591626,00.html (last accessed 4/8/17).

66. 'Could A Trump Presidency Be Pro-Israel And White Nationalist At The Same Time?', NPR, 21 November 2016, www.npr.org/2016/11/21/502841518/donald-trump-says-he-s-a-friend-of-israel-but-do-the-people-around-him-feel-the (last accessed 7/8/17).

67. 'Richard Bertrand Spencer', SPLC, www.splcenter.org/fighting-hate/extremist-files/individual/richard-bertrand-spencer-0 (last accessed 7/8/17).

68. The text is available on the website of The National Policy Institute.

69. 'Speechless Rabbi Admits Losing Argument Over Racism and Israel to White Supremacist Richard Spencer', 7 December 2016, http://forward.com/news/national/356363/speechless-rabbi-admits-losing-argument-over-racism-and-israel-to-white-sup/ (last accessed 4/8/17).

70. 'Where white nationalists and Zionists meet', *Deutsche Welle*, 19 May 2017, www.dw.com/en/where-white-nationalists-and-zionists-meet/a-38873676 (last accessed 7/8/17).

71. 'Netanyahu Launches Blistering Attack on EU: "Their Behavior Toward Israel Is Crazy"', *Haaretz*, 19 July 2017, www.haaretz.com/israel-news/1.802143 (last accessed 7/8/17).

72. 'Netanyahu's Bigheaded Euro-bashing in Budapest Is Bannon 101', *Haaretz*, 20 July 2017, www.haaretz.com/1.802275 (last accessed 7/8/17).

73. 'Netanyahu hails Orban's Hungary as an ally of Israel', *Financial Times*, 18 July 2017, www.ft.com/content/1652bef2-6bb4-11e7-bfeb-33feoc5b7eaa (last accessed 7/8/17).

74. Theodor Herzl, *The Jewish State*, first published in 1896, and available online here: www.gutenberg.org/files/25282/25282-h/25282-h.htm (last accessed 7/8/17); 'Address by Foreign Minister Ehud Barak To the Annual Plenary Session of the National Jewish Community Relations Advisory Council', 11 February 1996, http://webcache.googleusercontent.com/search?q=cache:VV_mWQJT4QAJ:mfa.gov.il/MFA/MFA-Archive/1996/Pages/FM%2520Barak-%2520Address%2520to%2520NJCRAC%2520-%2520Feb%252011-%25201996.aspx+&cd=20&hl=en&ct=clnk&gl=us (last accessed 7/8/17).

75. 'Israel PM: illegal African immigrants threaten identity of Jewish state', *Guardian*, 20 May 2012, www.theguardian.com/world/2012/may/20/israel-netanyahu-african-immigrants-jewish (last accessed 7/8/17).

76. 'Israel-based Journalist: EU/US Far Right Increasingly Finding Common Cause With Israel...And Vice-Versa', *Mideastwire Blog*, 29 March 2017, https://mideastwire.wordpress.com/2017/03/29/israel-based-journalist-euus-far-right-increasingly-finding-common-cause-with-israel-and-vice-versa/ (last accessed 7/8/17); 'Israel's Elbit Systems sees 2016 growth from Europe, Asia', Reuters, 22

March 2016, http://in.reuters.com/article/elbit-systems-results-idINKCN0WO27L (last accessed 7/8/17).

77. 'Could A Trump Presidency Be Pro-Israel And White Nationalist At The Same Time?' NPR, 21 November 2016, www.npr.org/2016/11/21/502841518/donald-trump-says-he-s-a-friend-of-israel-but-do-the-people-around-him-feel-the (last accessed 7/8/17).

78. 'How Steve Bannon and Breitbart News Can Be Pro-Israel – and Anti-Semitic at the Same Time', Forward, 15 November 2016, http://forward.com/news/israel/354402/how-steve-bannon-and-breitbart-news-can-be-pro-israel-and-anti-semitic-at-t/ (last accessed 7/8/17).

79. 'Republicans, Democrats sharply divided over Trump's Jerusalem decision', Middle East Monitor, 15 December 2017, www.middleeastmonitor.com/20171215-republicans-democrats-sharply-divided-over-trumps-jerusalem-decision/ (last accessed 3/1/18).

80. 'Congressional Israel Victory Caucus' launch by Republicans reinforces support for Israel', Washington Times, 27 April 2017, www.washingtontimes.com/news/2017/apr/27/congressional-israel-victory-caucus-launch-by-repu/ (last accessed 7/8/17); 'ZOA Supports Israel Victory Caucus, Seeking Support for Israel to Prevail Over Palestinian Arabs, Thereby Ending War', 13 July 2017, http://zoa.org/2017/07/10369301-zoa-supports-israel-victory-caucus-seeking-support-for-israel-to-prevail-over-palestinian-arabs-thereby-ending-war (last accessed 7/8/17).

81. 'A Knesset bloc unveils its plan for peace: Total Palestinian surrender', Jewish Telegraphic Agency, 10 July 2017, www.jta.org/2017/07/10/news-opinion/israel-middle-east/a-knesset-bloc-unveils-its-plan-for-peace-total-palestinian-surrender (last accessed 7/8/17); 'Anti-Muslim Activist Daniel Pipes and Congressmen to Launch 'Congressional Israel Victory Caucus', SPLC, 26 April 2017, https://www.splcenter.org/hatewatch/2017/04/26/anti-muslim-activist-daniel-pipes-and-congressmen-launch-%E2%80%9Ccongressional-israel-victory (last accessed 7/8/17).

82. 'Anti-Palestinian caucus divides pro-Israel camp on Capitol Hill', Al-Monitor, 27 April 2017, www.al-monitor.com/pulse/originals/2017/04/anti-palestine-caucus-congress-israel-camp.html (last accessed 7/8/17).

83. 'Bernie Sanders Signals Liberal Push To End Israel's Occupation – With Two States Or One', Forward, 2 March 2017, http://forward.com/opinion/364586/bernie-sanders-signals-liberal-push-to-end-israels-occupation-with-two-stat/ (last accessed 7/8/17).

84. Timothy Seidel (2016) 'Occupied territory is occupied territory': James Baldwin, Palestine and the possibilities of transnational solidarity, *Third World Quarterly*, 37:9, pp. 1644–60.

85. 'Freedom, Bound', https://freedom-bound.org/ (last accessed 7/8/17).

86. 'Where Zionism and the 'alt-right' meet', *Mondoweiss*, 28 July 2017, http://mondoweiss.net/2017/07/where-zionism-right/ (last accessed 7/8/17).

87. 'Israel's Allies Cannot Defeat BDS Alone – We Need Israel's Help', *Haaretz*, 22 June 2015, www.haaretz.com/opinion/.premium-1.662409 (last accessed 7/8/17).

88. 'Minister: I am concerned about decreasing US support for Israel', *Middle East Monitor*, 20 February 2017, www.middleeastmonitor. com/20170220-minister-i-am-concerned-about-decreasing-us-support-for-israel/ (last accessed 7/8/17).

89. 'Keeping pro-Israel politics bipartisan in an age of polarization', Jewish Telegraphic Agency, 19 June 2017, www.jta.org/2017/06/19/news-opinion/politics/keeping-pro-israel-politics-bipartisan-in-an-age-of-polarization (last accessed 7/8/17).

90. 'How long could Israel survive without America?', *Newsweek*, 14 July 2017, www.newsweek.com/how-long-could-israel-survive-without-america-636298 (last accessed 7/8/17).

91. 'Public Uncertain, Divided Over America's Place In The World', *Pew Research Centre*, 5 May 2016, www.people-press.org/2016/05/05/5-views-of-israel-and-palestinians/ (last accessed 7/8/17).

92. 'Israel Maintains Positive Image in U.S.', Gallup, February 15 2017, http://www.gallup.com/poll/203954/israel-maintains-positive-image.aspx (last accessed 16/3/17).

93. 'Repairing the U.S.-Israel Relationship', Council on Foreign Relations, November 2016, www.cfr.org/report/repairing-us-israel-relationship (last accessed 7/8/17).

Chapter 5

1. 'Why Israel Fears the Boycott', *New York Times*, 31 January 2014, www.nytimes.com/2014/02/01/opinion/sunday/why-the-boycott-movement-scares-israel.html (last accessed 16/8/17).

2. 'BDS is antisemitism, pure and simple', *Jerusalem Post*, 6 February 2017, www.jpost.com/Opinion/BDS-is-antisemitism-pure-and-simple-480761 (last accessed 16/8/17).

3. 'What is BDS?', BDS Movement website, https://bdsmovement.net/what-is-bds (last accessed 11/8/17).
4. Ibid.
5. '"Our Struggle Needs Many Tactics" by Nelson Mandela', South African History Online, www.sahistory.org.za/archive/our-struggle-needs-many-tactics-nelson-mandela (last accessed 11/8/17).
6. See the BDS Movement annual round-ups for 2013-2016, https://bdsmovement.net/news/round-bds-successes-2013, https://bdsmovement.net/news/amazing-things-we-achieved-together-2014, https://bdsmovement.net/news/bds-full-2015-round, https://bdsmovement.net/news/2016-bds-impact-round-up (last accessed 11/8/17).
7. 'Veolia completes withdrawal from Israel, in victory for BDS campaign', *Middle East Monitor*, 29 August 2015, www.middleeastmonitor.com/20150829-veolia-completes-withdrawal-from-israel-in-victory-for-bds-campaign/ (last accessed 11/18/17); 'BDS Marks Another Victory As Veolia Sells Off All Israeli Operations', BDS Movement, 1 September 2015, https://bdsmovement.net/news/bds-marks-another-victory-veolia-sells-all-israeli-operations (last accessed 11/8/17).
8. 'BDS victory in Ireland, as CRH ditches Israeli cement firm', *Middle East Monitor*, 9 January 2016, www.middleeastmonitor.com/20160109-bds-victory-in-ireland-as-crh-ditches-israeli-cement-firm/ (last accessed 11/8/17); 'G4S requested UK intervene after Israeli minister's criticism', *Financial Times*, 24 January 2017, www.ft.com/content/7a0deof8-e152-11e6-9645-c9357a75844a (last accessed 11/8/17) and 'Global Security Company G4S deepens ties with Israeli apartheid. Boycott G4S!', BDS Movement, 27 July 2017, https://bdsmovement.net/news/global-security-company-g4s-deepens-ties-israeli-apartheid-boycott-g4s (last accessed 11/8/17).
9. G4S was described as 'extracting itself from reputationally damaging work, including its entire Israeli business', see 'G4S shares plunge as cost of UK asylum services hits profits', *Financial Times*, 9 March 2016, www.ft.com/content/72789bbe-e5cf-11e5-bc31-138df2ae9ee6 (last accessed 11/8/17).
10. See for example: 'Dutch pension fund ABP divests from two Israeli arms companies', *Middle East Monitor*, 4 July 2014, www.middleeastmonitor.com/20140704-dutch-pension-fund-abp-divests-from-two-israeli-arms-companies/ (last accessed 11/8/17), 'Denmark's largest pension fund blacklists firm over links to Israeli occupation', *Middle East Monitor*, 14 December 2015, www.

middleeastmonitor.com/20151214-denmarks-largest-pension-fund-blacklists-firm-over-links-to-israeli-occupation/ (last accessed 11/8/17), 'US church divests from Israeli banks', *Electronic Intifada*, 13 January 2016, https://electronicintifada.net/blogs/ali-abunimah/us-church-divests-israeli-banks (last accessed 11/8/17), 'Mennonite Church to divest in protest of Israeli policies', Associated Press, 6 July 2017, www.yahoo.com/news/mennonite-church-divest-protest-israeli-policies-203325459.html (last accessed 11/8/17).

11. 'Israel slams U.N. body's call for 'blacklist' of settlement companies', Reuters, 24 March 2016, www.reuters.com/article/us-israel-palestinians-un-idUSKCN0WQ2LM (last accessed 11/8/17).

12. 'Israeli Companies Leaving West Bank in Apparent Response to Boycott Pressure', *Haaretz*, 27 March 2016, www.haaretz.com/israel-news/.premium-1.711096 (last accessed 11/8/17).

13. 'US Student Victories in the Boycott, Divestment, & Sanctions Movement', National Students for Justice in Palestine, www.nationalsjp.org/bds-victories.html (last accessed 11/7/17).

14. 'British students' union passes BDS resolution', Jewish Telegraphic Agency, 2 June 2015, www.jta.org/2015/06/02/news-opinion/israel-middle-east/british-students-union-passes-bds-resolution (last accessed 11/8/17).

15. '"Defining political issue of our time": NYU grad student union overwhelmingly votes to boycott Israel over violations of Palestinian human rights', *Salon*, 22 April 2016, www.salon.com/2016/04/22/one_of_the_defining_political_issues_of_our_time_nyu_grad_student_union_overwhelmingly_votes_to_boycott_israels_violation_of_palestinian_human_rights/ (last accessed 11/8/17).

16. 'Britain's largest student union endorses BDS', *Middle East Monitor*, 15 December 2016, www.middleeastmonitor.com/20161215-britains-largest-student-union-endorses-bds/ (last accessed 11/8/17).

17. 'AAAS votes in historic decision to support boycott of Israeli academic institutions', www.usacbi.org/2013/04/aaas-votes-in-historic-decision-to-support-boycott-of-israeli-academic-institutions/ (last accessed 11/8/17), 'Another Association Backs Israel Boycott', *Inside Higher Education*, 1 December 2015, www.insidehighered.com/news/2015/12/01/national-womens-studies-association-joins-israel-boycott-movement (last accessed 11/8/17), 'A Commitment by UK Scholars to Human Rights in Palestine', www.commitment4p.com (last accessed 11/8/17).

18. 'Israeli academics face growing boycott pressures', Associated Press, 1 February 2016, www.apnews.com/0886467ef4614ed2b53e352 d5d8aa745 (last accessed 11/8/17).

19. 'Cultural Boycott', BDS Movement, https://bdsmovement.net/ cultural-boycott (last accessed 11/8/17).

20. 'Nearly 1,000 UK Artists Commit to Cultural Boycott of Israel', *Hyperallergic*, 17 February 2015, https://hyperallergic.com/183208/ nearly-1000-uk-artists-commit-to-cultural-boycott-of-israel/ (last accessed 11/8/17).

21. 'When Nicole Krauss Was Bullied in Jerusalem for Being a U.S. Jew', *Haaretz*, 30 May 2014, www.haaretz.com/opinion/.premium-1.596222 (last accessed 11/8/17).

22. 'The Quiet Boycott: When Israeli Art Is Out', *Haaretz*, 8 January 2015, www.haaretz.com/.premium-1.635914 (last accessed 11/8/17).

23. 'Michael Bennett explains why he refuses to go to Israel as "an ambassador of good will"', *USA Today*, 11 February 2017, http://ftw. usatoday.com/2017/02/michael-bennett-nfl-israel-government-trip-not-going-why-letter-world-seahawks-stills-palestine-ali (last accessed 11/8/17).

24. 'To combat BDS, now's the time for financial Zionism', *Times of Israel*, 11 June 2012, http://blogs.timesofisrael.com/to-combat-bds-nows-the-time-for-financial-zionism/ (last accessed 11/8/17).

25. 'Netanyahu Postpones Ministerial Forum on BDS Threat Over Bennett Row', *Haaretz*, 29 June 2014, www.haaretz.com/israel-news/. premium-1.571146 (last accessed 11/8/17).

26. 'Israel boycott movement is antisemitic, says Binyamin Netanyahu', *Guardian*, 18 February 2014, www.theguardian.com/world/2014/ feb/18/israel-boycott-movement-antisemitic-netanyahu (last accessed 11/8/17).

27. 'Palestinians: Netanyahu Speech Effectively Ends Negotiations', *Haaretz*, 4 March 2014, www.haaretz.com/israel-news/1.577941 (last accessed 11/8/17).

28. 'Israel intimidated by boycott threat to apartheid status quo', *New Arab*, 10 June 2015, www.alaraby.co.uk/english/comment/2015/6/10/ israel-intimidated-by-boycott-threat-to-apartheid-status-quo (last accessed 11/8/17).

29. 'Israel brands Palestinian-led boycott movement a 'strategic threat', *Guardian*, 3 June 2015, www.theguardian.com/world/2015/jun/03/ israel-brands-palestinian-boycott-strategic-threat-netanyahu (last accessed 11/8/17).

30. 'Justice Minister: BDS movement is a terror organization', *Arutz Sheva*, 18 September 2016, www.israelnationalnews.com/News/News.aspx/217985 (last accessed 11/8/17).

31. 'Israel Developing Tools to Fight on Social Media Battlefront', *Bloomberg*, 13 February 2017, www.bloomberg.com/news/articles/2017-02-13/israel-developing-tools-to-fight-on-social-media-battlefront (last accessed 11/8/17).

32. 'Netanyahu, Lapid Play Politics Over BDS, Stand in Way of Real Fighters', *Haaretz*, 8 March 2016, www.haaretz.com/israel-news/.premium-1.707763 (last accessed 14/8/17).

33. 'The Lobby', Al Jazeera, www.aljazeera.com/investigations/thelobby/ (last accessed 14/8/17).

34. 'Cabinet embroiled in battle over Israeli goods boycott', *Financial Times*, 15 February 2016, www.ft.com/content/8f963eb2-d405-11e5-829b-8564e7528e54 (last accessed 14/8/17).

35. 'Covertly, Israel prepares to fight boycott activists online', Associated Press, 17 February 2016, www.apnews.com/0601a79f13e041b9b5b312ec73063c98 (last accessed 14/8/17).

36. 'Israel mulls new strategy on muzzling its critics', *Electronic Intifada*, 6 May 2013, https://electronicintifada.net/blogs/ben-white/israel-mulls-new-strategy-muzzling-its-critics (last accessed 14/8/17).

37. 'New Israeli plan calls for more "intelligence" gathering to disrupt BDS movement', *Electronic Intifada*, 1 June 2013, https://electronicintifada.net/blogs/ben-white/new-israeli-plan-calls-more-intelligence-gathering-disrupt-bds-movement (last accessed 14/8/17).

38. 'Action Plan for Combating Antisemitism 2015 and Beyond', http://mfa.gov.il/MFA/AboutTheMinistry/Conferences-Seminars/GFCA2013/Documents/GFCA2015Booklet.pdf (last accessed 14/8/17).

39. 'Cabinet embroiled in battle over Israeli goods boycott', *Financial Times*, 15 February 2016, www.ft.com/content/8f963eb2-d405-11e5-829b-8564e7528e54 (last accessed 14/8/17).

40. 'Battle over calls to boycott Israel goes global', AFP, 20 April 2016, www.yahoo.com/news/battle-over-calls-boycott-israel-goes-global-025020068.html (last accessed 14/8/17).

41. 'UN Envoy Danon lauds anti-BDS successes', *Ynet*, 17 November 2016, www.ynetnews.com/articles/0,7340,L-4880517,00.html (last accessed 14/8/17).

42. 'A New Boycott Battle', *Inside Higher Education*, 11 August 2017, www.insidehighered.com/news/2017/08/11/does-bill-against-israel-boycott-pose-threat-academic-freedom (last accessed 14/8/17).

43. 'Nearly 50 Senators Want to Make It a Felony to Boycott Israel', *The Nation*, 4 August 2017, www.thenation.com/article/nearly-50-senators-want-to-make-it-a-felony-to-boycott-israel/ (last accessed 14/8/17); 'Senator Gillibrand pulls support for Israel Anti-Boycott Act', *Electronic Intifada*, 3 August 2017, https://electronicintifada.net/blogs/josh-ruebner/senator-gillibrand-pulls-support-israel-anti-boycott-act (last accessed 14/8/17).

44. 'A New Boycott Battle', *Inside Higher Education*, 11 August 2017, www.insidehighered.com/news/2017/08/11/does-bill-against-israel-boycott-pose-threat-academic-freedom (last accessed 14/8/17); 'Civil Rights Groups to Congress: Oppose Unconstitutional Israel Anti-Boycott Act', *Palestine Legal*, 9 August 2017, http://palestinelegal.org/news/2017/8/9/civil-rights-groups-to-congress-oppose-unconstitutional-israel-anti-boycott-act (last accessed 14/8/17); 'The First Amendment Protects the Right to Boycott Israel', ACLU, 20 July 2017, www.aclu.org/blog/speak-freely/first-amendment-protects-right-boycott-israel (last accessed 14/8/17).

45. 'Israel fights BDS: Ego, suspiciousness, dispersed responsibilities and narrow political interests', *Yediot Ahranoth*, 23 February 2016, www.facebook.com/permalink.php?story_fbid=588916987939223&id=150236278473965 (last accessed 14/8/17).

46. 'Anti-BDS Legislation in the United States', *Palestine Legal*, http://palestinelegal.org/legislation/ (last accessed 14/8/17); 'Anti-BDS Legislation by State', *Palestine Legal*, http://palestinelegal.org/righttoboycott (last accessed 14/8/17).

47. 'A Multiple Front War', *Newsweek Middle East*, 27 April 2016, http://newsweekme.com/israel-a-multiple-front-war/ (last accessed 14/8/17).

48. Ibid.

49. 'Penal populism and the BDS movement after Security Council Res. 2334', *openDemocracy*, 30 January 2017, www.opendemocracy.net/luigi-daniele/penal-populism-and-bds-movement-after-security-council-res-2334 (last accessed 14/8/17).

50. 'The First Amendment Protects the Right to Boycott Israel', ACLU, 20 July 2017, www.aclu.org/blog/speak-freely/first-amendment-protects-right-boycott-israel (last accessed 14/8/17).

51. '"Militant leftwing" councils to be blocked from boycotting products', Press Association, 3 October 2015, www.theguardian.com/society/2015/oct/03/conservatives-stop-militant-leftwing-councils-boycotting-products (last accessed 14/8/17).

52. 'A Multiple Front War', *Newsweek Middle East*, 27 April 2016, http://newsweekme.com/israel-a-multiple-front-war/ (last accessed 14/8/17).

53. 'Diluted UK government position on 'Israel boycott ban' follows public outrage', BDS Movement, 18 February 2016, https://bdsmovement.net/news/diluted-uk-government-position-'israel-boycott-ban'-follows-public-outrage (last accessed 14/8/17).

54. 'Victory For Local Democracy', *Ethical Consumer*, 27 June 2016, www.ethicalconsumer.org/latestnews/entryid/2169/victory-for-local-democracy.aspx (last accessed 14/8/17).

55. 'Government suffers defeat in court by Palestine campaigners over boycott, divestment and sanctions', Palestine Solidarity Campaign, 22 June 2017, www.palestinecampaign.org/government-suffers-defeat-court-palestine-campaigners-boycott-divestment-sanctions/ (last accessed 14/8/17), 'Campaigners win legal challenge over government's 'anti-democratic' pension regulation', War on Want, 22 June 2017, www.waronwant.org/media/campaigners-win-legal-challenge-over-government's-anti-democratic-pension-regulation (last accessed 14/8/17).

56. 'Pro-Israel group loses High Court ruling over councils' boycott resolutions', *Middle East Monitor*, 28 June 2016, www.middleeastmonitor.com/20160628-pro-israel-group-loses-high-court-ruling-over-councils-boycott-resolutions/ (last accessed 14/8/17), 'Israel boycott ban: Three councils cleared of anti-semitism over Israeli goods boycott', *Independent*, 28 June 2017, www.independent.co.uk/news/uk/israel-boycott-ban-three-councils-cleared-of-anti-semitism-over-boycott-of-israeli-goods-a7107691.html (last accessed 14/8/17).

57. 'According to the Court of Cassation, freedom of expression does not authorize the call to boycott Israeli products', *AURDIP*, 1 November 2015, www.aurdip.fr/according-to-the-court-of.html (last accessed 14/8/17).

58. 'France's criminalisation of Israel boycotts sparks free-speech debate', AFP, 21 January 2016, www.france24.com/en/20160120-france-boycott-israel-bds-law-free-speech-antisemitism (last accessed 14/8/17).

59. 'France now more repressive of boycott calls than Israel', *Electronic Intifada*, 4 November 2015, https://electronicintifada.net/blogs/ali-abunimah/france-now-more-repressive-boycott-calls-israel (last accessed 14/8/17).

60. Ibid.

61. 'Defying court ruling, French figures call for Israel boycott', *Electronic Intifada*, 20 January 2016, https://electronicintifada.net/blogs/ali-abunimah/defying-court-ruling-french-figures-call-israel-boycott (last accessed 14/8/17).

62. 'Dozens of Spanish cities declaring themselves "Free of Israeli Apartheid"', BDS Movement, 8 September 2016, https://bds movement.net/news/dozens-spanish-cities-declaring-themselves-free-israeli-apartheid (last accessed 14/8/17).

63. 'Penal populism and the BDS movement after Security Council Res. 2334', *openDemocracy*, 30 January 2017, www.opendemocracy.net/luigi-daniele/penal-populism-and-bds-movement-after-security-council-res-2334 (last accessed 14/8/17).

64. 'Dutch government follows Sweden in affirming right to boycott Israel', *Middle East Monitor*, 26 May 2016, www.middleeastmonitor. com/20160526-dutch-government-follows-sweden-in-affirming-right-to-boycott-israel/ (last accessed 14/8/17); 'Lawmakers in Spain endorse right to boycott Israel', *Electronic Intifada*, 3 July 2017, https://electronicintifada.net/blogs/ali-abunimah/lawmakers-spain-endorse-right-boycott-israel (last accessed 14/8/17).

65. 'Groundbreaking statement by 200 European Legal Scholars Upholds the Right to BDS for Palestinian Rights', BDS Movement, 8 December 2016, https://bdsmovement.net/news/groundbreaking-statement-200-european-legal-scholars-upholds-right-bds-palestinian-rights (last accessed 14/8/17); 'BDS impact round up for 2016', BDS Movement, 28 November 2016, https://bdsmovement. net/news/2016-bds-impact-round-up (last accessed 14/8/17).

66. 'Behind Brand Israel: Israel's recent propaganda efforts', *Electronic Intifada*, 23 February 2010, https://electronicintifada.net/content/behind-brand-israel-israels-recent-propaganda-efforts/8694 (last accessed 16/8/17).

67. 'After Gaza, Israel Grapples With Crisis of Isolation', *New York Times*, 18 March 2009, www.nytimes.com/2009/03/19/world/middleeast/19israel.html?_r=0 (last accessed 16/8/17).

68. 'Israel's cuisine not always kosher but travelling well', *Sydney Morning Herald*, 22 May 2011, www.smh.com.au/entertainment/restaurants-and-bars/israels-cuisine-not-always-kosher-but-travelling-well-20110521-1ey1s (last accessed 16/8/17).

69. 'Delegitimization and Criticism: Driving a Wedge', Reut Institute, 1 April 2010, http://reut-institute.org/en/Publication.aspx?Publication Id=3814 (last accessed 16/8/17).

70. 'Penal populism and the BDS movement after Security Council Res. 2334', *openDemocracy*, 30 January 2017, www.opendemocracy.net/luigi-daniele/penal-populism-and-bds-movement-after-security-council-res-2334 (last accessed 16/8/17).

71. 'Israeli Supreme Court upholds the law prohibiting calls for boycott against Israel and the settlements in the West Bank', *Adalah*, 15 April 2015, www.adalah.org/en/content/view/8525 (last accessed 16/8/17).

72. 'Senior Israeli minister: Make BDS activists in Israel "pay a price"', +972 *Magazine*, 16 June 2016, https://972mag.com/senior-israeli-minister-says-working-to-make-bds-activists-in-israel-pay-a-price/120084/ (last accessed 16/8/17).

73. 'Israel imposes travel ban on BDS co-founder Omar Barghouti', *Electronic Intifada*, 10 May 2016, https://electronicintifada.net/blogs/ali-abunimah/israel-imposes-travel-ban-bds-co-founder-omar-barghouti (last accessed 16/8/17), 'BNC Statement on Israel's Ongoing Campaign to Silence Omar Barghouti & Repress BDS', BDS Movement, 22 March 2017, https://bdsmovement.net/news/bnc-statement-israels-ongoing-campaign-silence-omar-barghouti-repress-bds-movement (last accessed 16/8/17).

74. 'The war on Israeli BDS supporters', +972 *Magazine*, 4 August 2017, https://972mag.com/the-war-on-israeli-bds-supporters/129093/ (last accessed 16/8/17).

75. 'Israel challenges BDS at home and beyond', Al Jazeera, 4 August 2017, www.aljazeera.com/indepth/features/2017/08/israel-challenges-bds-home-170803044045108.html (last accessed 16/8/17).

76. 'Israel's Travel Ban: Knesset Bars Entry to Foreigners Who Call for Boycott of Israel or Settlements', *Haaretz*, 7 March 2017, www.haaretz.com/israel-news/.premium-1.775614 (last accessed 16/8/17), 'New Guideline Permits Israel to Deny Entry to Visitors Over "BDS Activity"', *Haaretz*, 6 July 2017, www.haaretz.com/israel-news/.premium-1.799805 (last accessed 16/8/17).

77. 'BDS activists prevented from boarding flight to Israel', Jewish Telegraphic Agency, 24 July 2017, www.jta.org/2017/07/24/news-opinion/israel-middle-east/bds-activists-reportedly-prevented-from-boarding-flight-to-israel (last accessed 16/8/17).

78. Brian Klug, 'The collective Jew: Israel and the new antisemitism', Patterns of Prejudice, Vol. 37, No. 2, (June 2003) Routledge (Taylor & Francis Group), www.academia.edu/740230/The_collective_Jew_Israel_and_the_new_antisemitism (last accessed 16/8/17).

79. 'Shifty antisemitism wars', *openDemocracy*, 22 April 2016, www.opendemocracy.net/can-europe-make-it/ben-white/shifty-antisemitism-wars (last accessed 16/7/17).

80. 'Anti-Zionism is the new anti-Semitism, says Britain's former chief rabbi', *Newsweek*, 3 April 2017, www.newsweek.com/jonathan-sacks-anti-semitism-anti-zionism-bds-israel-labour-442978 (last accessed 16/8/17).

81. '3D Test of Anti-Semitism: Demonization, Double Standards, Delegitimization', Jerusalem Centre for Public Affairs, www.jcpa.org/phas/phas-sharansky-f04.htm (last accessed 16/8/17).

82. 'Israeli minister: Criticizing Israel is the new anti-Semitism', *Washington Post*, 4 May 2016, www.washingtonpost.com/news/worldviews/wp/2016/05/04/israeli-minister-criticizing-israel-is-the-new-anti-semitism/ (last accessed 16/8/17).

83. 'Emmanuel Macron says anti-Zionism is a new type of anti-Semitism', *Independent*, 17 July 2017, www.independent.co.uk/news/world/europe/emmanuel-macron-anti-zionism-anti-semitism-israel-jewish-state-france-president-racism-attacks-a7844711.html (last accessed 16/8/17).

84. 'The "new antisemitism"', *openDemocracy*, 29 September 2015, www.opendemocracy.net/mirrorracisms/antony-lerman/new-antisemitism (last accessed 16/8/17).

85. 'The Myth of the New Anti-Semitism', *The Nation*, 15 January 2004, www.thenation.com/article/myth-new-anti-semitism/ (last accessed 16/8/17).

86. 'Labour and the legacy of antisemitism', Oxford University Press, 13 May 2016, https://blog.oup.com/2016/05/labour-legacy-anti semitism-vsi/ (last accessed 16/8/17).

87. 'British Labour Party Scandal Illustrates Zionism's Main Problem', *Haaretz*, 3 May 2016, www.haaretz.com/opinion/.premium-1.717700 (last accessed 16/8/17).

88. Jewish Voice for Peace, *On Antisemitism* (Chicago: Haymarket Books, 2017), p. 2.

89. 'American Jewish Establishment Stifles Free Speech to Silence Zionism's Critics', *Haaretz*, 7 December 2016, www.haaretz.com/opinion/.premium-1.757284 (last accessed 16/8/17).

90. The text of the draft working definition can be found on the site of the European Parliament Working Group on Antisemitism, www.antisem.eu/projects/eumc-working-definition-of-antisemitism/ (last accessed 16/8/17).

91. 'Israel lobby uses discredited anti-Semitism definition to muzzle debate', *Electronic Intifada*, 28 September 2012, https://electronicintifada.net/content/israel-lobby-uses-discredited-anti-semitism-definition-muzzle-debate/11716 (last accessed 16/8/17).

92. 'Israel lobbyists finally concede that EU has ditched anti-Semitism 'definition'', *Electronic Intifada*, 5 December 2013, https://electronicintifada.net/blogs/ben-white/israel-lobbyists-finally-concede-eu-has-ditched-anti-semitism-definition (last accessed 16/8/17).

93. 'Action Plan for Combating Antisemitism 2015 and Beyond', http://mfa.gov.il/MFA/AboutTheMinistry/Conferences-Seminars/GFCA2013/Documents/GFCA2015Booklet.pdf (last accessed 17/8/17).

94. '2015 Top Ten Worst Anti-Semitic/Anti-Israel Incidents', Simon Wiesenthal Centre, www.wiesenthal.com/site/apps/nlnet/content2.aspx?c=lsKWLbPJLnF&b=9240795&ct=14809459 (last accessed 17/8/17).

95. '2016 Top Ten Worst Anti-Semitic/Anti-Israel Incidents', Simon Wiesenthal Centre, www.wiesenthal.com/atf/cf/%7B54d385e6-f1b9-4e9f-8e94-890c3e6dd277%7D/TT_2016REPORT.PDF (last accessed 17/8/17).

96. 'IHRA Definition of Antisemitism', The Kantor Center for the Study of Contemporary European Jewry, http://kantorcenter.tau.ac.il/ihra-working-definition-antisemitism-2016 (last accessed 17/8/17).

97. 'Human Rights Activists Celebrate Multi-Country Adoption of New Definition of Antisemitism', Algemeiner, 1 June 2016, www.algemeiner.com/2016/06/01/human-rights-activists-celebrate-multi-country-adoption-of-new-definition-of-antisemitism/ (last accessed 17/8/17); 'Seminar: Turning words into action to address anti-Semitism', OCSE, 16–17 June 2016, www.osce.org/odihr/254346?download=true (last accessed 17/8/17).

98. 'IHRA Adopts Definition of Anti-Semitism', The Louis D. Brandeis Centre, 1 June 2016, http://brandeiscenter.com/blog/ihra-adopts-definition-of-anti-semitism/ (last accessed 17/8/17).

99. 'Antisemitism in 2016 – Overview, Trends and Events', Israeli Ministry of Diaspora Affairs, www.mda.gov.il/EngSite/Lists/HomePageBanner3Icons/Attachments/1/reportENG.pdf (last accessed 17/8/17).

100. 'B'nai B'rith Commends The International Holocaust Remembrance Alliance For Adopting Working Definition Of Anti-Semitism', B'nai B'rith, 7 June 2016, http://www.bnaibrith.org/press-releases/-bnai-

brith-commends-the-international-holocaust-remembrance-alliance-for-adopting-working-definition-of-anti-semitism (last accessed 17/8/17).

101. 'AJC Praises International Holocaust Remembrance Alliance Action on Anti-Semitism', AJC, 26 May 2016, www.ajc.org/site/apps/nlnet/content3.aspx?c=7oJILSPwFfJSG&b=8451793&ct=14851275 (last accessed 17/8/17).

102. 'By limiting criticism of Israel, Theresa May's new definition of anti-Semitism will do more harm than good', *Independent*, 12 December 2016, www.independent.co.uk/voices/anti-semitism-theresa-may-new-definition-jewish-council-holocaust-society-israel-criticism-palestine-a7470166.html (last accessed 17/8/17).

103. Wiesenthal Centre to French Interior Minister: 'Cancel "Israel Apartheid"' Conference at Paris University as Threat to Public Order and a Danger to the Jewish Community", 16 February 2012, www.wiesenthal.com/site/apps/nlnet/content2.aspx?c=lsKWLb PJLnF&b=7929811&ct=11630447 (last accessed 17/8/17).

104. 'Wiesenthal Center – Other Universities Should Follow British University's Cancellation of "Israel Apartheid Week"', 21 February 2017, www.wiesenthal.com/site/apps/nlnet/content.aspx?c=lsKWL bPJLnF&b=8776547&ct=14985817 (last accessed 17/8/17).

105. 'A definition of antisemitism', UK government website, 30 March 2016, www.gov.uk/government/speeches/a-definition-of-anti semitism (last accessed 17/8/17).

106. 'Sir Eric Pickles speech at the Inter-parliamentary Coalition for Combating Antisemitism Conference', UK government website, 21 March 2016, www.gov.uk/government/speeches/sir-eric-pickles-speech-at-the-inter-parliamentary-coalition-for-combating-antisemitism-conference (last accessed 17/8/17).

107. 'Will Britain's new definition of antisemitism help Jewish people? I'm sceptical', *Guardian*, 28 December 2016, www.theguardian.com/commentisfree/2016/dec/28/britain-definition-antisemitism-british-jews-jewish-people (last accessed 17/8/17).

108. 'Fight antisemitism and defend free speech', Jewish Socialists' Group, 30 July 2017, www.jewishsocialist.org.uk/news/item/fight-antisemitism-and-defend-free-speech (last accessed 17/8/17).

109. 'Antisemitism in 2016 – Overview, Trends and Events', Israeli Ministry of Diaspora Affairs, www.mda.gov.il/EngSite/Lists/Home PageBanner3Icons/Attachments/1/reportENG.pdf (last accessed 17/8/17).

110. 'Free Speech Advocates Warn that Anti-Semitism Bill Could Make Activism a Civil Rights Violation', *Forward*, 5 December 2016, http://forward.com/news/355903/free-speech-advocates-warn-that-campus-anti-semitism-bill-could-make-palest/ (last accessed 14/8/17).

111. Ibid.

112. Tweet posted by @ADL_National on 2 December 2016, https://twitter.com/ADL_National/status/804778450074697728 (last accessed 17/8/17).

113. 'Oppose H.R. 6421/s. 10, the Anti-Semitism Awareness Act of 2016', ACLU, www.aclu.org/letter/oppose-hr-6421s-10-anti-semitism-awareness-act-2016 (last accessed 17/8/17), 'Nearly 60 Jewish Studies scholars and hundreds of Jewish students oppose misguided Anti-Semitism Awareness Act', 8 December 2016, https://jewishvoiceforpeace.org/nearly-60-jewish-studies-scholars-hundreds-jewish-students-oppose-misguided-anti-semitism-awareness-act (last accessed 17/8/17).

114. 'University of California softens anti-Semitism statement', Reuters, 24 March 2016, www.reuters.com/article/us-california-discrimination-idUSKCN0WQ03F (last accessed 17/8/17).

115. 'University of California Adopts Statement Condemning Anti-Semitism', *New York Times*, 26 March 2016, www.nytimes.com/2016/03/27/us/university-of-california-adopts-statement-condemning-anti-semitism.html (last accessed 17/8/17).

116. 'IHRA Adopts Definition of Anti-Semitism', The Louis D. Brandeis Centre, 1 June 2016, http://brandeiscenter.com/blog/ihra-adopts-definition-of-anti-semitism/ (last accessed 17/8/17).

117. 'Should a major university system have a particular definition of anti-Semitism?', *Jewish Journal*, 22 June 2015, http://jewishjournal.com/opinion/175207/ (last accessed 17/8/17).

118. 'The Working Definition of Antisemitism – Six Years After', The Stephen Roth Institute for the Study of Contemporary Antisemitism and Racism, http://kantorcenter.tau.ac.il/sites/default/files/proceeding-all_3.pdf (last accessed 17/8/17).

119. 'On U.S. Campuses, When Does anti-Israel Become anti-Semitic?', *Haaretz*, 23 May 2015, www.haaretz.com/jewish/features/1.657753 (last accessed 17/8/17).

120. 'Labour members "in denial" over antisemitism, Board tells Chakrabarti inquiry', *Jewish Chronicle*, 10 June 2016, www.thejc.com/news/uk-news/labour-members-in-denial-over-antisemitism-board-tells-chakrabarti-inquiry-1.58764 (last accessed 17/8/17).

121. 'List of Consumer Boycotts', Ethical Consumer, www.ethical consumer.org/boycotts/boycottslist.aspx (last accessed 17/8/17).

122. Artists for Palestine UK, https://artistsforpalestine.org.uk/reasons-not-to-boycott/ (last accessed 17/8/17).

123. 'Stephen Hawking joins academic boycott of Israel', Guardian, 8 May 2013, www.theguardian.com/world/2013/may/08/stephen-hawking-Israel-academic-boycott (last accessed 17/8/17).

124. Remarks of Lawrence H. Summers, Columbia Centre for Law and Liberty, 29 January 2015, http://larrysummers.com/wp-content/uploads/2015/01/AcademicFreedomAndAntiSemitism_FINAL1-2.pdf (last accessed 17/8/17).

125. 'How Long Can Distinction Between Anti-Zionism and Anti-Semitism Survive?', Forward, 4 April 2016, http://forward.com/opinion/337349/how-long-can-distinction-between-anti-zionism-and-anti-semitism-survive/ (last accessed 17/8/17).

126. 'Shami needs to draw red lines over antisemitism', Jewish Chronicle, 23 June 2016, www.thejc.com/comment/comment/shami-needs-to-draw-red-lines-over-antisemitism-1.59386 (last accessed 17/8/17).

127. 'The Left has toxic attitudes to Israel', Telegraph, 1 May 2016, www.telegraph.co.uk/news/2016/05/01/the-left-has-toxic-attitudes-to-israel/ (last accessed 17/8/17).

128. Institute for Jewish Policy Research, July 2010, http://www.jpr.org.uk/documents/Committed,%20concerned%20and%20conciliatory:%20The%20attitudes%20of%20Jews%20in%20Britain%20towards%20Israel.pdf (last accessed 17/8/17); City University London, www.city.ac.uk/__data/assets/pdf_file/0008/295361/Israel-Report-FINAL.PDF (last accessed 17/8/17).

129. 'Anti-Semitism – Thought or Deed?' The Institute for Race Relations, 21 April 2016, www.irr.org.uk/news/anti-semitism-thought-or-deed/ (last accessed 17/8/17).

130. 'Anti-Semitism watchdog CST "abusing" mandate to defend Israel', Electronic Intifada, 12 August 2014, https://electronicintifada.net/blogs/ben-white/anti-semitism-watchdog-cst-abusing-mandate-defend-israel (last accessed 17/8/17).

131. 'Stop meeting anti-Semites, Jewish leader warns Corbyn: Community chief says Labour party is losing their trust', Daily Mail, 22 March 2016, www.dailymail.co.uk/news/article-3503641/Stop-meeting-anti-Semites-Jewish-leader-warns-Corbyn-Community-chief-says-Labour-party-losing-trust.html (last accessed 17/8/17).

132. 'Board says British Jews "concerned and uncomfortable" over Cameron's comment on illegal settlements encircling East Jerusalem',

Jewish Chronicle, 26 February 2016, www.thejc.com/news/uk-news/board-says-british-jews-concerned-and-uncomfortable-over-cameron-s-comment-on-illegal-settlements-encircling-east-jerusalem-1.60580 (last accessed 17/8/17).

133. 'Board attacks Glasgow council over Palestinian flag raising', *Jewish Chronicle*, 19 August 2014, www.thejc.com/news/uk-news/board-attacks-glasgow-council-over-palestinian-flag-raising-1.56197 (last accessed 17/8/17).

134. 'Jews furious at church exhibition featuring Israeli checkpoint', *Times*, 17 September 2016, www.thetimes.co.uk/article/jews-furious-at-church-exhibition-featuring-israeli-checkpoint-5vqkfxtqp (last accessed 17/8/17).

135. 'The Myth of the New Anti-Semitism', *The Nation*, 15 January 2004, www.thenation.com/article/myth-new-anti-semitism/ (last accessed 16/8/17).

136. 'On Anti-Palestinianism and Anti-Semitism', *The Magnes Zionist*, 14 April 2016, www.jeremiahhaber.com/2016/04/on-anti-palestinianism-and-anti-semitism.html (last accessed 17/8/17).

137. 'Why Rabbi Sacks Is Wrong: Palestinians Don't Have to Be anti-Semites to Be anti-Zionists', *Haaretz*, 6 April 2016, www.haaretz.com/opinion/.premium-1.713040 (last accessed 17/8/17).

138. 'Boycott Is the Only Way to Stop the Israeli Occupation', *Haaretz*, 1 May 2016, www.haaretz.com/opinion/.premium-1.717090 (last accessed 17/8/17).

139. 'Netanyahu Tells Knesset Panel: We Have Defeated the BDS Movement', *Haaretz*, 25 July 2016, www.haaretz.com/israel-news/1.733113 (last accessed 17/8/17).

Chapter 6

1. 'Islamic Jihad prisoner Khader Adnan ends hunger strike', *The Australian*, 23 February 2012, www.theaustralian.com.au/news/world/islamic-jihad-prisoner-khader-adnan-ends-hunger-strike/news-story/11654420eec849ccf0abd74eb3f05b05 (last accessed 8/11/17).

2. 'Addameer Calls for Continued Solidarity with Palestinian Prisoners as Mass Hunger Strike is Launched', *Addameer*, 18 April 2012, www.addameer.org/news/addameer-calls-continued-solidarity-palestinian-prisoners-mass-hunger-strike-launched (last accessed 8/11/17); 'Hunger strike movement for Palestine develops rapidly', *Electronic Intifada*, 11 October 2011, https://electronicintifada.net/

blogs/adri-nieuwhof/hunger-strike-movement-palestine-develops-rapidly (last accessed 8/11/17).

3. 'Palestinian prisoners end hunger strike', *Guardian*, 14 May 2012, www.theguardian.com/world/2012/may/14/palestinian-prisoners-end-hunger-strike (last accessed 8/11/17); 'Palestinian hunger strike deal reached', Al Jazeera, 15 May 2012, www.aljazeera.com/news/middleeast/2012/05/2012514153120630951.html (last accessed 8/11/17).

4. 'Mass hunger strike tests Palestinian unity', *Electronic Intifada*, 26 April 2017, https://electronicintifada.net/content/mass-hunger-strike-tests-palestinian-unity/20296 (last accessed 8/11/17).

5. 'Palestinian prisoners in Israel suspend hunger strike', Al Jazeera, 27 May 2017, www.aljazeera.com/news/2017/05/palestinian-prisoners-israel-suspend-hunger-strike-170527074751097.html (last accessed 8/11/17).

6. 'Palestinians observe general strike in solidarity with hunger-striking prisoners', *Ma'an News Agency*, 22 May 2017, www.maannews.com/Content.aspx?id=777210 (last accessed 8/11/17); *Arab 48*, 22 May 2017, https://goo.gl/iI2jZv (last accessed 8/11/17).

7. 'How Palestinian Hunger Strikes Counter Israel's Monopoly on Violence', *Al-Shabaka*, 12 May 2016, https://al-shabaka.org/commentaries/palestinian-hunger-strikes-counter-israels-monopoly-violence/ (last accessed 8/11/17); 'A timeline of Palestinian mass hunger strikes in Israel', Al Jazeera, 28 May 2017, www.aljazeera.com/indepth/interactive/2017/05/timeline-palestinian-mass-hunger-strikes-israel-170510130007023.html (last accessed 8/11/17).

8. *Al-Shabaka*, 12 May 2016.

9. 'Khader Adnan: No food without freedom', Al Jazeera, 17 February 2012, www.aljazeera.com/indepth/features/2012/02/201221715355300838.html (last accessed 8/11/17).

10. 'Fighting new Nakba in the Negev', Al Jazeera, 17 July 2013, www.aljazeera.com/indepth/opinion/2013/07/201371711611253362.html (last accessed 8/11/17).

11. Ibid.

12. 'Palestinian national strike to stop Israel's "Prawer plan" ethnic cleansing', *Electronic Intifada*, 15 July 2013, https://electronicintifada.net/blogs/linah-alsaafin/palestinian-national-strike-stop-israels-prawer-plan-ethnic-cleansing (last accessed 8/11/17).

13. 'Palestinians Unite to Rage Against Prawer Plan', *Middle East Monitor*, www.middleeastmonitor.com/20140123-palestinians-unite-to-rage-against-prawer-plan/ (last accessed 8/11/17).

14. 'Israeli police attack large anti-Prawer protests in Haifa', *Ma'an News Agency*, 30 November 2013, www.maannews.com/Content. aspx?id=652745 (last accessed 8/11/17), 'Activists hold 'day of rage' protests against Prawer Plan', +972 *Magazine*, 30 November 2013, https://972mag.com/activists-stage-day-of-rage-protests-against-prawer-plan/82706/ (last accessed 8/11/17).

15. 'While Prawer is frozen...', *Adalah*, 15 May 2014, www.adalah.org/en/content/view/8276 (last accessed 8/11/17).

16. 'A New Wave of Palestinian Youth Activism in Response to Israeli Prawer Plan', 19 August 2013, www.momken.org/?mod=articles &ID=5693 (last accessed 8/11/17).

17. '"We won": Al-Aqsa Mosque reopened to all Palestinians', Al Jazeera, 28 July 2017, www.aljazeera.com/news/2017/07/al-aqsa-prayers-pass-peacefully-weeks-unrest-170728145643875.html (last accessed 8/11/17).

18. 'Al-Aqsa: Palestinians killed as Jerusalem protests rage', Al Jazeera, 21 July 2017, www.aljazeera.com/news/2017/07/al-aqsa-palestinian-killed-jerusalem-protests-rage-170721113840496.html (last accessed 8/11/17).

19. 'The battle for al-Aqsa 'has just started'', Al Jazeera, 22 August 2017, www.aljazeera.com/indepth/features/2017/08/battle-al-aqsa-started-170820051352459.html (last accessed 8/11/17).

20. '"No sweeter feeling": Palestinians party after Israelis leave Aqsa site', *Middle East Eye*, 27 July 2017, www.middleeasteye.net/news/there-no-sweeter-feeling-palestinians-hail-victory-al-aqsa-747348862 (last accessed 8/11/17).

21. 'Al-Aqsa protests unified us and showed us a new way to resist occupation', *Middle East Eye*, 28 July 2017, www.middleeasteye.net/columns/al-aqsa-protests-unified-us-and-showed-us-new-way-resist-occupation-746810309 (last accessed 8/11/17).

22. 'Israel Concerned: Abbas' Health Deteriorating as West Bank Simmers', *Haaretz*, 31 July 2017, www.haaretz.com/israel-news/1.804074 (last accessed 8/11/17).

23. 'Young Palestinians sound off on current unrest, Israeli occupation', Al Jazeera America, 14 October 2015, http://america.aljazeera.com/articles/2015/10/14/young-palestinians-sound-off-on-current-unrest-israeli-occupation.html (last accessed 8/11/17).

24. 'Palestine's Inconvenient Rebels', *7iber*, 13 October 2015, www.7iber.com/politics-economics/palestines-inconvenient-rebels/ (last accessed 8/11/17).

25. 'Palestinian Youth Revolt: Any Role for Political Parties?', *Al-Shabaka*, 23 November 2015, https://al-shabaka.org/roundtables/palestinian-youth-revolt-any-role-for-political-parties/ (last accessed 8/11/17).

26. 'Looking for a Leadership with a Strategy', *Al-Shabaka*, 19 March 2012, https://al-shabaka.org/roundtables/looking-for-a-leadership-with-a-strategy/ (last accessed 8/11/17); 'Palestinian Political Disintegration, Culture, and National Identity', *Al-Shabaka*, 15 March 2016, https://al-shabaka.org/commentaries/palestinian-political-disintegration-culture-and-national-identity/ (last accessed 8/11/17); 'Focus On: PLO and Palestinian Representation', *Al-Shabaka*, 31 August 2017, https://al-shabaka.org/focuses/focus-plo-palestinian-representation/ (last accessed 8/11/17); 'Talking Palestine: What Frame of Analysis? Which Goals and Messages?' *Al-Shabaka*, 12 April 2017, https://al-shabaka.org/commentaries/talking-palestine-frame-analysis-goals-messages/ (last accessed 8/11/17).

27. 'Palestine Strategy Group', www.palestinestrategygroup.ps/328-2/ (last accessed 8/11/17).

28. 'Towards New Strategies For Palestinian National Liberation', Oxford Research Group, 1 August 2011, www.oxfordresearchgroup.org.uk/publications/briefing_papers_and_reports/towards_new_strategies_palestinian_national_liberation (last accessed 8/11/17).

29. 'How Palestinians can reverse Israel's divide and conquer tactics', +972 *Magazine*, 5 September 2017, https://972mag.com/how-palestinians-can-reverse-israels-divide-and-conquer-tactics/129577/ (last accessed 8/11/17).

30. 'Roundtable on Palestinian Diaspora and Representation', *Jadaliyya*, 11 September 2012, www.jadaliyya.com/pages/index/6082/round table-on-palestinian-diaspora-and-representat (last accessed 8/11/17).

31. 'The Palestinian Issue: Dangers, Threats and Strategic Options', The Jerusalem Fund, 12 March 2015, www.thejerusalemfund.org/4036/the-palestinian-issue-dangers-threats-and-strategic-options (last accessed 8/11/17).

Chapter 7

1. Olmert warns of 'end of Israel', BBC News, 29 November 2007, http://news.bbc.co.uk/1/hi/world/middle_east/7118937.stm (last accessed 7/11/17).

2. Albie Sachs, 'The Future Constitutional Position of White South Africans: Some Further Ideas', January 1990, http://dullahomar institute.org.za/about-us/our-historical-publications/the-future-of-constitutional-position-of-white-south-africans.pdf/view (last accessed 7/11/17).

3. 'The Lawmaker Who Thinks Israel Is Deceiving the Palestinians: "No One Is Going to Give Them a State"', *Haaretz*, 28 October 2017, www.haaretz.com/israel-news/.premium-1.819291 (last accessed 7/11/17).

4. 'Defense Minister Ya'alon: I am not looking for a solution, I am looking for a way to manage the conflict', *+972 Magazine*, 16 October 2014, https://972mag.com/defense-minister-yaalon-i-am-not-looking-for-a-solution-i-am-looking-for-a-way-to-manage-the-conflict/97761/ (last accessed 7/11/17).

5. 'What We Must Do', Azmi Bishara, 3 April 2008, http://azmibishara.com/Publications/Articles/2008/What-we-must-do.aspx (last accessed 7/11/17).

6. Meron Benvenisti, *Sacred Landscape* (Berkeley, CA: University of California Press, 2002), p. 335.

7. M. El-Fadel, R. Qubaía, N. El-Hougeiri, Z. Hashisho and D. Jamali, 'The Israeli Palestinian Mountain Aquifer: A Case Study in Ground Water Conflict Resolution', *The Journal of Natural Resources and Life Sciences Education*, Vol. 30, (2001).

8. Virginia Tilley, *The One-State Solution* (Ann Arbor, MI: The University of Michigan Press, 2005), p. 64.

9. Ibid., p. 91.

10. 'Political Agency for Palestinian Return', *Al-Shabaka*, 3 July 2013, https://al-shabaka.org/roundtables/political-agency-palestinian-return/ (last accessed 7/11/17).

11. Alessandro Petti, Sandi Hilal, Eyal Weizman, *Architecture After Revolution* (Berlin, Germany: Sternberg Press, 2013), p. 39.

12. 'Israel Displaced 67% of Palestinians in 1948', *Palestine News Network*, 22 June 2017, http://english.pnn.ps/2017/06/22/israel-displaced-67-of-palestinians-in-1948/ (last accessed 7/11/17).

13. 'Palestinians in purgatory: Eternally displaced', *Qantara.de*, 9 December 2016, https://en.qantara.de/content/palestinians-in-purgatory-eternally-displaced (last accessed 7/11/17).

14. 'Roundtable on Occupation Law: Part of the Conflict or the Solution? (Part III: Ahmed Barclay and Dena Qaddumi)', *Jadaliyya*, 22 September 2011, www.jadaliyya.com/pages/index/2703/

roundtable-on-occupation-law_part-of-the-conflict- (last accessed 7/11/17).

15. 'High Court Rejects the Right of Ikrit Refugees to Return Home', *Haaretz*, 27 June 2003, www.haaretz.com/high-court-rejects-the-right-of-ikrit-refugees-to-return-home-1.92437 (last accessed 7/11/17).

16. 'Restitution: a Major Component in Durable Solutions', BADIL, 20 October 2003, www.badil.org/en/publication/press-releases/17-2003/768-press-318-03.html (last accessed 7/11/17).

17. Faris ed. p. 204.

18. 'Right of Return Conference at Boston University: Realizing Return In Practice', *Jadaliyya*, 28 May 2013, www.jadaliyya.com/pages/index/11908/right-of-return-conference-at-boston-university_re (last accessed 7/11/17).

19. 'A report from the BADIL-Zochrot joint actions: Practical Approaches to Refugee Return', *Zochrot*, May 2011, http://zochrot.org/en/article/54466 (last accessed 7/11/17).

20. Ibid.

21. 'Competition for Reconstruction of the Destroyed Palestinian Villages', Palestine Lands Society, www.plands.org/en/news/competition-poster (last accessed 7/11/17), 'BZU graduate wins competition on reconstructing destroyed Palestinian villages', Birzeit University, 14 September 2017, www.birzeit.edu/en/news/bzu-graduate-wins-competition-reconstructing-destroyed-palestinian-villages (last accessed 7/11/17).

22. 'Planning Al-Awda: Re-Imagining the Spatial Contours of Israel-Palestine', *Arena of Speculation*, 18 May 2011, https://arenaofspeculation.org/2011/05/18/planning-al-awda-re-imagining-israel-palestine/ (last accessed 7/11/17).

23. 'The Democratic Constitution', *Adalah*, www.adalah.org/uploads/oldfiles/Public/files/democratic_constitution-english.pdf (last accessed 7/11/17).

24. Saree Makdisi, *Palestine Inside Out: An Everyday Occupation* (New York, NY: W. W. Norton, 2008), p. 284–5.

25. Ibid., p. 285.

26. Mazen Masri, *The Dynamics of Exclusionary Constitutionalism: Israel as a Jewish and Democratic State* (Oxford: Hart Publishing, 2017), p. 197.

27. Ali Abunimah, *One Country* (New York: Henry Holt & Company, 2006), p. 109, 110.

28. 'The One State Declaration', 29 November 2007, https://electronicintifada.net/content/one-state-declaration/793 (last accessed 7/11/17).

29. Anglo-American Committee of Inquiry, http://avalon.law.yale.edu/20th_century/angch01.asp (last accessed 7/11/17).

30. 'A Plan For The Future Government Of Palestine', US State Department, 4 June 1947, https://history.state.gov/historical documents/frus1947v05/d772 (last accessed 7/11/17).

31. 'A forgotten US vision for a single democratic state in Palestine', *Electronic Intifada*, 3 March 2017, https://electronicintifada.net/blogs/josh-ruebner/forgotten-us-vision-single-democratic-state-palestine (last accessed 7/11/17).

32. 'The Palestinian-Israeli Pulse: A Joint Poll', December 2016, www.pcpsr.org/sites/default/files/Table%20of%20Findings_English%20Joint%20Poll%20Dec%202016_12Feb2017.pdf (last accessed 7/11/17).

33. Karma Nabulsi, 'Justice as the way forward', in *Where Now for Palestine?* ed. Jamil Hilal (London: Zed Books, 2007), p. 250.

34. 'Palestinian-Israeli Pulse', Palestinian Centre for Policy and Survey Research, 1 August 2017, www.pcpsr.org/en/node/696 (last accessed 23/12/17).

35. Amos Oz, 'The Meaning of Homeland', in *Zionism: The Sequel*, ed. Carol Diament (New York, NY: Hadassah, 1998), p. 249.

36. Amos Oz, *In the Land of Israel* (New York, NY: Mariner Books/Houghton Mifflin Harcourt, 1993), p. 148.

37. Oz, *In the Land of Israel*, p. 148.

38. Adam Shatz, 'In Praise of Diasporism, or, Three Cheers for Irving Berlin', in *Prophets Outcast*, ed. Adam Shatz (New York, NY: Nation Books, 2004), p. xvii.

39. 'Israel as Refuge for the Jews', *The Magnes Zionist*, 30 March 2012, www.jeremiahhaber.com/2012/03/israel-as-refuge-for-jews.html (last accessed 7/11/17).

40. 'Israel's Nation-state Bill is Undemocratic', *Haaretz*, 11 May 2017, www.haaretz.com/opinion/.premium-1.788553 (last accessed 7/11/17).

41. 'Israel's definition of a "Jewish state"', Al Jazeera, 8 April 2013, www.aljazeera.com/indepth/opinion/2013/04/201344840244399.html (last accessed 7/11/17).

42. 'Israel: The Alternative', *New York Review of Books*, 23 October 2003, www.nybooks.com/articles/2003/10/23/israel-the-alternative (last accessed 7/11/17).

43. 'An Alternative Future: An Exchange', *New York Review of Books*, 4 December 2003, www.nybooks.com/articles/2003/12/04/ an-alternative-future-an-exchange/ (last accessed 7/11/17).

44. 'Israeli Jews and the one-state solution', *Electronic Intifada*, 10 November 2009, https://electronicintifada.net/content/israeli-jews-and-one-state-solution/8528 (last accessed 7/11/17).

45. 'Wanted, for crimes against the state', *Guardian*, 24 July 2007, www. theguardian.com/world/2007/jul/24/israel (last accessed 7/11/17).

46. Colin Shindler, *Triumph of Military Zionism: Nationalism and the Origins of the Israeli Right* (London: I. B. Tauris, 2009), p. 88.

47. 'For its survival, Israel must abandon the one-state option', *LA Times*, 7 March 2015, www.latimes.com/opinion/op-ed/la-oe-oz-two-state-solution-peace-israel-palestinians-20150308-story.html#page=1 (last accessed 29/10/17).

48. 'What the whites feared', *Politicsweb*, 11 November 2009, www. politicsweb.co.za/opinion/what-the-whites-feared (last accessed 7/11/17).

49. Sachs, 'The Future Constitutional Position of White South Africans: Some Further Ideas', January 1990, http://dullahomarinstitute.org.za/ about-us/our-historical-publications/the-future-of-constitutional-position-of-white-south-africans.pdf/view (last accessed 7/11/17).

50. 'The only alternative', *Al-Ahram Weekly*, 1–7 March 2001, http:// weekly.ahram.org.eg/Archive/2001/523/op2.htm (last accessed 7/11/17).

51. 'Israeli Jews and the one-state solution', *Electronic Intifada*, 10 November 2009, https://electronicintifada.net/content/israeli-jews-and-one-state-solution/8528 (last accessed 7/11/17).

52. Raef Zreik, 'When Does a Settler Become a Native? (With Apologies to Mamdani)', in *Constellations*, Volume 23, Number 3, (2016).

53. Yoav Peled, 'Zionist Realities', in *New Left Review*, 38, (March–April 2006), https://newleftreview.org/II/38/yoav-peled-zionist-realities-debating-israel-palestine (last accessed 7/11/17).

54. Virginia Tilley, 'The Secular Solution', in *New Left Review*, 38, (March–April 2006), https://newleftreview.org/II/38/virginia-tilley-the-secular-solution-debating-israel-palestine (last accessed 7/11/17).

55. 'What Comes Next: A secular democratic state in historic Palestine – a promising land', *Mondoweiss*, 21 October 2013, http:// mondoweiss.net/2013/10/democratic-palestine-promising/ (last accessed 7/11/17).

56. 'Zionism's own intellectual history includes early humanitarian Jewish thinkers who once argued passionately for sharing the land

with the 'Arabs'. Today, such early ideas may seem superfluous or useful only as moral band-aids allowing modern Zionism to claim its early good intentions. Yet, revived ... those old ideas offer some venerable resources to unravel the present formula of destruction, by suggesting the only stable conflict – the same solution finally accepted by all the Western democracies: democratization in one secular, democratic, civil nation-state". Tilley, *One Country*, p.133.

57. Steven Friedman, 'The Inevitable Impossible: South African Experience and a Single State', in *Israel and South Africa: The Many Faces of Apartheid* (London: Zed Books, 2015) p. 278.

58. Ibid., p. 288, 289.

59. Judith Butler, *Parting Ways: Jewishness and the Critique of Zionism* (New York, NY: Columbia University Press, 2012), p. 210.

60. 'How Jews Should Relate to Palestine', *The Magnes Zionist*, 3 February 2013, www.jeremiahhaber.com/2013/02/recognizing-palestine-as-homeland-of.html (last accessed 7/11/17).

61. 'Zionism without a Jewish State', *The Magnes Zionist*, 12 August 2007, www.jeremiahhaber.com/2007/08/zionism-without-jewish-state.html (last accessed 7/11/17).

62. 'The age of Trump spells the end of the Zionist dream', +972 *Magazine*, 7 February 2017, https://972mag.com/the-age-of-trump-spells-the-end-of-the-zionist-dream/125080/ (last accessed 7/11/17).

63. 'The State of Zionism', *The Nation*, 18 June 2007, www.thenation.com/article/state-zionism/ (last accessed 7/11/17).

64. 'On the day Yafa's refugees return – Zochrot 2010', www.youtube.com/watch?v=Fbp2Ep9BXpQ (last accessed 7/11/17).

65. Condoleeza Rice, *No Higher Honor: A Memoir of My Years in Washington* (London: Simon & Schuster, 2011), p. 243.

66. 'American Attitudes on the Israeli-Palestinian Conflict', https://sadat.umd.edu/sites/sadat.umd.edu/files/american_attitudes_on_israel-palestine.pdf (last accessed 7/11/17).

67. Edward Said, *The End of the Peace Process* (London: Granta Publications, 2000), p. 312.

68. Edward Said, *The Question of Palestine* (London: Vintage, 1992), p. 181.

69. 'The Single-state Solution Is Already Here', *Haaretz*, 17 October 2015, www.haaretz.com/opinion/.premium-1.680882 (last accessed 7/11/17).

70. Mourid Barghouti, *I Saw Ramallah* (London: Bloomsbury, 2004), p. 23.

71. Ibid., p. 119.

72. Said, *The Question of Palestine*, p. 69–70.

Index